EVERY ☆ THING ☆ ☆ PROSPERS

Discard

M THE PLANTATION OF MARIGNY

The Port of New Orleans

Books by
HAROLD SINCLAIR

The Port of New Orleans
Years of Illusion
Westward the Tide
The Years of Growth
American Years
Journey Home

THE LEVEE - NEW ORLEANS.

Wharf scene of the Port of New Orleans in 1883.

THE PORT OF
New Orleans

By
HAROLD SINCLAIR

Doubleday, Doran & Company, Inc.
GARDEN CITY　1942　NEW YORK

PRINTED AT THE *Country Life Press,* GARDEN CITY, N. Y., U. S. A.

917.63

7349

"For Sidney"

Author's Note

THAT THIS VOLUME is not and was never intended to
be a formal history of the city of New Orleans should be
obvious to the most casual reader. Not here will the reader
find any year-by-year record of city budgets, candidates for
mayor, or much of anything else that may be had by recourse
to the city's department of vital statistics.

This is, rather, *one* account of New Orleans as a city, with
especial reference to its importance as an American seaport
and its relationship to the rest of the Mississippi Valley. A
realistic account, if you will, with the moss-grown legends for
the most part left undisturbed in the pages of other, and perhaps better, writers—moth-eaten legends which writers in
these days repeat largely in order to create an opportunity
for demolishing them. Legends sprout easily in the romantic
soil of the Crescent City—and flourish amazingly. In modern
New Orleans the glib tourist guides (could they be lineal
descendants of the original romanticists?) add their word-of-
mouth bit to the printed collections. There was, for instance,
the guide who was showing two matronly ladies the points of
interest around Jackson Square, when one of them, out of the
blue, asked, "By the way, do you know where Anthony Adverse lived when he was in New Orleans?" Whether or not

the guide had ever heard of the celebrated Adverse is beside the point; in any case he didn't miss a beat. "Yes, ma'am," he said. "I'm glad you mentioned that—he lived right up there on the second floor, in that corner apartment!"—and pointed to an upper corner of one of the Pontalba Buildings. Who can say but what the truth of this, too, may become established by time?

In any work of this character which concerns a subject with a record as lengthy and complex as New Orleans', the writer is faced with the problem of what to leave out—for want of space if for no other reason. The choice here has, of course, been mine, but the intention has been to omit what seemed likely to be of least interest to the general reader; that is the reader interested in the collective character and activities of the city as opposed to the individuals concerned.

New Orleans has been called, and properly, one of America's three most interesting cities, and because this is so almost every facet of its life, past and present, has been written about in detail—sometimes in more detail than the subject matter has warranted. For those who are interested there are volumes on New Orleans' cookery, convivial drinks, morals, pirates, first families, politicians, genuinely distinguished public figures, architecture, artists, antiques, and ancestry. These items are for Orleanians and others who have the time and inclination for such matters. *This* particular item is for those who prefer New Orleans but not so much of any one part of it.

Now that this book is finished, from the writer's point of view at least—he hopes not the reader's—it appears that there is much in it which seems, inferentially at least, hypercritical. I should like to say that wherever that impression is strongest, wherever New Orleans suffers from what are perhaps unjust comparisons, it is in order to present the city's character as it might appear to the observer with the average point of view— that is to say the point of view which, on the evidence, one must assume was prevalent in the United States of the corresponding period. I am of course responsible for the expression

Author's Note

(and interpretation) of that point of view, but I insist that it is not necessarily always my own personal and private view. My own opinion is not important in any case. But as I think about it now, and of necessity have thought of it throughout the process of writing these pages, it occurs to me that I for one would not have New Orleans one whit different, had I the choice. New Orleans, like any city or any man, is the sum of all its parts, its failures as well as its successes, its averages and eccentricities.

I haven't the least doubt that even the least diligent searcher can find errors aplenty in these pages. But whatever the errors of commission are, I wish the finder of them as much pleasure in the discovery as I had in the process of making them.

For in various ways aiding and abetting the work which went into these pages I wish to thank J. S. W. Harmanson, Lynn Covert, Rudd Fleming, Dan Spaight, E. P. (Pat) O'-Donnel, John Herrman, John McClure, Albert Goldstein, and Artie Simon—and won't *he* be surprised at finding his name in a book!

HAROLD SINCLAIR

April 1942.

Contents

[xi]

Contents

Illustrations

The Port of New Orleans

PROLOGUE

THERE is the blue and empty immensity of the Gulf and
the sky, with perhaps a few soaring gulls bisecting the
sweeping curves of space, and there is the illusion that this is
the center of a vast emptiness. There are the gulls, perhaps one
or more other ships coming in—moving with almost dreamlike
slowness, a lone fisherman's lugger in the blue distance, and
you *know* that there, only a few miles to the north, lies the
Mississippi Valley and the Continental United States.

You move closer to the still unseen land and this feeling of
space and emptiness persists, but it is not all illusion.

The bar pilot's launch comes alongside, the pilot climbs
aboard, and again you know that you are coming in; here is
even further proof. But still there is no land, no faintest line
of demarcation between earth and sea.

Then presently there is the great brown flood of the Mississippi mingling with the blue of the Gulf, the vast discharge
dividing at the mouths of the passes, but eventually all veer-
ing westward with the prevailing Gulf current. Here the
greatest of all river systems comes to its final end, dumping
the water and topsoil of nearly half a continent into the Gulf
of Mexico. The U.S. Engineers—specifically the Corps of
Engineers, U.S. Army—can tell you the exact figures, down

[1]

to the last gallon of water and ton of sediment, but all that is of no consequence here. This is a matter for the imagination. That chunk of drift log floating idly, purposelessly past— months ago it was, perhaps, a tall sycamore on the green shore of the Wabash in Indiana or the Big Sandy in Kentucky; months from now it may be salt-encrusted driftwood on a lonely beach in Brazil—or somewhere on Africa's Ivory Coast.

Straight ahead now is one of the channels of the Mississippi itself: the main light towers at the pass entrance; the jetty lights; the neat buildings of the light tenders, and the pilot station.

These individual entrances to the great river are not especially impressive to the eye, for after all there are five of them, and the discharge of the Mississippi into the Gulf is so divided. But they are impressive to the mind, for you know what this final climax was originally a part of. South Pass is about seven hundred and fifty feet wide, and Southwest Pass twenty-four hundred feet at its maximum, although above Head of Passes, where the Mississippi is its individual self, it is far wider. Even so, however, it is not as wide a river as the average riverman will inform the uninitiated. At any given point between Head of Passes and New Orleans the width is popularly supposed to be "about a mile"; as a matter of fact, it seldom reaches a width of more than three quarters of a mile in this stretch— just about the width of the Ohio River above Cairo. Vastly more depth and volume it has, yes, but not breadth visible to the eye, and if this be heresy one can only refer the doubting to the figures of the U.S. Engineers, who know more about the Mississippi than anyone else on earth.

For a moment you wonder a little, for obviously these structures here, since they do not float, must be built on something. And then you see that they are built on land—or on what passes as land in this watery wilderness. It is flat and green, almost level with the water, and there is even an illusion about all this too. For the earth is only partly earth; the rest is water. There is just enough solidity to support piling, and

Prologue

thus piling is what every man-made thing here is built upon; otherwise it must of necessity float.

All this—the lights, the jetties (of which more elsewhere), the pilot station—is technically part of the Port of New Orleans. And yet New Orleans the city is one hundred and ten miles, more or less, upstream.

On the charts, the Mississippi and its Lower Delta appear very much like an uprooted tree. The river and the land on either side form the trunk; the lower channels, or passes, from Head of Passes to the open Gulf, the dangling roots. Too, the charts indicate five passes by name: Pass à l'Outre, Northeast Pass, Southeast Pass, South Pass, and Southwest Pass. But in these later days only the last two are maintained at ocean vessel depth by the Engineers. The others are used by small craft native to these waters, but otherwise they are silted up, unlighted, and without pilot service.

If your vessel enters by way of Southwest Pass, you will drop the bar pilot at Pilot Town and take aboard the river pilot in his stead; if by way of South Pass, you will make the exchange at Port Eads.

In these days a trim, businesslike gray Coast Guard tug is moored somewhere near the Pilot Town wharf, and equally trim, businesslike sailors in the wheelhouse train their glasses on your passing vessel. Upriver or down, in another moment the tug's radio will be reporting your passing—reporting it somewhere.

And here also every man-made thing stands on stilts or piling, not even excepting the oil storage tanks, though in truth you can't *see* the piling on which the latter rest. Here, too, children grow to the age of five or six before knowing the feel of solid land underfoot. There is a tale—possibly but not necessarily apocryphal—of the five-year-old who was taken upriver to Venice for the first time; but once on solid land he became so wildly frightened that his parents had to return him to the launch and it was months before he could be induced to try the experiment again.

[3]

The Port of New Orleans

Above Head of Passes the land lies flat, green, and treeless on either side, walls between the brown current of the river and the blue water of the Gulf, and in places the land seems no more than a few hundred yards across. Ships moving in the Gulf outside give you the unsettling impression that they are sailing over dry land, though you know that can't possibly be true. Here and there cattle graze contentedly on the river banks. Strange, that—and yet, why not? The land here is good for little else. The grass is lush and richly green; the waterways make natural fences; and here and there cattle chutes run down to the river's edge, so that the way-freight boats may transport the animals to and from their watery pastures.

You pass wing dam after wing dam—fencelike rows of piling extending varying distances out from the banks, each with its warning light at the river end. Their purpose is to control this mighty current's vagaries, and they are many; to put it exactly where the Engineers want it, and keep it there. It is a wondrous knowledge of the ways of the Mississippi these Engineers have, and hardly less amazing the manner in which they put that knowledge to practical use. This was not always so, but after Captain James B. Eads showed them the first path they found the rest of the way themselves.

This is a liquid, lonely world and the settlements, what few there are of them, lie far apart. Yet this Delta country teems with a life, at once primitive and modern, peculiarly its own; a life almost unknown to the outside world of headlines and neon glitter, almost unknown even to New Orleans itself, which it nourishes in so many ways. It is a land weird, sinister, and unfriendly to the unsympathetic stranger, but to the initiated it has a rare and exotic quality all its own, a quality unmatched by any other place in the United States.

There is the strange beauty of moss-streamered live oaks in fog so thick you can almost gather it with a bucket; and in windy, sun-filled days when the clouds, in arrays of colors beyond naming or white as growing cotton, march up from

Prologue

the Gulf in towering, tumbled mountain ranges; and everywhere the earth is endlessly green. Death can lurk underfoot—alligators, water moccasins, canebrake rattlers—while overhead live many of the loveliest of American birds. And always and above all, the mighty central theme of the Delta symphony, there is the river. Fur trappers—the uninformed can scarcely believe that this semi-tropical region is *the* great fur-producing area of North America—oystermen, fishermen, cattlemen, and their families, live much as they did a century ago or longer. Of course they use gas engines in place of sail rigs, use the radio and modern firearms and fishing gear, but these are only incidentals. The primary objectives of their lives have changed but little. For these people, or most of them, New Orleans the city begins and ends at the markets and supply stations for their needs, the levee and its immediate environs. Their own world is the Delta, its canebreaks and thick jungle growth, and its almost endless waters.

So in many ways this land is as unchanged as when La Salle, above Head of Passes, buried the leaden plate which is supposed to have been inscribed:

In the reign of Louis the Great, 9th April, 1682, Robert Cavalier, with Seigneur de Tonti, Reverend Father Zenobio, member of the Recollect order, and twenty Frenchmen, first navigated this river from the village of the Illinois and made the passage of the mouth, 9th April, 1682.

The river has changed the *shape* of the land many times and in many ways since then; but the character of the land is little different. Men spend lifetimes learning to know only a small part of this bayou country intimately, and even now men disappear as though by magic, leaving no apparent trace behind them.

Here, too, are the weird contrasts between the old and the new. In the swamps at night the gases from the oil wells burn with a bright orange flame, from wells drilled with fantastically modern equipment, while alligators drowse in the

[5]

muddy waters only a few yards away. The U.S. Engineers combat the river with machines almost beyond the imagination of a seventeenth-century La Salle. Sulphur is forced from below the waters with machinery at least as imaginative as that conceived by the comic-strip artists, and the brown surface of the Mississippi is roiled by the high-speed propellers of the Navy's latest model torpedo boats. The newest thing in oil-burning ocean vessels pass within a few yards of the levees, their superstructures towering high above the cabins, the fish-and-oyster houses, and the live oaks, and yet on the shores of the bayous there is jungle growth as thick and impenetrable as any on the headwaters of the Nile or Amazon.

From Head of Passes to the bend where Forts Jackson and St. Philip once stood the Mississippi performs a feat which, for it, is really remarkable: it runs for about twenty miles in an almost straight line. Here it turns west (or approximately west) for about a mile, then north again at Bolivar Point, and from here on is its real tortuous self. Here, too, the land broadens and the Gulf is less frequently in sight. The population becomes a little more dense but hardly more visible, and there are still few places that can be called towns; a general store, an oil dock, a post office, but still not proper towns. Rich names there are here, too, though frequently they refer to a roughly defined area rather than to a specific place—Buras Settlement, Cubits Gap, the Jump, Pointe Coupée, Devils Flats, Grand Prairie, Little Texas, Point à la Hache, Poverty Point, Battleground Plant, a host of others that roll off the tongue as easily. And here too the river begins to acquire the names by which it has been known since there were rivermen to coin names: Tropical Bend, Jesuits Bend, English Turn—this last a hairpin bend in really proper Mississippi style.

Naturally there are reasons, some of them fascinating to the delver in historical minutiae, for all these place names, though their cataloguing does not properly belong here. But English Turn deserves some special mention. Not long after the first French settlement on the Gulf coast, the British, seldom missing an opportunity to profit at the expense of someone else, sent two armed vessels to explore the mouths of the Mississippi, with a view to future settlement. Captain Bar, commanding the expedition, was becalmed at this particularly difficult bend—as was many another vessel after his—could not proceed, and lay there for days.

Bienville, on one of his regular exploring jaunts in the Delta, came upon Captain Bar by accident. Learning that Bar was not really sure that this *was* the Mississippi, Bienville assured him emphatically that it was not, that the great river lay much farther to the west. Whether Bar really believed Bienville, or whether he was bored and disgusted with his long becalming and looking for any excuse to get away, is now impossible to say. But at any rate he accepted Bienville's word, dropped down the river to pick up his other ship, and figured no more in the saga of the Mississippi. So today this hairpin bend is still English Turn and geographically is almost as well known as Algiers Point.

(Indicative, too, of the French governmental attitude of the time toward the colonies is another incident connected with this visit of Captain Bar's. Accompanying Bar was a Frenchman named Secon, an emissary from those French Protestant families who, after the revocation of the Edict of Nantes in 1684, had emigrated to Carolina. Protesting against Catholicism as state religion but still, oddly enough, desiring to live under France politically in Louisiana, providing they were allowed freedom of conscience, Secon handed Bienville a memorial from some four hundred French Carolina families to that effect; and Bienville duly forwarded it to the Count de Pontchartrain, colonial administrator for the regency. In time the persons concerned were haughtily informed that the French sovereign had not driven these Protestants from his kingdom in order that they might make a republic in America. It is probable that Bienville, privately, at least, cursed his bad luck, for if there was any one thing he needed in Louisiana it was sober, industrious colonists who would do something remotely resembling work. So Louisiana's loss was British Carolina's gain.)

Overhead a swan, incredibly white against the blue of the sky, floats slowly, and on a sand bar near the shore stands a flock of pelicans; all facing the same way, they are stock-still, like an audience absorbed in action on a stage. There are trees along the banks now, mostly willows that gradually increase in size as you move upstream, and at night the burning gases from the oil wells are torches in the swamps.

Then presently, on the west bank, there is the village of Venice—appropriate name for a town in this watery landscape. It is no more than a hamlet, yet to the stranger it seems an important landmark in this semi-floating world where there are no mountain peaks, no smallest hills or jutting headlands, hardly even a church spire. Geographically, too, Venice is important in the Delta, for here, some eighty miles below New Orleans, the only road on the west bank of the river ends—and on the east bank there is no road at all for many more miles upstream. Back there behind Venice is one of the choice orange-growing districts of Louisiana, though little of that may be seen from the river. Nowadays most of the crop goes to New Orleans by truck, and while rivermen on the way-freight boats grumble at the loss, there is little else they can do about it; for besides being faster the trucks eliminate transfer charges at the New Orleans docks. These rivermen are among the last to face economic annihilation by way of fast trucks on paved roads ashore; they have their place but yearly it grows smaller.

This Delta population is perhaps as strange a racial mixture as may be found in America, where strange mixtures are taken for granted. Here are Cajuns—speaking their astonishing brand of un-French—Negroes of all shades and bloods, Portuguese, Slavonians, Dalmatians, Italians, Filipinos, Spanish, even occasional Chinamen. Time, their comparative isolation, and one of the primal urges have combined to mix them more than one usually expects even in a cosmopolitan America, but that is not to say that they are completely and indiscriminately mixed, nothing of the sort. Yet here there is not so much of the racial cleavage, the group apartness, which is frequently visible even in a city as comparatively small as New Orleans. Probably the primitive state of some phases of Delta life accounts for at least part of this, for in the American wilderness racial opposites have almost always gotten along together.

On the west bank of the river, farther upstream, are the wharfs of Port Sulphur, with the monster plant itself behind them. And all this, too, is a miracle of modern engineering. Here is the largest sulphur-producing plant in the world, built on the quivering swampland and tearing its raw product from far down in these watery depths. Louisiana, and thus New Orleans, has engineering genius to thank for much, for without it a vast amount of her richest natural resources could never have been utilized.

And so, presently, New Orleans the city.

The first view of it is likely to be at once impressive and disappointing. It is impressive because mile on mile of almost solid docking space, row on row of battleship-gray warehouses—their street names lettered on the river side—great modern grain elevators, grain and bulk goods conveyors, banana cranes, cotton sheds, repairs yards and dry docks, shipping from all the world—though usually with vessels in the Central and South American trade predominating—how can this be anything but impressive? The disappointment lies in the fact that from here this is about *all* you can see of New Orleans. Not from here, the throbbing economic heart of the port, will you see much of the enchanting, romantic New Orleans of the tourist guidebooks and Chamber of Commerce folders. But perhaps it is presumptive to assume that this is a disappointment. The romance is here, too, but it is that of the romantic realist who can sense the overtones in the commonplace and everyday—rusty tramps with ugly, business-like guns fore and aft under loose canvas jackets; battered old packets still working the Lower Coast trade; ferries huff-huffing softly back and forth between Algiers and the foot of Canal Street—Eads Square—as they have for more than a century; the long, green lines of bananas pouring upward from the holds of vessels at the Erato and Julia Street wharves—some 45,000 stems per ship; the mingled odors of sacked coffee, molasses, and tarred cordage; the thousand-and-one details of a busy port life; and the ageless, restless, persistent brown current of the river complementing the busy yet frequently leisurely activity of New Orleans the city, gateway to half a continent. And beside all this the lace-embroidered half legends of the French Quarter are likely to seem more than a little pallid.

For the possible disappointment there are several reasons, and the first is the imprisoned river itself. The docks and warehouses are just high enough to cut off all view of the main portion of the city from any but the tallest of ship bridges, since the city lies below the normal level of the river and beyond the wide levee. The Mississippi is a mighty stream here, but even so it is not wide enough to permit docks to be built at right angles to the stream, as is common in most deepwater ports. Not only that—docks built at right angles into the Mississippi, providing slips for the largest vessels, would probably cause this current to do weird and unpredictable things. Thus the docking sheds parallel the stream—incidentally eliminating the need for tugs in mooring even the largest ocean vessels—and form a wall between New Orleans and its river.

Then, too, the city has no sky line of consequence. There is a scant handful of mildly tall buildings in the downtown business section, a few towering factory chimneys, here and there a notable church spire, the bell tower at one of the universities —all of which adds up to little when compared with New York's Manhattan or Chicago's lake front along Michigan Avenue. The last reason is the great, sweeping curve of the river, which gives New Orleans its second name of Crescent City. Coming upstream, the river points directly at the heart

of the city, swings abruptly around the point which is Algiers
—once an independent town but now a part of New Orleans—
and then goes into its great looping bend, so that at no single
point on the entire water front can the whole foreshore of
New Orleans be seen at one time.

All this, of course, was not true of original French New
Orleans. That lay, and the so-called French Quarter still lies,
on the outside of the bend of which the inside is Algiers Point,
the latter a piece of geography known to seamen the world
over. When the Place d'Armes, now Jackson Square, faced
the open Mississippi, the view toward and from the Square
was more than a little impressive, indeed it had in it something
of majesty.

Time was, and not so many years ago, when the miles-long
rows of docks did not altogether hide city and river from
each other. The docks lay above and below the foot of Canal
Street, with a long stretch of broad, open levee in between,
and the levee was one of the city's most popular promenades.
There was always the kaleidoscopic view of moored and moving shipping, water-borne sights and sounds and smells from
the near and far places of the earth, and New Orleans liked
to look at its river. It is also, of course, the river of Baton
Rouge and Natchez, of Vicksburg, Memphis, Cairo, St. Louis,
and Quincy, of Dubuque, St. Paul, Minneapolis, and a thousand-and-one little landings in between. Once it was known
as "Old Man Shreve's River" and as "Eads' River," and La
Salle thought to call it St. Louis rather than Mississippi. But
always for Orleanians it has been "our" river—and who would
chide them too much for such a harmless proprietorship?

With the need for more dock space the natural tendency
seemed to be to close up the levee in the center. So it was
done, and thus New Orleans—on the New Orleans shore as
opposed to the more sparsely populated west bank—except for
an occasional gap such as that at the foot of Canal Street, was
fenced off from its river. Probably it couldn't be helped, but
it is something of a pity that more of New Orleans the city

can't be seen from what is beyond doubt one of the truly great river fronts of the world.

Behind her Chinese wall of levee lies the city of New Orleans. She has been called one of America's three most charming cities, and she is—but she doesn't really care much. She is something like a once-lovely belle grown old—a little fat and wrinkled and dilapidated, still charming when she wants to be, but withal a little bored, her appetites jaded, her soul a little tarnished by overmuch sin, pleasant and otherwise, ready on occasion to turn and snarl without cause at her flatterers.

She is in some ways more like New York than any other city in America, and yet she boasts a smaller population than, say, Milwaukee. Few cities in America are so outwardly religious, yet few have tolerated, even delighted in, so many forms of earthly sin. She is a Marseilles or a Shanghai, American style, shot through with overtones of Christy Minstrels, the *code duello*, white steamboats on a chocolate-colored river, coffee and cotton, wine in cobwebbed bottles, vine-festooned patios, and Basin Street jazz. In a sense she is the living heart of the Deep South, yet in many ways she is hardly as Southern as Evansville, Indiana.

She is, in short, New Orleans.

CHAPTER I

Empire and the French

WHEN La Salle, in the inscription on his leaden plate, used the phrase "from the village of the Illinois," he was probably not referring to any exact spot in that part of the American continent. For Illinois to the early French meant that vast area of land which lies north of the mouth of the Ohio River and on both sides of the Mississippi. In all their explorations the French naturally followed the lines of least resistance, that is, the waterways, and in time they came to have a very fair knowledge of the main streams in the Mississippi Valley. But from necessity they often had very vague notions of what lay beyond the banks of the streams, and thus the area called Illinois was ill-defined. Nevertheless, this Illinois country was important in the French scheme of things. It was the keystone of the great arch which was to stretch, and for a time did, from the mouth of the St. Lawrence to the mouth of the Mississippi. And to insure it Fort Chartres, on the east bank of the Mississippi below the site of present St. Louis, was built. Next to the Citadel at Quebec, Chartres was planned to be the strongest fortification in the Western Hemisphere, and it was in the very heart of the Illinois country, the center of the keystone.

All this, of course, was long after the time of La Salle, but his work in the Mississippi Valley was largely responsible for these later plans. And it is worth mentioning in passing that as plans there was nothing wrong with these. Indeed in the New World neither the Spanish nor the British ever planned so all-inclusively or with such foresight. The eventual failure of these plans, and the gradual loss of all French holdings in America, was largely due to inept colonial administration in France; it was seldom the fault of the men on the ground here. A great many of the latter knew what had to be done in order to preserve French gains, and, let alone, would probably have done it. But traditional obedience to the crown and its delegates in authority was also strong with them, and in the long run that tradition, plus ineptitude and the, at that time, more important European political horse-trading, eventually finished them for good and all in the New World.

But when La Salle used the word "Illinois" he unwittingly symbolized the link which in the future, regardless of French losses, would bind the Mississippi Valley to the city of New Orleans; make it the great outlet for which, in that future, men on the Upper Ohio, the Missouri, the Wabash, the Kanawha, and countless other rivers of the Northern valleys would be willing to fight, even though they themselves had never been within a thousand miles of the city.

After his journey to the mouth of the Mississippi, La Salle returned to Canada and from there went on to France with his enthusiastic report. At home he was well received and promised a great deal, but, like most of the men who were really making an effort to establish France in the New World, was actually given little more than encouragement. After a time he again came to Canada and renewed his activities in the great valley, always with the thought of founding a permanent settlement in what would be the best possible spot. He failed, though through circumstances which reasonably can be called no fault of his own. Before he could determine his ideal site he was shot and killed by a soldier in one of his own parties, who had a fancied grievance against the man who had come so far and accomplished so much for France in the New World.

Characteristically enough, the Court of France, represented then in the person of Louis XIV, did little—except perhaps talk—about the matter of Louisiana for some fifteen years.

The connection between the Catholic Church and French exploration in America is a matter for endless and fascinating speculation, though in general the best reason for it was probably the close relationship between the Church and the French crown; that and the fact that the Church was genuinely anxious to extend its spiritual domain and thought of America as a fertile field, as of course it was. (Few will deny that the influence of the priesthood in early America was, in general, anything but good.) However that may be, there was not a French explorer of note—unless it be the luckless Radisson, who was never much in favor at Versailles—whose name is not linked with one or more members of the priesthood. Father Marquette was something of an explorer in his own right, and every schoolboy knows—or should know—the story of Marquette and Joliet. Father Hennepin was another. And La Salle himself, before coming to America for the first time, was a member of the Jesuits; in fact, he failed to inherit property from his parents at their death because he was connected with the Jesuit order and therefore civilly dead.

In his account of the passage of the Mississippi mouth La Salle mentions one Father Zenobio by name, and among the "twenty Frenchmen" there was at least one other priest, a Father Athanase, who accompanied La Salle on his further explorations and later was to return to the Gulf coast.

Dozens of such instances could be cited, but the point is that wherever went the flag of France, there, too, went the cross—and not following the flag but beside it. And at least partially because of that the Church was to have a powerful voice in the affairs of Louisiana and New France as long as the French—and Spanish—ruled politically in any part of America. Whether this was a good or bad thing is not worth arguing here. The point is made only to show an odd, and it may be a revealing, contrast between French and British exploration and settlement in the New World.

In 1698 the French crown, having finished temporarily with the wars in Europe, decided to take up the unfinished business of Louisiana. The first expedition numbered about three hundred souls—one company of marines, about two hundred alleged settlers, most of whom had lately been mustered out of the Canadian service, and some women and children. The party sailed from France in two ships, the whole under the command of Pierre le Moyne, Sieur d'Iberville.

Iberville was one of the brothers Le Moyne, had commanded troops successfully in Canada, and had volunteered to take up the work La Salle had been forced to abandon. Three more of the Le Moynes were to figure in the affairs of Louisiana: Sauvolle and Bienville, who came with Iberville on this first journey, and Chauteague. Bienville, at the time a midshipman of perhaps twenty, was cast in the same character mold as La Salle and was to live and serve Louisiana much longer than any of his brothers.

Also accompanying this first expedition was that same Father Athanase, member of the Recollects, who had been with La Salle; and he probably served as guide as well as spiritual confessor.

Having touched at the Spanish settlement of Pensacola, at Cat Island and the Chandeleurs, the two ships anchored at Ship Island in the Bay of Biloxi in February of 1699. As soon as temporary shelters were erected, Iberville, Bienville, Father Athanase, and a party set out in search of the Mississippi. Coming on the great river—a blind man could hardly miss it—they met Indians who had relics of La Salle. Iberville, in spite of Father Athanase's insistence, was not quite convinced that this was the Mississippi, but he was satisfied when the Indians further exhibited a letter composed by Tonti and a prayer book in which another of La Salle's men had written.

Thus having "discovered" the Mississippi for the second

time—or fourth if you count De Soto and De Pineda—Iberville
sent Bienville to make the passage of the river to the Gulf,
while he himself turned in the other direction and discovered
Lakes Maurepas and Pontchartrain—which he named, and
the Rigolets, the narrow gut of water which ties Lake Pontchartrain to Lake Borgne and thus to the Gulf itself.

Shortly thereafter both parties successfully returned to
Ship-Island, and it was decided that a more or less permanent
settlement be made on the shore of Biloxi Bay, near the mouth
of the Mobile River. Why here, rather than somewhere on
the Mississippi, the record does not make clear; but here it
was. (Probably the chief reasons were solid land and its prox-
imity to the Gulf and the open sea, for Bienville had traversed
the hundred-odd miles down-river from Pontchartrain to the
Gulf and so knew how non-existent high land, even *dry* land,
was in the Delta.)

A fort of sorts was erected and cannon mounted, and in
May Iberville sailed for France to report progress.

These first colonists were a hardened, toughened lot in the
sense that almost all had seen service in the French armed
forces, either in Canada or on the Continent, and such service
in itself was a hardening process. They had to be tough in
order to survive at all, and no doubt their womenfolk were
comparable. But they were not thieves, cutthroats, and pimps
as were so many of the founders of the first families of
Louisiana who arrived during the next three decades. No
doubt some of them were only one step ahead of the jailer,
but certainly by no means even a majority of them were. As
colonists in a new and almost unknown land they had faults in
plenty. They were not only unskilled but lazy as well and
had no intention of providing for themselves by working—
at least not as long as the French government was willing to
supply them from home. They were willing to pick up what
wealth might be lying about on the ground, but that was
about the extent of their ambition. Thus their failings in some
ways were many, but by and large they were not criminals.

The Port of New Orleans

In December, Iberville returned from France, bringing appointments for his brother Sauvolle as governor of the province, and for Bienville as lieutenant governor. Informed by Bienville of Captain Bar's late visit to the Mississippi, Iberville thought it best to establish still another settlement on the great river itself, so there would be no argument about prior claims should the British again attempt to move in. Accordingly, Fort Iberville was built some miles below English Turn, and a garrison installed there under the command of Bienville. Thus the first real French settlement on the Lower Mississippi. It is a lonely enough place even now; in the year 1700 it must have been one of the most isolated spots in the entire Western Hemisphere.

The settlements on Biloxi Bay—a few people still remained on Ship Island—were located on what was unquestionably the most sterile land on the entire Gulf coast, but apparently that was quite satisfactory with all concerned. They weren't there for agricultural purposes anyway, so what did the land matter? Rather the colonists dallied with schemes for hunting gold and silver which wasn't there; a plan to domesticate buffaloes and raise them for their *wool;* and searching for pearls and precious stones which also were non-existent. All of which, obviously, got them exactly nowhere economically.

Sauvolle died in 1701 and was automatically succeeded by Bienville, who, in spite of natural sorrow at his brother's death, was undoubtedly glad to get away from the watery isolation of Fort Iberville. He was to continue as governor, and a good one considering all the troubles he had to deal with, until 1713. In the meantime he was to spend months and years in exploring the Mississippi and its endless tributaries, in making friends with the innumerable Indian tribes and acting as referee in their continual disputes among themselves, and in keeping his own people in some sort of order. In many ways the tangible results of Bienville's first twelve years as governor were almost nil, yet the fact that he survived at all is a tribute to his stamina and leadership.

Empire and the French

More than once, when supply ships failed to arrive from France, the colonists were on the verge of starvation—in a land potentially overflowing with plenty. As rainy season followed rainy season they learned to expect the appalling and never-failing floods that erased old landmarks and sometimes changed the face of the country almost overnight. From its earliest beginnings Louisiana understood what a transportation blessing its waterways were—the present state of Louisiana has just under 5,000 miles of navigable waters—but certainly the blessing was not unmixed. The Indians were in a continuous state of war somewhere, though for the most part not with the French, and disease periodically ravaged the settlements. Sauvolle's death occurred in the summer of 1701 and the following autumn about half the colony perished of disease in one form or another. Iberville, the eldest of the Le Moyne brothers, died of yellow fever, that scourge of the tropics, in San Domingo in 1704, and thus young Bienville had his private sorrows as well as his public troubles.

The death of his two brothers in so short a period could have made Bienville hate the New World, but he did not. Death in far places seldom leaves men with a neutral feeling. Either they despise the place and want no more of it or determine to stay and make it pay for the loss, and Bienville chose the latter course.

When floodwaters inundated the settlement on the shore of Biloxi Bay, the village was moved to the west bank of the Mobile River, farther upstream, though a small garrison was maintained at the old site. At about the same time another settlement was made on Massacre (later Dauphine) Island. Thus within a comparatively few years the French had founded five settlements on the Gulf coast and the Mississippi, apparently to no good purpose whatever. The colonists divided their resources and energies, spent days and weeks of valuable time in merely communicating with each other, and in general accomplished little beyond a precarious existence.

At least part of this decentralization, however, was the fault of the government in France, which thought to extend its authority by creating as many points of settlement as possible. Bienville and the others could do little about this policy except follow orders as best they might.

It was ten years after the French settlement of the Gulf coast when the first non-French vessel arrived to trade with the colony. A Spaniard from Havana put in with a cargo of provisions, brandy, and tobacco. Thereafter there was a smattering of trade with the Islands, mostly San Domingo and Martinique, and with the Spanish in West Florida—but it never amounted to a great deal in this period. By this time, too, a certain amount of fur came down from the Ohio Valley, to pass through the hands of traders in the Gulf settlements. There were French traders in the Ohio Valley who found the Gulf coast more convenient than the stations on the Great Lakes, and doubtless, too, some of them had personal reasons for avoiding the Northern posts.

Too, wandering French traders, priests, and missionaries maintained more or less continuous contact between Louisiana and Canada. Their journeyings were sporadic and irregular, but someone was always moving up or down the Mississippi, passing word-of-mouth communication all along the far-flung line from Quebec to Head of Passes. There was always the sea traffic between the Gulf settlements, France, and the Caribbean Islands, so Louisiana was lonely but hardly isolated.

The Church saw to it that the spiritual needs of the colonists were well taken care of, new priests being sent out at fairly frequent intervals, and the government looked after practically everything else.

It was about the middle of this first decade that the earliest shipment of "twenty-three poor girls," otherwise inmates of the houses of correction in Paris, was sent to the colony. That they found husbands, almost before they could get ashore, goes without saying, and the Church, possibly looking to the future reputation of the first families of Louisiana, made certain that the marriages were consummated legally as well as otherwise, if not immediately then as soon as possible.

Many a comment, ribald and otherwise, has been made about these girls transported by the French government, but it is difficult to resist still another. It seems that shipment of these girls—and this, at this late date, is by no means an evaluation of their collective character; they *may* have been misjudged—is a lucid commentary on what the French government thought of its colonists. In other words, they were sent what they were thought to deserve.

Thus in 1712, some thirteen years after its first settlement, the province of Louisiana had a population of less than four hundred, including some twenty Negroes and the clergy, scattered in several tiny hamlets. Their buildings were little more than hovels; they were alternately stricken by disease and hunger; they had no commerce or agriculture worth mentioning; and their morals were no better than might have been expected.

Yet lest the human picture seem too one-sided, consider some of the contributing circumstances. The climate was unhealthful, as it more or less continued to be for over a century and a half. The swampy land with its stagnant waters, continual floods, and millions of snakes and alligators, was something totally outside the experience of the average European. With the exception of the knowledge of the country picked up from friendly Indians, they had to learn everything from scratch—and there was a great deal to learn about living in Louisiana. The Indians fought continually among themselves, and occasionally with the French, and once during this thirteen-year period Dauphine Island was raided by a privateer from Jamaica. Furthermore, the colonists, in their general activities, were but following the orders of the French crown.

So perhaps the scales were not so far out of balance after all. Given time, the French would manage—and did. Of all the Europeans in America they got on best with the Indians—

with the possible exception of the Quakers, who, after all, were a religious sect and not a nationality. And, above all, the French were adaptable—as witness the fact that they peopled both the northern and southern extremes of the North American continent.

CHAPTER II

Louisiana Becomes a Business

BY 1712 it was evident even to the French government that
Louisiana as an investment in colonization was producing
nothing but red ink, and accordingly it was decided something should be done about it.

The solution for the time being seemed to lie in the proposition of one Anthony Crozat, who had a high opinion of
Louisiana in spite of the fact that he had never seen it. So the
colonial administration made a contract with Crozat, under
the terms of which he was in effect to take over the province
of Louisiana lock, stock, and barrel. This contract, with
certain reservations, was to remain in force for a period of
fifteen years. In general Crozat was granted the sole right to
all commerce in Louisiana; only he, or his agents, could export
goods from France to the colony, carry on trade with the
Indians, mine precious metals, and till the soil for profit, import Negroes into the colony as slaves, and carry on shipping.
In short, all the presumably profitable business of Louisiana
was given into his hands. Government in general was to be
administered by the king's officers, but they were to co-operate with Crozat's agents in every possible way—which meant
in practice that even government would be administered in
the interests of Crozat. The Church only was to retain its cur-

rent status, there being no apparent profit in that direction. Crozat was to have the use of all physical property then owned by the crown in Louisiana. In addition the cost of supporting the king's officers and garrison, fixed at ten thousand dollars per annum, was to be paid directly to Crozat in France, he to pay in goods, at a profit, in the colony. This last provision, however, was to expire at the end of nine years, after which time Crozat was to assume this expense himself. In return for all this Crozat was to pay the French crown a set portion of all gold, silver, other precious metals and stones recovered in the colony through his efforts.

On the surface this appeared to be a sort of dream grant, a proposition in which everything was in favor of the grantee, with practically no strings attached; it looked as though he couldn't possibly lose. But Crozat didn't know Louisiana. It turned out that he could, and did, lose a considerable fortune.

La Mothe Cadillac, whose name is well known in the annals of Canada, was selected to manage Crozat's affairs in the colony, thus to all intents and purposes succeeding Bienville as governor, though the latter remained as head of those who were still directly in the king's service. Naturally Bienville did not relish the apparent demotion, and his displacement was volubly resented by the other colonists, but he himself seems to have accepted the situation with good grace.

Crozat was a businessman and made no pretense of thinking of the colony as anything other than a business enterprise. He wanted the colony to prosper and was willing to do all he could to see that it did, but he was whipped almost before he began.

In the first place, he expected to do a considerable business with the Spanish ports—Pensacola, Havana, Tampico, and Vera Cruz—as he knew the colonists had had some traffic with these places in the past. He planned to retain this trade and enlarge it, but other people thought otherwise. At the solicitation of the British, out to thwart the projects of the French wherever possible, these ports were closed to Crozat by the Spanish. Thus the first blow to his expectations.

Mining, of course, was another project dear to the hearts of Crozat and Cadillac, and the latter was elated when a man named Dutigne arrived from Canada, bringing with him samples of fine silver ore which he said had been found near Kaskaskia, the French settlement near the later site of Fort Chartres on the Upper Mississippi. With much secrecy Cadillac and a small party set out on the long journey up the river. Arriving at Kaskaskia, he discovered that his ore samples, while undoubtedly silver, had merely been left as curiosities by a Spaniard who was passing through the region. Cadillac's chagrin must have been monumental, and there was little more said about silver mining during his remaining stay on the Gulf coast.

During this period the Indian alarums and excursions were practically continuous, and Bienville had his hands full in that direction. And as time moved on the bad feeling between Bienville and Cadillac did not abate. Crozat's own force in Louisiana, that is men primarily loyal to his interests, was small. The balance of the population was exactly as it had been before, had little personal interest in Crozat's affairs, and insisted on regarding Bienville as their leader in spite of the fact that Crozat's orders read otherwise. Probably Cadillac's exasperation was natural enough in the circumstances, but the situation didn't make for harmony in general.

About this time, too, a vessel from Martinique and one from La Rochelle arrived at Dauphine Island to trade, but under the terms of Crozat's charter neither of them was allowed to land goods—another example of how commerce in the colony was being hamstrung by the existing arrangement.

Cadillac, under urgent orders from Crozat, made every attempt to trade with the Spanish, by land to the west as well as by sea, but was completely unsuccessful. Apparently the Spanish preferred to do without rather than do business with the French under the circumstances. But the final straw was a cargo of luxury goods that was sent to Vera Cruz in the mistaken belief that it would, at last, be allowed to land. Cadillac had reason to believe it would be. But the Spanish answer was still a cold and emphatic "No." This cargo was said to be worth two hundred thousand dollars at cost in France, and there was nothing to do but return it to Biloxi Bay. There it was turned over to Crozat's employees and the soldiery in lieu of considerable sums of money owed them by Crozat, though the merchandise was undoubtedly better suited to Regency châteaus in France than the rude hovels of Louisiana. The resultant outcry was great, but Crozat's aggregate losses for the five-year period were even greater, and this last bad bargain was all he could stand. Thus in August of 1717 he surrendered his charter, probably heaving a mighty sigh of relief when government allowed him to retreat from his obligations so easily.

In the meantime Bienville had erected Fort Rosalie at Natchez on the Mississippi and Fort Toulouse inland above Lake Maurepas, had been made a Knight of the Order of St. Louis, and vastly increased his prestige among Indians and colonists alike. Through the efforts of Crozat and his associates the population of the province had increased to about seven hundred, including all ages, sexes, and colors, but the general status of trade and agriculture was almost unchanged—that is, there was very little of either.

In September, after Crozat's release, Louisiana was rechartered to the party known variously as the Western Company, the Mississippi Company, and the Compagnie des Indes. The terms of the charter were similar to Crozat's, though even broader in scope, and was to run for twenty-five years, during which period the company specifically engaged to bring in six thousand whites and three thousand Negroes.

There was, however, one important difference between this venture and Crozat's. The latter had operated as a private individual, whereas the Western Company was a corporation, authorized to issue an *unlimited* amount of stock. The shares had a par value of about one hundred dollars and were offered for sale to aliens as well as French citizens.

In spite of Crozat's obvious failure there seemed to be a vast number of people in Europe who were still eager to believe and invest in the future of Louisiana—and not a few of them were small people, as always hunting a safe place to invest their small savings. On the whole, the affairs of the company were managed prudently enough until that celebrated Scots blue-sky promoter, John Law, began to spread out and got a foothold in the basic financial affairs of France. Whereupon the shares of the Western Company really boomed—a few shares were supposed to make one rich almost overnight. The truth was that the Western Company merely happened to be a useful pawn in the game of speculation; almost any other investment attractive to the imagination would have done as well. Fortunes were made and lost—on paper—overnight, and the eventual result was the collapse of the so-called Mississippi Bubble, and with it the whole financial structure of France; a collapse whose effects were felt over half of Europe. All this, of course, was to occur in the future. But oddly enough Louisiana itself, the original inspiration for the Bubble, was not greatly affected by its bursting. The wild speculation, the buying and selling, and the tumult and shouting, occurred elsewhere, and when it was all over the land and people of Louisiana were there just as before.

When the Western Company's first three ships arrived on the Gulf coast in February 1718, bringing three companies of infantry and sixty-odd new colonists, they also carried Bienville's reappointment as governor—which was no bad start for the company, since the population in general was as well pleased as Bienville himself.

The company knew from Crozat's experience that there was little to be gained from mining or expected trade with the Spanish, and accordingly an attempt was made to establish an agriculture. To further this plan large grants of land, on both sides of the Mississippi, were made to various individuals in France, one of the terms being that the grantee furnish enough settlers to operate the land. Grants were also made on other river fronts, and to groups as well as individuals. One of the largest, a tract twelve miles square on the Arkansas River, was given to John Law. So far the intent was good, but the actual practice of agriculture didn't work out well in the beginning. As usual, the settlers shipped by the landed proprietors were mostly of inferior quality—it was at this period that the company began scouring the French prisons and brothels for prospective emigrants—and they couldn't see working hard for masters who were so far away. Furthermore, the climate, in the growing seasons especially, was not conducive to hard work, and the settlers were unfamiliar with the soil and methods of planting. So, as a possible solution to the problem, a year or two later, about 1720, two company ships brought five hundred Negroes from the west coast of Africa and the slave agriculture system was launched in Louisiana.

In the meantime, in 1718, Bienville had determined upon the site of the future Nouvelle Orleans, laid out the rough outlines of a town, cleared some ground, and erected a few crude buildings—including a warehouse for company stores. The place lay on the left bank of the Mississippi at the point where the Indians usually left the river for the portage to the head of Bayou St. John, the stream, or backwater, which flows into Lake Pontchartrain.

Thus New Orleans, as nearly as can be determined, was actually founded in 1718—though the exact year is an arbitrary choice still open to argument. But it was hardly the auspicious affair Orleanians of the present like to believe. In the Cabildo there is a life-size painting of Bienville and his men, Bienville, with a draughtsman at his elbow, laying out the lines of the future city of New Orleans. Presumably the city thereafter sprang into life full blown. It makes a pretty picture but could hardly be farther from the truth. Presumably Bienville did keep a small garrison there from the time of the city's founding, a sort of intermediate post between the Mississippi settlements and those on Biloxi Bay; but it was a number of years before anyone—except Bienville, of course—considered it seriously as a place for permanent settlement. Every other official of the Western Company and the government—and the two were practically synonymous—disliked La Nouvelle Orleans as a site for anything.

France having again declared war on Spain, it was also necessary for Louisiana to go to war against the near-by Spanish settlements. The fact that for some time the French and Spanish settlers on the Gulf coast had been on rather good terms personally and had several times helped each other in emergencies made no difference. Bienville, as governor, was occupied with this senseless business for some months, and the matter of New Orleans had to wait on more important affairs. As far as the Gulf coast was concerned the war lasted but a short time, and as usual ended with no visible net gain for either.

The war over for the time being, Bienville renewed his campaign to move the headquarters of the colony to New Orleans, but again without much success. An inundation of the embryo town by the Mississippi, plus the destruction done by a minor hurricane, gave Bienville's opponents a lever for argument, and the company officers in France were positive in their orders that the permanent headquarters should be fixed on Biloxi Bay, even though they had fostered agricultural projects and Biloxi Bay was the worst possible place for those. Thus outnumbered, Bienville perforce gave way; but he did not—call it vision or what you will—lose sight of New Orleans as an eventual objective.

With the use of slave labor agriculture was looking up, and at intervals more and more blacks were brought in—as were also several more shipments of "poor girls." Most, if not all, of them found husbands, and at any rate none of them had trouble in finding a livelihood. Slave labor apparently proving a remedy for one of the country's ills, the colony's officers requested that no more convicts or "vagabonds" be sent them. The king's council so decreed, but one Louisiana historian remarks dryly that the edict did not include females, so the "poor girls" continued to arrive at intervals for some years.

During this period also some four hundred and fifty German settlers (Alsatians really), in two groups, arrived in the colony, one group having suffered terrible losses by death and disease on the long voyage. The first shipment was destined for Law's grant on the Arkansas, and there they originally went; but eventually they returned to the immediate environs of New Orleans and became a most useful adjunct to the town. They had not the volatile imagination and color of the French and other nationalities, but New Orleans usually had an oversupply of those qualities anyway.

It was about this time, too, that Pauger, an engineer in the employ of the Western Company who is generally credited with the design of original New Orleans, made a general survey of the Lower Mississippi and the passes. His report of this survey to Bienville is more than a little interesting because of a later development in the life of New Orleans and the Mississippi.

Pauger noted, as almost any observant person might, that driftwood from upstream lodged along the riverbanks, accumulated smaller wood and mud, and eventually became land of a sort—land solid enough, at least, to channel the river at ordinary level. (Because of this natural process the banks of the Mississippi, contrary to the habits of most rivers, were almost invariably higher than the land behind them. This was true only in the Delta country, of course, not farther upstream.) Why not, Pauger suggested, aid this process and guide the river along *one* of the passes, then close off the others by sinking old vessels and otherwise damming them? Thus the increased velocity of flow in the one pass would automatically create a clear channel there—for already getting a vessel of any size in and out of the mouths of the big river was a problem. (The Mississippi, incidentally, is the only major river in the world which is narrower in its lower channel than in its upper reaches. The vastly greater depths near its mouths accommodate the increase in volume of flow.) Pauger's theory was a simple application of the laws of hydraulics and was quite correct. Nevertheless, it was more than a hundred and fifty years before James B. Eads controlled the passes with a somewhat modified application of Pauger's idea.

Bienville had repeatedly been at odds with both the local and European officers of the Western Company, and because these others represented the profit interest of the company Bienville was frequently overruled. At least one cause of dissension was the company's insistence that a settlement be made on Atchafalaya Bay or some other likely spot west of the Mississippi and Bienville's consistent opposition to such a plan. He believed that the settlements were too far extended already and campaigned steadily for New Orleans as the logical central location of a permanent settlement.

He was, about 1722, to get his wish—for a number of reasons which are too complicated to go into here. At any rate, the commissioners in France restored him as president of the council—although still governor his disfavor with local company officials had caused his removal from the general governing body of the colony—and directed him to move the principal establishment of the province to New Orleans. He lost no time carrying these new orders into effect—lest someone change his mind again.

The original French city as designed by Pauger—though some authorities give credit to De la Tour—was eleven squares along the river front and six squares deep. It was bounded on the upriver end by Custom House Street; on the lower end by Barracks Street; on the land side by a jungle growth which eventually became Rampart Street; and on the river side by the Quai, or landing ground. Chartres Street was at that time the first thoroughfare away from the river to bear a name, there being one full square between it and the Quai. Each square measured three hundred feet in either direction and was laid off in twelve lots, the lots in general being divided among those residents on the ground. The streets were narrow —they measured thirty-two French feet—and still are, and were laid off in straight lines at right angles to each other. The whole town was surrounded by a moat—later each square was to be so treated for drainage purposes—and a palisade of sharpened poles, though it seems probable that neither the palisade nor the drainage moat was built along the riverside. Unlike most frontier towns of the period, there was apparently no attempt made at real fortification. Probably cannon were mounted along the Quai and in the vicinity of the parade ground called the Place d'Armes, but the palisade apparently served more as a fence than as a defensive wall.

Thus New Orleans, some four years after its actual founding, began to resemble a town of sorts, but in its early beginnings it was a miserable place. The priest, Father Charlevoix, who visited here in the early 1720s, so described it—and Charlevoix was well accustomed to the roughness of frontier settlements in general. He described New Orleans as containing about one hundred rude cabins, "placed without much order," a large wooden warehouse, two or three dwellings which would not have adorned a village—though it is noticeable that he distinguishes between these last and the cabins. There was also a storehouse which had once served as a chapel, though now a rude shed served that purpose—a good indication all around that the business of the Western Company was the most important in the colony; indeed at the moment it *was* the colony.

This statement too pretty well disposes of the grandiose words attributed to Bienville at the time of the founding of the city: "Here, we shall build the church. Here, the seat of government"—apparently the buildings uppermost in his mind; or at least the ones uppermost in the minds of future chroniclers of the event. One wonders a little, though, at Charlevoix's statement that the cabins were "placed without much order." For the town was laid out in orderly squares from the beginning and a map made in 1728, a few years later, indicates that almost all the buildings fronted neatly on the streets. This map leaves a definite impression of order everywhere in the town, though of course it is possible that the cartographer was mainly interested in doing a neat job on his map. However, original New Orleans did have one characteristic which was utterly different from any other town of its time in America. As the population increased, however slowly, it showed no tendency to expand outward, whereas most American towns spread all over the landscape if given a chance. The American wanted elbow room and breathing space, even though it was only in the area immediately about his own dwelling. But the French were gregarious and content to fill up the vacant spaces in their original town. It may have been that the town with all its discomforts was preferable to the jungle which lay just outside the original town limits; or perhaps this was an example of French logic: there was room enough in the town and the town was made for living—why then go outside it? At any rate, it was years before the population spilled over the limits of the original city.

The town was subject to regular floods spring and fall and sometimes in between seasons. Just outside the palisade, and frequently inside it, were multitudes of rattlesnakes, alligators, and croaking frogs of gigantic stature. Yellow fever was a frequent visitor and malaria as common as a bad cold, perhaps more so. The heat in summer was tropical and enervating, and in winter the damp cold struck to the very marrow. Geographically, it was one hundred and ten miles upriver from the sea. Still, the town was a reality and a beginning had been made; those were the important things.

CHAPTER III

The Western Company also Fails

THE FIVE-YEAR PERIOD between 1725 and 1730 was the busiest and most eventful New Orleans had seen to date and there was certainly no lack of excitement, though not all of it was pleasant. (It has been said that the history of New Orleans and Louisiana, like that of Paris and France, is synonymous, and as a generality the statement is true enough, for certainly the first century and a half of Louisiana's history revolved about New Orleans.)

Agriculture was gaining a slow foothold in the colony, and there were attempts to cultivate rice, indigo, figs, tobacco, and oranges—all with somewhat indifferent success. The Western Company, in spite of its hedging in other directions, still believed there were precious metals to be had somewhere in its vast domain, and in truth there were, though not the sort the French had in mind. At any rate, the company still sent out parties of miners and they prospected far up the Mississippi and into the valleys of the Missouri and Illinois rivers. Of course they found no ores of consequence, but the excursions provided the French with an increasing geographical knowledge of the great valley.

During this period, too, the company commissioners in France had a regular orgy of legislating for the supposed

The Western Company also Fails

benefit of the colony. They fixed the prices of commodities, including rice, tobacco, brandy, wine, and Negroes, and made rules and regulations for almost every possible move of the colonists. A copper coinage was created and made legal tender in the stores of the company, and Bienville promulgated a Black Code—patterned after the *Code Noir* of San Domingo—for the strict regulation of the growing slave population. Since nearly all of the slaves were at most only a few years removed from the African jungles it is probable that, assuming the necessity of slavery as an institution, strict regulation was really necessary. And while penalties for breaking any provisions of the Black Code, especially those dealing with personal relations between blacks and whites, were severe, the blacks in turn were protected from undue oppression, to a certain extent and for a while, on the part of their white—or black!—masters.

From the beginning Negro slavery in New Orleans and Louisiana had curious features that endured until the Civil War and did not entirely disappear until long after that. Almost from the beginning of slavery as an institution in Louisiana, there had been free Negroes. Many of them achieved their free status for reasons purely charitable or humanitarian, but the vast majority of them were free solely because of their white blood. There was only one way the offspring of a black could acquire white blood, and while it is usually assumed that this white blood came from the staff side, such was not always the case—to assume as much would be to assume a very large miracle indeed. Of course this phenomenon was more or less true of all the slave South, as it was true also of all the Caribbean islands, but nowhere else in the United States did it ever reach such astounding proportions as in New Orleans. At the beginning of the Civil War there were in New Orleans no less than ten thousand of these "free people of color," who were neither slaves nor citizens in the ordinary sense, and it was necessary, in the years between the Louisiana Purchase and the Civil War, to compile a whole set of laws for their benefit, or, more properly, their regulation. Had it not been for the upheaval of the Civil War, there is no knowing to what social state the situation might have eventually led. It was commonplace for *free* blacks to own slaves of their own, and a curious law provided terms under which these same free blacks could voluntarily become slaves to either white or black masters.

Not a part of the Black Code but a product of the same wave of legislation were the laws expelling all Jews and forbidding their future residence in the colony. With the exception of a few favored Jews who later flourished under the Spanish regime, the race was excluded from the province until after the coming of the Americans in 1803. Probably these anti-Jewish edicts had their roots in religion, since during both the French and Spanish occupation the practice of any but the Catholic religion was strictly forbidden by law—and Catholicism and Judaism were more fundamentally opposed than Catholicism and many other faiths.

Nor were the practical details of Catholicism neglected.

About this time a division of religious authority was made, and it lasted until long after the Western Company had been forgotten. The ministry from the mouth of the Mississippi to the Illinois country was entrusted to the Capuchins. The Carmelites were given the districts east and northeast of New Orleans, and farther north in the Illinois country, including the Wabash and Lower Great Lakes regions, the Jesuits were supreme in spiritual authority.

The company further undertook to underwrite much of the Church's expense in the colony. Churches, chapels, and dwellings were provided for the use of the clergy, plus transportation from France and certain emoluments after their arrival in Louisiana. In return the clergy was to serve the outlying posts as well as the general population and the army, plus the usual missionary work among the Indians. (This work among the tribes was to redound not only to the glory of the Church in general but to the practical benefit of

The Western Company also Fails

the French colonists and the Western Company in particular, and among the Indians it succeeded as well as any such work ever did.)

To the Jesuits, who had a much greater distance to travel in order to reach the scenes of their endeavors, certain property in New Orleans was given. They were granted ten arpents of land on the Mississippi below New Orleans and allowed to acquire slaves on the same terms as the planters and other inhabitants, but they were *not* allowed to perform any ecclesiastical functions locally without special permission from the superior of the Capuchins. In the beginning the Society of Jesus accepted these restrictions gracefully and for them New Orleans was supposed to be only a transfer point on the long road to the Ohio Valley and beyond. But as time passed and New Orleans appeared to need more spiritual firmness than the Capuchins could or would give, the Jesuits couldn't resist taking a hand. The result was a prolonged feud between the two orders which ended only when, in 1764, the Pope's Order of Expulsion banned the Jesuits from all territory controlled by France, Spain, and Naples. But the society was shortly reorganized and before long, and thereafter, wielded more influence than ever in New Orleans.

To provide for the education of a growing population of young females and for the maintenance of the hospital—then as now an important New Orleans institution—an agreement was made in France between the company and the Ursulines of Rouen. Bienville is generally credited with the plan, but it was the company commissioners in France who carried it forward. Three principal Ursuline sisters were involved: Marie Françoise Tranchepain St. Augustine, Mary Ann Le Boulanger St. Angelique, and Mother Catherine Brussoli of St. Armand. These, accompanied by a number of novices and servants, sailed from France in February 1727, in the ship *Gironde*. There are accounts of that voyage which seem to be, and probably are, unbelievable. The ship was supposed to have encountered terrible storms, been attacked by pirates—

during which engagement all the ladies except the nuns donned male attire and helped work the ship—and later went aground at Dauphine Island, where the *Gironde* was forced to jettison most of her cargo. At the mouth of the Mississippi the passengers were, for some reason—possibly northerly winds prevented the *Gironde* from making the entrance of the passes —transferred to pirogues for the balance of the journey to New Orleans, which required fifteen days. Two weeks from the passes to New Orleans, even by pirogue, seems remarkably slow time, but at any rate the trip from France had consumed six months and in the sea transport of the eighteenth century that, with most of the more vivid details omitted, must have been harrowing enough in itself.

On their arrival they were quartered in a house at a corner of Bienville and Chartres streets—probably Bienville's house, as he was once more being relieved as governor and this time was going home to France himself. By 1730 the company had erected suitable convent buildings near the river at the foot of Ursulines Street, where the order maintained its headquarters for some ninety-four years, when it was moved to a new location farther down on the river front. Fortunately the convent was one of the few important buildings spared by the great fire of 1788, when so much of New Orleans as the French had built it was destroyed, and after the Ursulines moved to their new location the older building served for many years more as the seat of the Archbishop of Louisiana. For almost two hundred years the Ursulines were responsible for the operation of Charity Hospital, which has grown from a rude hovel paid for out of the savings of a grateful sailor in 1735 into one of the great hospitals of the South. They set up the first orphanage in the city, after the Natchez massacre in 1729; operated the first New Orleans school for girls; and in general have served the city without too much regard for race, color, or political persuasion.

In the meantime John Law's fantastic career in France had come to a close with the crash of the Mississippi Bubble, and

The Western Company also Fails

France once more faced temporary financial ruin. It was neither the first time nor the last that some John Law, Scot or Frenchman, was to get France into the same kind of trouble. Of course the Western Company, like the rest of France, was in serious financial straits, but it still had tangible assets, Louisiana itself if nothing else, and so continued to function. With the crash came the inevitable shake-up in personnel and in this same year, 1727, one Périer, a lieutenant in the French navy, was named to replace Bienville as governor. He arrived in the autumn and Bienville left for France almost immediately.

Perhaps Bienville was glad to go. He was far from being an old man and yet he had spent some thirty years of his active life in Louisiana. He had seen his brothers die here in the same service, and certainly he himself must have been one of the few remaining original colonists of Louisiana. Place of disease, hunger, and violent death that it was, he must have become attached to it or he wouldn't have stayed on as he did. Other men had not, and he needn't have.

As governor in Bienville's place Périer seems to have been reasonably successful, and one thing especially stands out in his administration: he built the first flood-protection levees at New Orleans in an attempt to get the city out of the practically continuous mud. (Some historians say that Bienville was responsible for the levee, but the weight of the evidence seems to rest with Périer.) As complete protection for the town the first levees were far from being a success, but they were a beginning and must have been, with the tools available, a very considerable job of work. The city's eleven squares along the river front, including the streets in between, occupied something less than a mile, and Périer's levee was fifty-four hundred feet long. It was a puny bulwark against the mighty power of the Mississippi, which even now causes the U.S. Engineers sleepless nights in spite of the fact that it is leveed from Cairo to below New Orleans and controlled in a dozen other ways as well. And Périer's levee was built almost altogether with men and shovels, for there were very few work animals in the Louisiana of that day. In fact, horses and cattle were so scarce that among the edicts of the company commissioners was one which decreed the death penalty for a person *killing or wounding* the domestic animals of another. So this mile-long levee was no mean undertaking.

New Orleans and Louisiana had other troubles. One of the first bad hurricanes of record struck and the devastation, especially among crops almost ready to harvest, was considerable. But one of the hurricane's effects was an almost perfect example of the old "ill-wind" adage. For while the storm apparently had destroyed the rice crop it had in reality picked it up and replanted it over a wider area, so that the following growing season produced a far more abundant crop than the planters could possibly have made themselves.

Louisiana was learning, too, what inflation, following Law's adventures in French finance, could do to an economy that was none too stable anyway. New Orleans, like all French outposts, was flooded with fiat paper currency, the value of which changed with the arrival of each fresh batch of news from home, and the real value of debts, profits, and losses varied accordingly.

John Law's departure from France—his name is bound to recur frequently in this part of New Orleans' story—meant also that he had abandoned his grants on the Arkansas. No more supplies being forthcoming, most of Law's German settlers came down the Mississippi in a body, petitioning the colony's officers in New Orleans for passage to Europe. Whether the colony was unwilling or unable to furnish them passage is of little consequence now, but passage they didn't get. Instead, most of the Germans accepted small land grants of their own on the Mississippi above New Orleans and turned the fertile land into highly productive truck gardens from which they supplied the needs of the city. Regularly on Saturday nights during the growing seasons they dropped downstream, their pirogues loaded with produce, and at sunrise on Sunday morning spread their wares for sale along the new levee. The famous French Market of today stands almost exactly on the ground where these homesick Alsatians first sold their garden truck. A small garrison was established at the settlement upstream and it was soon known as the German Coast. In time most of these Alsatians, through intermarriage and lack of further German immigration, lost most of their racial identity, but their original settlement is still known as the German Coast of New Orleans.

Up to this time the French had in general been on good terms with most of the Indian tribes of the great valley, the one consistent exception being the Chickasaws. Of course there had. been occasional friction with other tribes but these breaches had soon been healed. But not so with the Chickasaws. They simply wanted no part of the French or any other whites and never made any bones about their feelings in the matter.

Now the Chickasaws, with a plan not unlike the later Conspiracy of Pontiac among the Great Lakes tribes, determined to wipe out Louisiana before it could become still stronger. Accordingly, they connived with what other tribes they could trust and managed to hide their plans from those other tribes which were almost certain to be pro-French. If the plan had been strictly adhered to the tribes might well have devastated Louisiana completely. But the Indians had almost always been poor allies of each other, and in this instance one of the belligerent tribes, the Natchez, attacked too soon, having been provoked by the stupid conduct of the French commandant at Fort Rosalie in the Natchez country. Even so, too soon or not, some two hundred Frenchmen were killed and about two hundred and fifty women and children made prisoners. The Indians did not, however, molest any of the slaves in the settlements, and some effort was made to induce them to join the warring tribes against the whites.

Of course the massacre was a terrible blow to the province at large, and when a half-starved refugee reached New Orleans with news of it Périer at once sent a ship to France for aid. In the meantime he gathered his own scattered troops and their Indian allies and prepared to do what he could against the attacking tribes, though he doubted he had the strength to deal with what appeared to be a general uprising.

Fresh troops were sent from France, though it was six long months after the beginning of hostilities when they arrived, and then they were fewer than Périer had hoped for. The fighting and slaughter continued in one place and another—though New Orleans itself was never attacked—for more than two years. At the end of that time the Indians were temporarily checked rather than vanquished, and the cost to the colony and the Western Company in men, money, and munitions was very great. For a time New Orleans swarmed with the widows and orphans of men lost in distant fighting, and this, too, was a heavy burden on a people already none too well off.

So in the end the experience of the Western Company was almost what Crozat's had been: they simply couldn't get a profit out of Louisiana, try as they would. The immediate excuse was the Natchez massacre and the Indian wars that followed, though these events probably served merely to hasten the end. The company had not made money in Louisiana and now was a good time to admit it. At any rate, the company surrendered its charter in January of 1732, after some fourteen years of effort in Louisiana. Thereupon all company property again reverted to the crown and, politically at least, the colony was about where it had been thirty years earlier.

But not quite. For one thing, the population, while still not large, had increased greatly. In spite of disease, war, desertions from the army, and natural deaths, the population had grown to some five thousand whites and two thousand Negroes. The increase during the Western Company's tenure had been about 1,000 per cent; few other settlements in America could boast of a like increase during the same period.

Furthermore, the physical property had increased accordingly. Provision had been made for regular court administration and a code of laws established. The Church had an efficient organization which, while not large, was capable of expanding indefinitely as the need arose. There was trade, limited but still operating, in rice, indigo, tobacco, furs of all kinds, and some lumber, plentiful in Louisiana, for the Caribbean islands.

It has been said that, while the Western Company eventually failed, Louisiana as a whole made more real progress during its regime than at any other period of the French occupation. Comparatively speaking, that may be true, although such generalities are usually only partly valid. It does seem true that the company left the colony with most of the basic elements of future prosperity—except perhaps the drive and enterprise necessary on the part of the population as a whole. Those qualities they almost never had to the extent which characterized the folk in New England and the Middle Atlantic colonies of the British. One answer is to blame the climate—and the slave system induced by the climate—though probably there were many other factors equally important.

As a matter of policy, and a pretty good one at that, Negro slaves were not molested by the Indians either during the Natchez massacre or afterward. A good many were taken "prisoner" by the Indians, or released from their previous captivity; it all depends on the point of view. In many ways the Negroes, most of them not more than a few years away from the jungle, must have been psychologically closer to the Indians than to the whites, and the Indians made strong efforts to enlist the Negroes as allies—a sort of "What-can-you-lose-but-your-chains?" theory. Such an alliance seemed logical, yet there was a link of understanding missing somewhere, and no Negro-Indian coalition was ever successful in America. One such attempt was made on New Orleans during the troubles of the early 1730s, but as far as successful revolt was concerned it came to nothing. Some of the stronger spirits among the captured—or released—Negroes planned an uprising of the plantation gangs along the river above New Orleans. But a Negro woman revealed the plot to French authority and the black ringleaders—four men and a woman—were executed promptly and their heads mounted on poles at the principal entrances to New Orleans. The punishment may have been severe but it was also effective, and it was a long time before the city again worried about black violence.

The surrender of the Western Company's charter and the continued Indian troubles made Louisiana's general situation more precarious than ever. Since Périer had been more or less the Western Company's man, and because he had failed dismally against the warring Indians, his recall was almost inevitable. And in his place it was only natural that government, once more responsible for the colony, should turn again to Bienville, the one man in France who might possibly be able to manage a chaotic Louisiana.

So Bienville the veteran was in 1733 to return for another ten years as governor—and in the end he probably wished he had let well enough alone. He inherited the Indian troubles, among other things, from Périer, and seems to have lost his own original prowess with the tribes—or perhaps the Indians, some of them at least, had learned that the whites were not necessarily invincible. At any rate, about the best Bienville could do with the tribes during his last period as governor was a draw.

The Indian troubles tended to make New Orleans a more important center of population, and Bienville found the city more disorderly and harder than ever to control. The convict and criminal element brought in by the Western Company hadn't changed its character in the least; in fact, it was just coming into its natural element and beginning to give New Orleans a violent coloration that it was never to lose altogether.

New Orleans in the 1730s was already well on its way to acquiring the collective character which in time was to make it famous—or infamous—in all the Seven Seas. In the first place, it was the southern sea outlet for the French Empire in North

The Western Company also Fails

America. As a seaport it was oddly and illy situated, but port it was and is. And the life which flowed into it from the Caribbean islands and from the North was picturesque and colorful. It had at once a ready-made underworld and a powerful religious organization; a well-established Negro slavery, a very poor and a wealthy class, for in spite of the fact that Crozat and the Western Company had been supposed to control all trade in the colony, as usual a number of individuals had contrived to do very well by themselves. Also it was beginning to acquire a heterogeneous floating population which is so characteristic of seaports that are both old and geographically important. Furthermore, its government had been of a military character, alternately harsh in the extreme, corrupt, or hopelessly inefficient in the small matters which help a society function evenly. It was a miniature city of strange contrasts, with the possibilities for future good and evil about even. Already the subtle delicacies and extreme violences of French and Spanish temperament existed side by side, and were more or less taken for granted.

Soldiers, courtesans, the clergy, *voyageurs* from the wilderness valleys, sailors from every port in the Caribbean, slaves of all hues, Indians, mad dogs, alligators, and bullfrogs were equally commonplace sights in the muddy sewers which passed as streets. Aristocrats from the allegedly best families in France rubbed shoulders with recent graduates of the Paris jails and brothels and black savages but a few months from the Ivory Coast. There was no middle or artisan class and neither Boston, New York, Baltimore, nor Charleston could boast such a polyglot population.

In short, New Orleans almost from the beginning possessed all the elements which in time would make her sister city to Marseilles, Shanghai, and all the other bawdy and corrupt anchorages of the oceans.

CHAPTER IV

Pomp in the Wilderness

BY 1743, ten years after his last return to New Orleans, Bienville was ready to quit for good. He had spent forty years of his life in the swamps of his adopted country and the final ten years had been, for him, by far the worst of the lot. New Orleans had been indifferent toward his efforts during this last decade and his enemies—he'd always had them—had done what they could to discredit him; the colonial administration at home had followed few or none of his suggestions for improvement of the province; and his ill success with the Indians persisted. Manifestly his failures during this last period were not all his fault, but he naturally received the blame, and his lengthy explanations were considered little more than lame excuses for his shortcomings. Most colonial administrations have short memories, and that of France was never an exception.

Getting on in years—he was now sixty-five—and realizing that as governor he was doing less than well, Bienville asked to be relieved. The French government showed its feeling in the matter by honoring his request promptly. And while he never again returned to New Orleans, Bienville was to live long and before his death was once more to figure in the affairs of his adopted city, though to no good purpose.

Pomp in the Wilderness

Bienville was succeeded as governor by Pierre Rigaut, Marquis de Vaudreuil, and with his coming New Orleans entered upon a new phase of her already gaudy existence.

While it is true that the activities of the Western Company increased the total population of Louisiana, it is also true that after the withdrawal of the company the population decreased. But this decrease was most noticeable in the outlying sections of the province, where the Indian depredations had been worst, and the population of New Orleans increased accordingly. The already cited Indian troubles were responsible for some of this increase, but there was also another reason of importance. The company had managed to keep its ex-convicts and thugs somewhat scattered, but when the company withdrew these elements naturally and immediately gravitated toward New Orleans. Many of them had been denied the gregarious pleasures of a metropolis too long and proceeded to let off steam.

Thus when the Marquis de Vaudreuil took over he received an especially choice selection of citizens—which didn't worry him in the least. In fact, from the record one can almost say with certainty that for most of his purposes De Vaudreuil got exactly the kind of citizenry he would have taken by choice—for a corrupt citizenry is naturally the kind most easily plundered and manipulated by a corrupt government.

De Vaudreuil—and according to contemporary accounts his lady as well—was a fascinating scoundrel with just enough good qualities to make him believable. Son of a former Canadian governor general and member of one of France's most powerful families, the marquis apparently believed that colonial government existed solely for the personal enrichment of people like himself. (Though, after all, Louisiana *had* been operated as a profit-making enterprise before and so Vaudreuil wasn't being original. The only difference was that with him it was mostly all profit and government was paying the costs.) But he believed, too, that the people should have some compensation, so his first effort was to try to turn New Orleans into a sort of Little Versailles of the Swamps.

The personal establishment of the governor was modeled after the French court and its activities regulated accordingly. Nicety in dress and the small courtesies, complicated manners, and hypocritical moral standards were the order of the day—and incongruous these things must have been against the rude and brawling background of New Orleans. He filled public offices with his relatives, farmed out the privileges and duties of government wherever it was possible to do so at a profit, and by virtue of his office had a hand in a variety of private businesses.

The troops were undisciplined and spent a large part of their time brawling in the unregulated taverns and pothouses. Many of the army officers openly supported mistresses who were more or less forced upon what respectable society there was, and at least one of De Vaudreuil's critics claimed that the marchioness sold narcotics openly from the governor's house, frequently dispensing them herself if her aides weren't available. De Vaudreuil profited largely from deals in supplies for the garrison, and his subordinates tried to see to it that the soldiery did most of their drinking in alehouses profitable to the governor.

Aside from all this the governor quarreled continually with other officials who were more or less honest—or at least claimed to be. One of these was Rouvillière, the Intendant-Commissary, who wrote home long, acrimonious letters concerning De Vaudreuil's conduct. At least some of this may have been a case of the pot and the kettle, for the governor wrote equally bitter letters about the affairs of his Intendant-Commissary.

Regardless of whose fault it was, there was little of either law or order in New Orleans during De Vaudreuil's regime —and after. It has been maintained, and with reason, that the ultimate character of the city was formed during this period, and if that is not altogether true a precedent was certainly set. It was during De Vaudreuil's time, too, that the feud between the Jesuits and Capuchins got well under way, and this also didn't induce the laity to behave any better.

Eventually matters became so bad that even De Vaudreuil was convinced that the situation was getting completely out of hand. Accordingly, in 1751, a stiff set of police regulations was put into effect. Herbert Asbury, however, writes that these regulations were not necessarily for the public good in particular.* They were a form of control, yes, but intended mainly for the use of De Vaudreuil and his cohorts, a club over the heads of those who didn't want to play ball the governor's way. Taverns and houses of ill fame, for instance, were closed by the military—only to reopen as soon as financial arrangements were made with the right people.

The more important of the original and later French settlers were of no great value in creating a social balance between a corrupt government and an equally corrupt lower class. While not necessarily corrupt in the political sense themselves, this Creole stratum—now well into the second generation—was forming the traits which eventually would distinguish them as a class. More than a few of them were becoming wealthy, or at least well to do; but, on the other hand, they were poorly educated if at all, bigoted and intolerant, contemptuous of ideas beyond their own narrow mental horizon, arrogant, and intemperate. They cared nothing for the responsibilities of government and equally little for the welfare of those less fortunate than themselves. Their main interests were sports, gambling, and the maintenance of the social status quo. They were well on their way toward creating that ruling class of the American South whose every action and thought were contrary to all logic, not even excepting its own; a ruling class which has been explained in a hundred ways by both its apologists and its bitterest enemies and still remains to a certain extent an enigma. And while all this is a part of the record, it is only fair to say that most of

*Asbury, Herbert. *The French Quarter*. New York, 1936.

their faults were part and parcel of the accepted social pattern of the time. They considered themselves the elite of Louisiana and there is no reason why their standards of conduct should have been any higher than the examples set by the same elite of France, Britain, and Spain.

Nevertheless, and in spite of the obvious hindrances, there was commerce of a sort in New Orleans. Poorly situated in relation to the sea as it was—especially so considering the motive power of the sea craft of the time—it was, for better or worse, the natural outlet of the great valley. And there were always men in New Orleans who considered trade the most important thing in life, and it is well to remember that New Orleans was but a part of the province of Louisiana, the boundaries of which had never been defined. The great money product of the Upper Mississippi and its tributaries was fur, and that part of it which didn't go out by way of the St. Lawrence had to come down-river to the Gulf. The firm of Maxent, Laclede & Company of New Orleans was given exclusive rights to the fur trade with "the savages of the Missouri," a phrase which gave them plenty of latitude in their trading activities. Pierre Laclede took charge of the business in the field and eventually founded St. Louis. In spite of later changes in government Laclede remained for many years the largest trader in the Missouri area, and the annual fur trade which flowed from St. Louis through New Orleans was estimated at £80,000, no mean sum for the time. New Orleans served as the transfer point, and as such achieved its first commercial importance. Later cotton, rice, indigo, lumber, and food products were to replace fur as the trade staple, but New Orleans continued to take its toll in brokerage, wharfage, and forwarding fees.

It is something of a pity that so much of the city's history must be discussed in terms of the records of governors and generals and other such elite, rather than those of the man in the street; but it is with such as these that most of the contemporary records deal, so the affairs of the lesser folk must be largely inferred.

Thus in 1753 the Marquis de Vaudreuil was relieved as governor by Louis Billouart de Kerlerec, a French naval captain. But it would be a mistake to suppose that De Vaudreuil was removed because of his failures; that would have defied all precedent except in rare cases like that of a comparatively friendless Bienville. As reward for maintaining a corrupt government in Louisiana De Vaudreuil was made governor general of Canada.

Upon his arrival—with the usual entourage of deserving relatives—De Kerlerec gave an expansive party, a sort of greeting to the populace and bon voyage to De Vaudreuil. But this social outburst was his last for a long time. With the departure of De Vaudreuil, Kerlerec was in short order to learn what a nightmare he had inherited. The populace was lawless and dissolute; the garrison—what was left of it— slovenly and unruly; the provincial treasury not only empty but pledged for debt. Furthermore, Kerlerec's new Intendant-Commissary, Rochemore, was of the same stripe as De Vaudreuil and immediately cast his lot with the ex-appointees of the marquis, whom Kerlerec had promptly thrown out of office. As if this were not enough the British were penetrating further into the Ohio Valley and trying to win over the Indians by inciting them against the French border settlements. Kerlerec, an honest and sincere man, was naturally appalled by the situation thus placed in his hands and set about remedying it as well as might be. Of course the harder he tried the less popular he became.

By pledging his salary and personal credit the governor managed to fortify the city after a fashion, but even then he didn't have sufficient troops to man his makeshift fortifications. The bulk of the garrison, bad as it had been, had moved to Canada with De Vaudreuil, and Kerlerec's pleas to France for money and men were for the most part ignored.

In the meantime, in 1755, the Seven Years' War—called in

America the French and Indian War—began, and almost from the beginning the French luck was bad. French empire in the New World, thanks largely to the stupidities of government at home, was on the way out. As a matter of fact, New Orleans was not then threatened in the military sense, but Kerlerec, as a naval man, knew that if and when the Northern provinces fell, the future of Louisiana under France would be worth nothing. New Orleans could never stand against the British navy, and the city was the key to all Louisiana.

Since actual warfare never remotely approached the more settled portions of Louisiana, there was no very strong feeling about the war or its outcome in New Orleans. Weary and defeated Frenchmen from the Northern valleys drifted into the city with their tales of woe, yet Orleanians in general were too busy to worry about such distant affairs. But Kerlerec was aware of what was happening and he must have felt abandoned indeed.

The French and Indian War and its consequences are an important part of the history of the United States, but its immediate effect upon New Orleans is more pertinent here.

Only in comparatively recent years has the fancy diplomacy involved in the transfer of Louisiana from France to Spain—and its later retransfer—been well understood. The ramifications are almost endless but, in brief and with some of the minor details omitted, it was like this:

According to the terms of the French surrender at Montreal in September 1760, Canada and its dependencies were ceded to the British, and within a year all the French posts as far west and southwest as Green Bay were taken over by the British. But the war was not yet over and in Europe, in August 1761, Spain promised to enter the war against England the following May 1762. France, however, needed help at once, not eight months later, and offered Louisiana in return for a loan and quick Spanish participation in the actual fighting. England, suspecting—or more likely knowing of—such a deal, took the lead by declaring war against Spain in January 1762.

Thus Spain was involved whether or no and before she had a chance to reflect.

The outlying possessions of Spain and France were no match for the British navy, and during the summer of 1762 the British took Havana, Martinique, St. Lucia, Granada, St. Vincent, and the Philippines. Under this continued hammering France was soon ready to quit, and as an inducement to such a move again offered Louisiana to Spain—but this time in return for getting *out* of the war. What Louisiana might think of the trade had no bearing on it. Spain agreed—she might as well salvage what she could from the wreckage—and in November 1762 Louisiana was secretly ceded to Spain. "Secretly" is the word commonly used in connection with the transaction, but it seems highly probable that Britain knew exactly what was going on—British Intelligence functioned then as now—and was agreeable. She must have been, for Spain and France were badly defeated and presumably Britain need not have chosen to recognize the validity of the Louisiana cession.

To Spain France gave "all the country known under the name of Louisiana, and also New Orleans with the island on which it stands." To those not familiar with the geography of Louisiana—and that might include a number of people who have lived there all their lives—this mention of New Orleans' "island" may sound a little ambiguous. Actually, the terms of the treaty were a little more specific: The center of the Mississippi River southward to a point in the center of Bayou Manchac—then a navigable stream connecting the Mississippi with Lake Maurepas, a line through the center of Bayou Manchac and thence through Lake Maurepas, Lake Pontchartrain, and the Rigolets to Lake Borgne, this last a freshwater name for an arm of the Gulf—thus was defined the actual eastern boundary of the province of Louisiana. And so bounded, New Orleans literally stands on an island.

Britain, of course, was to have the right of free navigation of the Mississippi, though under these boundary terms the last one hundred and fifty miles of the great river lay entirely within Spanish territory. There always was the bone of contention in the West: free access to the mouths of the Mississippi.

Thus by a deal made over the council tables of Europe, Louisiana, French by birth, tradition, and inclination, became half Spanish, half British, with New Orleans going into the first pot. And while it has long since ceased to be a cause for any sort of mourning, with Louisiana went the last foot of French territory on the American continent.

Ponder now a series of odd things said to be fact. The "secret" cession of Louisiana took place in 1762. The definitive treaty validating the cession was signed in February 1763, and in June of this latter year L'Abadie, for the time being last French governor of Louisiana, arrived to succeed Kerlerec —who, incidentally, was welcomed home by being given a term in the Bastille. Yet the record says that, except for the vaguest of rumors, New Orleans did not learn of its changed status until 1764. It seems more than a little incredible!

Granting that L'Abadie did not know of the secret treaty, he *must* have known of the treaty of February 1763. He arrived at New Orleans in June and, allowing a full three months for the voyage, more than enough time ordinarily, he would have left France in March at the earliest. He did not come to New Orleans alone, so even if *he* didn't know of the Louisiana cession, some of his entourage must have, or his ship's captain, at any rate *someone*, who would have spread the bad news. And if L'Abadie did know, then to all intents and purposes he accepted the governorship of a colony his country no longer owned. Furthermore, all during this period disgruntled Frenchmen, unwilling to live under British or Spanish rule on the Upper Mississippi, were drifting into New Orleans. Even granting that only part of these things were true, how could New Orleans remain so blissfully ignorant? It would be extremely interesting to know where in this diplomatic maze L'Abadie stood, and why.

Pomp in the Wilderness

The news did reach the city fully and officially in 1764, so says the record, and Orleanians discovered they had been Spanish subjects for a year and a half, though they were still being governed by a French officer who had received his appointment only within the last year.

Outwardly the populace was astounded and angered by the news. But, oddly enough, Orleanians were angry neither with the government which had summarily abandoned them nor the one which had inherited them; instead, they denounced the British who had defeated both an arrogant Spain and a fumbling, decadent France.

Yet even before the bad news had officially arrived in 1764 there had been a certain amount of unrest in the city. Perhaps Orleanians sensed something peculiar in L'Abadie's governing—or lack of it—and accordingly a group of prominent merchants and planters petitioned the governor for a little more attention to matters of importance, chiefly commerce. L'Abadie replied by calling them seditious and insubordinate.

It has been somewhat the custom to assume that the New Orleans of the eighteenth century was of little or no commercial and financial importance, that only with the coming of the Americans after the Louisiana Purchase did she really become strong in these fields. In some ways these things were true. New Orleans never claimed to be a southern Boston or Philadelphia. In population she was little more than a village; she was lawless and lewd, badly built architecturally, and always subject to flood and pestilence. Furthermore, her wealthiest citizens did not think of their city as being primarily a commercial center. Yet when all these factors are considered, the extent of her financial and commercial strength was almost remarkable.

For one thing New Orleans always had, and that was the Mississippi River.

In 1763 indigo to the amount of 100,000 pistoles was exported—though that was a makeshift crop which was later almost abandoned commercially. She was also exporting rice, naval stores and lumber, especially cypress products, for cypress was beginning to be recognized as the fine wood that it is. Fur, of course, was always a staple. And all this was managed in spite of the fact that trade was terribly restricted between nations and national possessions. The French did business with the French, the Spanish with the Spanish, and the British wherever there were customers and the British navy.

It was during this period, too, that the Jesuit-Capuchin feud ended with the Order of Expulsion which removed the Jesuits from all territory controlled by France, Spain, and Naples. (Of course the Jesuits were still free to pursue their business in the *former* French territory east of the Mississippi, the territory which had been primarily theirs in any case.) The monks had accumulated a large amount of property in Louisiana, the bulk of it in New Orleans; and at the subsequent forced sale this property brought about $180,000, most of which was confiscated by the colonial government and should have gone far toward bolstering the beleaguered treasury. This forced sale and the amount involved is another commentary on the financial status of the New Orleans of the time. It was significant that the Jesuits could in some forty years accumulate such a property, perhaps even more significant that the New Orleans market could absorb such an offering. Transactions involving such sums, considering the size of the population, were little short of remarkable, for in 1769 the population of the city was officially 3,190, about a third of whom were slaves—or at least colored. Certainly the per capita wealth must have been at an all-time high.

In the meantime New Orleans had become Spanish, technically at least. And yet long after the terms of the treaty and the manner in which the transfer was to be affected were officially made public, Orleanians steadfastly refused to believe their eyes and ears. Such a thing simply *couldn't* be true. All this was merely an elaborate ruse to mask some plan for eventually undoing the dastardly British—and at times it appeared that such might really be the case. But it was true, all of it. As Frenchmen themselves perhaps Orleanians should have known!

CHAPTER V

Comic Opera in Spanish

WHEN GOVERNOR L'ABADIE DIED in 1765 and was succeeded by Charles Aubry, senior captain of the garrison, official transfer of the colony had not been consummated. But official notice of the cession had been given, the transfer presumably would take place eventually, and in the meantime there was little for Aubry to do except mark time. As for local and internal affairs of the colony, the governor had long been assisted in these by a Superior Council made up of local men, and now this group handled such matters almost altogether.

Early in 1765 a mass meeting was held in the Place d'Armes for the purpose of determining certain future conduct of the colony, and it is noteworthy that Orleanians, with certain of the near-by planters, took for granted that they spoke for the entire province. As usual certain merchants and influential planters were the moving spirits, and it was decided to petition the French government for colonial reinstatement. At this distance it seems a little odd that a small group of men in Louisiana, no matter how influential, supposed they could change a territorial agreement already made by France, Britain, and Spain. But there was no harm in trying, and the current status of Louisiana had been determined by a group of men not very much larger, though the comparison is hardly reasonable.

At any rate, a petition to that effect was addressed to the French government and Jean Milhet, a member of the Superior Council and one of the city's leading merchants, was appointed to deliver it in person. Upon Milhet's arrival in France he at once sought the help of Bienville, now in his eighties, and the old man agreed to make one last effort for Louisiana. Absolutely nothing came of this partnership; in fact, they did not even manage to present their case directly to the king, for Bienville had long since been without influence. Milhet, however, stayed on in France, still trying, and the fact that he *was* trying, plus Spain's reluctance to take over in Louisiana, strengthened the belief of Orleanians that the transfer was a gigantic fraud of some sort.

But late in the summer of 1765 came a letter from Havana, addressed to the Superior Council. The letter was from Don Antonio de Ulloa, lately appointed governor of Spanish Louisiana, and informed the council that he would shortly arrive to take over. Thus at last it appeared that Spain intended to do something about its property. Presumably the Superior Council was resigned to the situation, or at least willing to await developments, for Ulloa's letter was at least a definite statement of intention.

Yet 1765 dragged to a close, January and February of the next year came and went, and still no Ulloa. New Orleans got along about as well as ever, but as time passed the populace again became restless. Which isn't surprising, all things considered. Almost three years had gone by, and, except for that one lone letter from Ulloa, Louisiana had not seen a single sign of Spanish officialdom.

There was another thing, too, which gave Orleanians food for thought, and that was the British traffic on the Mississippi under their very noses. The British had been a little slow in taking over some of the French posts on the Ohio and Mississippi but they were now making up for the delay. After a few minor differences with the Indians they had occupied the posts from Fort Pitt through Fort Chartres to Natchez and Mobile. As usual, the British then set about putting their business affairs in order and the great river, as always, was the natural highway. Coming and going around Algiers Point at New Orleans, they must have been amused at the unhappy, ambiguous state of western Louisiana, for certainly the British were well aware of it.

Ulloa, with some ninety men, arrived at last. On the fifth of March 1766 he came ashore over the levee and had his first look at the bedraggled Place d'Armes in a cold, drenching spring rain. Probably he was depressed by what he saw, though that doesn't begin to explain his behavior of the next two years—and Don Antonio's future conduct can only be described as astonishing. Some of this has been explained on the ground that, while he was a naval officer, Ulloa was also a scientist and so far more interested in science than in governing. All of which is true but hardly explains his apparent lack of even the simplest form of common sense.

The day Ulloa arrived, before the man could really find his land legs, Foucalt, Intendant-Commissary of the Superior Council, demanded to know what he intended to do about the depressed paper currency still circulating in the colony—there were seven million livres of it, worth only about a third of its face value. Since this was probably news to Ulloa, he said reasonably that, pending other instructions from Madrid, the money should continue to circulate as it had been. (Nearly a century later General Ben Butler of Massachusetts was to say the same thing about depressed Confederate currency.) That was about all he could truthfully have said, but immediately the folk took another stand: the money must be redeemed at par, and that at once. There was nothing like asking for a miracle.

Three days later a committee of merchants invited the governor to answer a series of questions concerning the future of the commercial interests. They wanted to know, they said, "how to direct their future actions." Now on the face of it that was a reasonable enough request. But, as put by the committee, the words could have been just a statement or a veiled, indirect threat. Ulloa chose to accept it as the latter—no doubt he had his reasons—and called the group insolent, imperious, and menacing. Probably the merchants were reasonable in their request, and Ulloa right about their surface temper.

The governor's first brush with the Superior Council was unfortunate for both parties. Aubry, anxious to follow his orders to the letter and still head of the garrison, was a member of the council—as Bienville had earlier been—but he did not dominate it. Foucalt and Lafrénière, the attorney general, were the council's leading spirits. They at once demanded to see Ulloa's credentials—a reasonable formality though probably none of them really doubted his authority. But a request would have served better than a demand, and in a moment of poor judgment Ulloa informed them that he was awaiting more troops before taking formal possession, and that in any case he expected to deal only with Aubry, the proper delegate of the French crown.

The unlucky Aubry was caught between two fires. He was willing and anxious to transfer the colony as per his instructions, but how could he when Ulloa refused to take it? Moreover, because he was forced to support Ulloa, no matter how eccentric the latter's methods, he put himself at cross-purposes with the Orleanians.

Apparently everybody was at fault. The Orleanians expected to be taken over by Spain, and if Ulloa had gone ahead matter-of-factly they would probably have taken his authority for granted and Ulloa would have had no use for more troops. In turn New Orleans misjudged Ulloa's intentions, which, in spite of his possibly mistaken methods, were really of the best; he wanted nothing so much as to get along amicably with everyone, but he just didn't know how to go about it. But the temper of the situation was being fixed, and neither side would admit being wrong, or even partially wrong.

The Port of New Orleans

Yet New Orleans did not forcibly resist Ulloa, for he had mentioned additional troops and no doubt did ask for them, and the Superior Council wanted no part of a Spanish army of reprisal. Of course they had no way of knowing that Ulloa wouldn't get the troops he probably asked for. Resistance consisted mainly in irritating the governor as much as possible in small ways. They ignored him socially, nothing he did was right, and when he did something constructive he was accused of merely trying to curry favor under false pretenses.

On the other hand, there was a good deal to be said for some of the New Orleans point of view. For one thing, Spanish colonial revenue laws, indeed all Spanish colonial laws, were notoriously harsh and confiscatory, as everyone knew, and fear of them was natural; everyone thinks of his purse if he has one. For another thing, Ulloa was attempting to act as governor without having formally assumed the office and its responsibilities. He traveled here and there in the more easily accessible parts of the province, sent a company of soldiers to establish fortifications near the mouth of the Missouri, and built a miserable little fort almost within musket shot of British territory above New Orleans. Furthermore, he arranged to pay the French garrison but insisted on leaving them under Aubry's command, with the French flag still flying above their barracks, while Ulloa's own troops were quartered separately under the Spanish flag.

It was a curious state of affairs indeed, but to add to the general confusion Ulloa, leaving his troubles and the colony to get along without him, took time out to return to Havana to be married. Not that there was anything wrong with marriage as such—it was the time and place Ulloa chose for it.

Late in 1767 Jean Milhet returned from France and his admission of final defeat only fanned French dislike of Ulloa and everything Spanish. Time drifted on. Nothing was done about the inflated currency—though unquestionably a solution of that had to come from Madrid—and the Spanish had failed to pay the debts they had assumed with the cession of the territory. Specie was scarce, all commercial ventures doubtful of success, and the busy British were taking a heavy toll of the trade in the northern valleys which had once been French. And to cap it all there came a rumor that a royal decree would soon forbid all trade with France and the West Indies, the backlogs of the New Orleans export trade.

The pot of open revolt was rapidly coming to a boil.

For the most part the planners of the minor uprising that followed were Orleanians, again presuming to act for all the colony, and some of them were members of the Superior Council itself. Lafrénière was one and Foucalt another. Jean and Joseph Milhet, merchants; Doucet, a *notarie;* Marquis, a Swiss-born officer of the French garrison; Caresse, Petit, and Poupet, well-known Orleanians; Joseph Villeré, Hardy de Boisblanc, and Balthasar de Masan, planters; and two youthful brothers, nephews of old Bienville, were the other chief conspirators. But curiously enough, perhaps through fear of treachery in the city itself, the men expected to do the actual shooting, if any, were recruited on the German Coast above New Orleans and from among the Acadians still farther upriver.

On the twenty-seventh of October Foucalt called a meeting of the Superior Council for the next day, and during the night the guns at the Tchoupitoulas Gate, at the upriver corner of the city—the same gate where years before the heads of revolting slaves had been displayed—were spiked. On the morning of the twenty-eighth the Germans and Acadians marched into the city. Stores and offices were closed, many of the populace joined the marchers, and the Place d'Armes was packed. Lafrénière, the Milhet brothers, and the lawyer Doucet made speeches, and it is recorded that six hundred persons signed a petition to the Superior Council, already in session and waiting for just such an excuse to act.

(Six hundred seems pretty strong; there probably weren't any more than that number in the city who could sign their names.)

Aubry had about one hundred and ten men at his disposal, but probably under the circumstances he didn't trust them too much. At any rate, he didn't use them to disperse the mob. He castigated Foucalt and Lafrénière verbally but of course that did little good, and under Aubry's protection Ulloa and his family boarded a Spanish frigate, which slipped her lines at the wharf and anchored again in mid-river. Ulloa's staff remained in his house, and while the mob surrounded it and made a lot of noise there was no real violence. The mob, probably fired by alcohol, the mob spirit, and the fact that the authorities made no attempt to disperse them, held together until the next day, when the French flag was raised in the Place d'Armes and the Superior Council, in response to the petition and over Aubry's protests, adopted a resolution ordering Ulloa to "leave the colony, and without delay."

Romancers have it that the cables of Ulloa's ship were cut during the night and he floated off toward the Gulf and Havana against his will. As a matter of fact, Ulloa did leave almost immediately, but he left in a French vessel and the Spanish frigate remained. There remained also most of the Spanish garrison and three of the governor's personal staff— Loyala, Gayarre, and Navarro.

Thus while the revolt began with a roar it ended with a very weak sigh. As soon as Ulloa's ship was out of sight the conspiring Orleanians, individually and collectively, rushed to explain matters to both the French and Spanish governments; and in their explanations and apologies they contradicted themselves and each other with almost every other sentence. At first there was some talk of setting up a republic in Louisiana, but that somehow became transformed into a begging plea to be taken back and forgiven by Louis XV. In fact, three Orleanians took such a plea to the French court in person, there to be coldly informed that the Spanish king, well aware of what had occurred, was planning to take steps of his own.

Time slipped away. The Spanish frigate remained in New Orleans until the following April, and the remaining Spanish garrison and government officials were entirely unmolested. Having revolted, the exuberant Creoles apparently didn't know what to do next; so, characteristically enough, they did nothing. Probably they convinced themselves in time that there really hadn't been any revolt after all. But they were due for a very rude shock on that score. Spain might be slow and awkward but she still believed in her own authority.

On a day late in July 1769 New Orleans was shocked from its sleepy complacency by the news that a Spanish fleet was off the mouth of the Mississippi. Marquis, the fire-eating Swiss captain, appeared in the Place d'Armes with a white republican cockade in his hat, and was joined there by Petit, who is supposed to have carried a pistol in either hand—visible symbols of revolt, presumably. Together they urged the people —eventually about a hundred gathered in the square to see what the shouting was for—to rise and defend their liberties. But the people didn't rise; instead they went home. Undoubtedly it was a hot day, and a hot July day in New Orleans is something to take the revolutionary ardor out of the strongest-willed patriot. Aside from that there seemed to be a great many Spaniards and enough cannon to cut New Orleans off level with the dust of the Place d'Armes.

After a while Petit and Marquis also went home.

The following day Aubry addressed the people in the Place d'Armes, promised they would be treated fairly, and ordered them to stay at home.

Lafrénière, Marquis, and Jean Milhet went down the river to meet and first present the respects of the populace to the Spanish commandant—and again certain Orleanians, probably those with guiltiest consciences, were taking a good deal on themselves. The Spaniard's reply was courteous if a bit sar-

donic, and he assured them that they would be treated justly
—though he also found time and a place for a few words about
sedition.

This commandant of the Spanish fleet was Don Alejandro
O'Reilly, an Irishman in the Spanish service who was reputed
to have gained favor because he had once saved the life of
the Spanish king, Charles III. O'Reilly was probably a loyal
enough Spanish subject but, in one sense at least, he was also
a mercenary and so knew that he must be zealous if he expected to maintain his position. Certainly he knew his own
mind and showed none of Ulloa's vacillation; in fact, he was
as direct as Ulloa was evasive.

The twenty-four Spanish ships, carrying twenty-six hundred troops, were three weeks making the torturous trip up
the Mississippi—a fair indication of the difficulties besetting
ocean vessels in that stretch of water. O'Reilly's army marched
over the levee into the Place d'Armes on the eighteenth of
August and, amid pomp and display never before seen in
muddy little New Orleans, the captain general formally took
over the province from Captain Aubry.

Thus six and one half years after the cession of the province
by France, Spain officially assumed control. Considering
every exigency of time, distance, and slowness of communication, that must have been a record of some kind.

New Orleans hadn't long to wait for Count O'Reilly to
act. Within three days after his arrival he had arrested twelve
of the original revolutionists, if they can be called by that
name. It wasn't necessary, from his point of view, to make
any preliminary investigation. Probably Ulloa in Havana had
given him all the information he needed.

Foucalt, who had been missed in the original roundup, was
arrested two days later. He pleaded that whatever he might
have done had occurred before the official Spanish occupation, and that therefore he was subject to French rather than
Spanish law. Oddly enough, O'Reilly agreed. Foucalt was
shipped to France, where he was tried and found guilty, and

subsequently served about a year in the Bastille. It seems strange that the others did not plead the same as Foucalt, for their circumstances were the same as his and would have been entitled to the same consideration. Perhaps the fact that they were not was a whim of O'Reilly's, who felt that the colony should have an object lesson in its own front yard.

Braud, the public printer, was arrested with the others but was released when he pleaded that he was obligated to print all public documents and so had no choice in printing the seditious resolutions.

Villeré died—or was killed—the day of his arrest. The official report says he died from a sudden madness, but possibly that was another way of saying he was killed while attempting to resist his guards.

The others were all summarily tried and convicted. Nicholas Lafrénière, Jean Noyan, Pierre Caresse, Joseph Milhet, and Pierre Marquis were sentenced to hang; the rest, except young Bienville, were given prison terms in Havana's Morro Castle and deprived of all but a small part of their property. In the end those sentenced to hang were instead executed by a firing squad in the Place d'Armes.

For one of the families involved the execution was more than an ordinary tragedy, for Noyan, one of Bienville's two young nephews, had lately married Lafrénière's daughter, who thus lost husband and father at the same time.

Louisiana historians have made much over the "barbarity," the "uncalled-for severity," the "bloody cruelty," of the treatment accorded the revolutionists, and because of it O'Reilly was given the sobriquet "Cruel" in Louisiana. Yet now it is hard to muster any great amount of sympathy for the condemned. There was no doubt whatever of their guilt, such as it was, and they went into the business originally with their eyes wide open—they knew full well what chances they were taking. They knew, too, that revolt was something not to be tolerated for a moment by either the French or Spanish governments; in fact, revolt and treason were among the few crimes almost certain of conviction and punishment. Further-more, the forebears of these same men fifty years earlier had decapitated Negroes who were merely *planning* revolt. Your Orleanian even today will plead violently that there was a difference, but to the disinterested observer it is hard to find any difference worth mentioning. And at any rate the whole business was part of the political pattern of the period and the racial temperament of the people involved.

Captain Aubry, for his part in the affair as a whole, was offered a high commission in the Spanish army. He refused it though perhaps would have fared better had he accepted. He sailed for France and his ship had already entered the Garonne when it was wrecked and Aubry drowned.

Strictly speaking, Count O'Reilly was never governor of Louisiana; he was a commissioner appointed to take over the province and put its tangled affairs in order. To that end he abolished the Superior Council and in its place set up the *cabildo*, a Spanish form of governing body. In some ways the cabildo had little real power; its members all had pompous titles but their duties and authority were mostly concerned with petty matters which in most governing bodies would have been handled by minor clerks. Actually the Spanish system of government organization tended to decentralize power *under* the governor and his top officials. There were hosts of lesser officials, their powers carefully limited and ex-actly described. So while there was a great deal of authority, not much of it was concentrated in one place. Sometimes it seemed that every other citizen was an official of some sort, charged with administering some special, minute portion of the multitudinous laws, and one of the most important rules was that these petty officials should not poach on each other's prerogatives. Until long after O'Reilly's time the great mass of Spanish law was not published in Louisiana, either for the benefit of lawyers or whoever else could read, so it was very common for the honest citizen to be jailed or fined

The Pontalba apartments facing on Jackson Square in New Orleans.

heavily for some offense of which he had never heard—and some of the alleged "crimes" would have been laughed at in many places, even in the eighteenth century. Penalties for infractions of religious laws were especially harsh.

As a matter of fact, the Spanish were addicted to government for its own sake. It was not an evil necessity to be endured, but a complete end in itself, and Louisiana under Spain was an excellent example of the genre.

While O'Reilly, Unzaga, and their successors levied a number of new taxes and many special license fees, the state income never remotely approached the cost of the government establishment. Usually the outlay was five or six times the amount of income and the per capita cost of government in Louisiana was astronomical in comparison with the same cost in any of the thirteen Atlantic colonies.

As soon as the cabildo and its subsidiaries were organized O'Reilly appointed Don Louis de Unzaga governor, though for a considerable time afterward O'Reilly remained in New Orleans and Unzaga functioned under him. Spanish became the official language of the state and the courts, though of course not the one spoken by the people. But on the whole the introduction of Spanish law was not as much of a hardship as the people of New Orleans had expected. In many ways it was more severe and arbitrary than the French code, provided greater punishment for smaller offenses, but the two had a common origin and the laws of marriage and inheritance —important in Louisiana—were not much different.

So while Spanish colonial government was generally considered to be harsh beyond necessity, the extent of the severity in practice always depended on the men who administered the law; and Louisiana and New Orleans, throughout the Spanish regime, were especially fortunate in this respect. They never had a Spanish governor who in any way could be considered tyrannical. When Spanish law conflicted with common sense or common practice, Unzaga and his successors either secured royal concessions or winked at infractions.

The Port of New Orleans

O'Reilly claimed that when he arrived in New Orleans British traders were making off with nine tenths of the town's profit, though unquestionably that was a great exaggeration. In any case, O'Reilly drove off the British and refused to allow their vessels to dock at New Orleans. (Perhaps it should be remembered that O'Reilly was Irish before he was Spanish, and so had his own feelings about the British in general.) But the French of New Orleans had few scruples about trading with their erstwhile enemies—a profit was a profit wherever you found it. So when Unzaga took over—O'Reilly with over half his original force left New Orleans in October 1770— he winked at British trade although British vessels were still not allowed to actually dock in New Orleans. But there were a dozen easy ways to get around a simple thing like that. In the direct New Orleans trade, for instance, two floating wharf boats, or stores, were tied up at the west bank of the Mississippi a little distance above the city proper. Since by slipping their cables the wharf boats could be free of Spanish territory— the river was free—British vessels loaded and unloaded from the floating wharves with impunity; technically, they were violating no law. For the benefit of upriver planters and other customers these same vessels were anchored just over the territorial line in Bayou Manchac or the river, and trading was as simple as crossing to the other side of Fifth Avenue— simpler, really, and a good deal safer. Certain New Orleans merchants, believing this clandestine trade deprived them of legitimate business, complained loudly to Unzaga, but the latter well knew that the majority of the populace were in favor of the practice, so allowed it to flourish. This out-of-bounds trade was so considerable that British merchants extended crop credit to French planters, and on that basis even sold them slaves in order that they might make their lands— on both banks of the Mississippi above New Orleans—more productive.

In the comparatively short space of seventy years New Orleans had become one of the most colorful and cosmopolitan capitals on the American continent. And yet when Unzaga took over it was still a badly built wooden town of some 3,200 souls, both free and slave. It contained about 500 buildings, none of them worth looking at twice, with most of them located on the four lateral streets nearest the water front—Chartres, Royale, Bourbon, and Dauphine—and the Quay itself. And New Orleans was even more a queer combination of filth and fastidious elegance, piety and open bawdiness, leisurely civilian life and stiff military pomp and display.

Geographically, it was the heart of a great trade area, potentially the sea outlet for half a continent, and its prominent merchants, brokers, and planters were fast becoming wealthy. Yet somehow the population refused to grow. In fact, at times it was necessary for government to restrict immigration in order that the general interests of the town might be served. Even after the Spanish occupation that government did not encourage immigration by its own people. In fact, Spain never encouraged mass immigration to its own possessions; she preferred to exploit the already resident population whenever possible. A few Spanish trickled into the city, of course, but for the most part they were of the wealthy or adventurer class.

There were exceptions, naturally, as for instance Don Almonaster y Roxas, who in time became not only the wealthiest man in the province but also, after the sailor Jean Louis whose meager savings established the first Charity Hospital, New Orleans' first philanthropist of note.

Almonaster leased the two squares on St. Ann and St. Peter streets, above and below the Place d'Armes, and soon turned the two blocks into the city's best shopping district. Years later, just before the Civil War, Almonaster's daughter, the Baroness de Pontalba, razed the buildings erected by her father and in their place had built the Pontalba Buildings, said to be the first real apartment buildings in the United States. Each building was a full block long, from Chartres to Decatur Street (Decatur Street had replaced the Quay as the first street away from the river), three stories high with a fourth-floor attic, and fronted on two sides of the Place d'Armes. In their heyday they were the most elegant living quarters in New Orleans, and though their interiors have seen many changes since, the buildings themselves are still landmarks in the old city and their outward appearance is little changed. The lovely iron-railed balconies, with the intertwined initials A-P—Almonaster-Pontalba—run full length of the block from Chartres to Decatur on both second- and third-floor levels, and for over ninety years the sidewalks, roofed by the balconies of the second floor, have provided pleasant shelter from New Orleans' withering sun and sudden tropical showers.

From these balconies one can look down into the greenery of Jackson Square (the old Place d'Armes), centering about the weathered equestrian statue of the general himself, or diagonally across the square toward the venerable façades of the Cabildo, the Presbytère, and St. Louis Cathedral facing the square on Chartres Street. At night the time-mellowed chimes of the cathedral count the hours, and in the river a little distance away freighters from a hundred ports hoot mournfully. It is a pleasant place, this little square which is, and was planned to be, the heart of the old French city, and this plot of earth has witnessed as much history in the making as any comparable spot in the United States.

CHAPTER VI

New Orleans and Another Revolution

BECAUSE New Orleans was Spanish at the time, it is often assumed that she had little or nothing to do with the American Revolution, but such is hardly the case. The role of New Orleans was hardly decisive, but it was interesting and had a real bearing on the war's eventual outcome.

The chief figure in the New Orleans phase of the war was Oliver Pollock, whose connection with the city antedated that of Count O'Reilly. Pollock, like O'Reilly an Irishman, had not been long in the Colonies—he came to Philadelphia from Coleraine, northern Ireland, in 1760—but before he was thirty he had made a name for himself in the West Indies trade. In 1768 he had settled more or less permanently in New Orleans and from there was doing business with both the Atlantic ports and the West Indies.

When O'Reilly landed in New Orleans his army was larger than the city's entire white population, and before long the feeding of such an organization became a major problem. Prices went out of sight and there was not enough food regardless of what the price might be. At a critical moment Pollock arrived from Baltimore in his ship *Royal Charlotte* with a cargo of flour—Baltimore's earliest export of consequence—which he shortly sold to O'Reilly at the latter's own price, and one very much below the current market. Properly grateful, O'Reilly gave young Pollock the privilege of free trade in Louisiana for his lifetime, and according to Pollock's own testimony the privilege was never violated nor proscribed by the Spanish.

So much is true—but there is a little more to the tale. Pollock is generally thought of as a shrewd Yankee trader who arrived in New Orleans at an opportune moment and by a clever piece of dealing received a nice concession from tough O'Reilly. Actually Pollock had fixed his headquarters in New Orleans during the previous year and he had known O'Reilly in Havana even before that. O'Reilly was Catholic and Pollock probably was, and the two had been introduced originally by a Jesuit priest. So while Pollock was lucky his was the luck of a man who has carefully prepared his preliminary steps.

Since O'Reilly had promptly chased all British merchants, except Pollock, from New Orleans, the latter's position was fortunate indeed. (For while Pollock is thought of as an American he was of course a British subject in 1769.) His friendship with O'Reilly and with later Spanish governors gave him advantages quite beyond the mere privilege of trading. Pollock stood higher in Spanish esteem than did most of his French competitors. The record does not so state specifically, but undoubtedly Pollock was the liaison man in many a deal between Orleanians and the British who waited to do business over the river. He supplied many of the needs of the Spanish garrison, was often entrusted with personal funds of Spanish officials for investment, and sometimes borrowed money from them himself. He dealt in all sorts of merchandise: manufactured goods from England and the Continent; slaves from Africa; flour and foodstuffs from Philadelphia and Baltimore. He operated a 500-acre plantation near Baton Rouge —this in *British* territory, of course; his employees traded far up the Mississippi, and he acted as agent in various enterprises for individuals and business concerns in the East. His nationality, and the fact that he was *persona grata* with Spanish officialdom, was naturally of the greatest possible aid in these ventures.

It has been said that at the beginning of the Revolution Pollock was the most prominent merchant in New Orleans, and while that may not be true he certainly belonged in the upper strata. At this time he was personally worth $100,000, and his credit was at least twice that. Furthermore, he had started with practically nothing—one of his early ventures had involved a mere ten barrels of flour—and whatever he had accumulated was the result of his own efforts, plus perhaps a little luck. And in 1776 he was still under forty years of age.

Like most of the Colonists who early called themselves Americans, Pollock's patriotism in the beginning was pretty much mixed up with his business interests; which is no criticism, actual or implied. There was hardly a Revolutionary figure to whom the same statement would not apply, for, patriot or not, a man must get a living some way. Thus while Pollock sacrificed his personal fortune and most of his commercial reputation in the American cause, he became involved in the first place through business interests and associates.

Before the year 1776 Pollock had purchased 1,500 acres of land near his own holdings for Willing & Morris (Thomas Willing and Robert Morris, both well known in Revolutionary annals) of Philadelphia. He did much other business for and with this same firm, and in 1776 held a balance of $42,000 in their favor.

In the years just before and after 1776 an American was a hard thing to define politically. Americans were more easily distinguishable for what they were against than what they were for. But the American cause, both in word and action, was Pollock's from the beginning, and from the beginning he was deeply involved.

American reasons for courting the favor of Spain were several. In the first place, Spain was one of the real powers in

North America, and it was to the advantage of the American cause that Spain, in the event she could not be secured as an ally, at least be kept neutral. And the Colonies *hoped* that she would be a friendly neutral, as indeed she was.

In order to secure this state of affairs, General Charles Lee, speaking for the Virginia Committee of Safety, wrote to Governor Unzaga in May 1776. He pointed out, naïvely enough in a way, that the interests of Spain and the Colonies nowhere conflicted, whereas those of Spain and Great Britain most certainly did; therefore it would be only common sense for Spain to go along with the revolting Colonies. (Of course at the time Lee was speaking the truth, for everyone knows that in their dim beginnings the Colonies would have been more than content with the independence of the Atlantic seaboard area. It was only later that they changed their minds.) Moreover, and more immediately, the Americans needed a place, not too far away, where they could secure badly needed munitions. A possibly friendly France no longer held American territory, and procurement in the French West Indies was largely out of the question because of the British navy. The Continental Army needed guns, powder, blankets, and medical supplies, and where on the Continent could it get these things except, perhaps, New Orleans?

Captain George Gibson and Lieutenant William Linn, with fifteen supposed traders, arrived in New Orleans with General Lee's letter in August 1776. New Orleans had its full quota of British spies, some of them ostensibly in the Spanish service, and Gibson and Linn were in considerable personal danger. The killing of a trader or two in a tavern brawl was still more or less commonplace in New Orleans, though admittedly it was better policed than during the French regime.

Whether by intention or luck, Lee's letter was entrusted to Pollock for delivery to Unzaga, and Pollock became a sort of unofficial agent for Virginia, and through her for the Colonies at large. This was quite agreeable to Pollock; in fact, he was more than ready to do whatever he could. The record does not say whether the aging Unzaga was impressed by the diplomatic representations of General Lee, but in any case Pollock was allowed to buy ten thousand pounds of powder for the use of the Colonies against Britain.

Linn and forty-three men—he had done some active though secret recruiting in New Orleans despite the hovering British —started up the Mississippi with nine thousand pounds of the powder in September. They successfully ran the gantlet of the British posts at Baton Rouge and Natchez but were forced to winter at Arkansas Post, on the Spanish side of the river. There Linn bought supplies for the winter and to last him during the rest of the journey to the mouth of the Ohio, and these supplies he paid for with a draft on Pollock in New Orleans.

In the meantime the British had learned about the powder shipment and their influence in New Orleans had caught up with Captain Gibson. After all, the town was little more than an overgrown village in size and strangers who stayed long were easily remarked. So in order to satisfy everybody Gibson was arrested and clapped in the *calabozo*, and there he had a very pleasant stay until such time as Pollock had a vessel ready to sail for Philadelphia. When the time came Captain Gibson was quietly released and embarked for the City of Friends, taking with him, carefully concealed about the ship, the remaining thousand pounds of powder.

At the beginning of 1777 Unzaga was succeeded by young Don Bernardo de Galvez, and the latter was even more friendly to the American cause than Unzaga had been. Aside from the friendly feeling Galvez already had, Unzaga presented Oliver Pollock to him as a man "in whom he might impose implicit confidence." The words are Pollock's own, written later in justification of his claims against a Congress that hated to pay its just bills. Galvez, son of the Viceroy of Mexico and nephew of the Spanish Secretary of State, immediately struck up a warm friendship with Pollock and did everything possible, even far beyond the limits of a strict neutrality, to aid him.

Galvez's first friendly act was to declare the Port of New Orleans open to American vessels and to permit American privateers to bring certain prizes into the same port for sale. The port was, however, to be a neutral refuge only, and American vessels—always excepting Pollock's, of course— were not to come in to trade. This action, though, was not entirely original with Galvez, since a royal decree of the previous autumn allowed such action to be taken, at discretion, in all Spanish ports. Spain had little reason to see Britain successful in anything she undertook.

In order to keep them out of British hands, American vessels off the mouth of the Mississippi were frequently subjected to mock seizure by the Spanish and later released. Once when an American ship was taken by the British the Spanish promptly seized every British vessel between Head of Passes and Bayou Manchac, the upper limit of Spanish territory on the east bank of the Mississippi. And Galvez let it be known, through Pollock, that money and munitions, and perhaps men, would be provided if the Americans decided to move against the British posts in West Florida and along the Mississippi. Pollock was in the thick of all this business, perfectly at home in New Orleans, and even suggested to Congress that he be allowed to recruit men in the city—Linn's small efforts in that direction had been *sub rosa* and for a special venture.

Pollock finally made himself so openly obnoxious to the British that the governor of Pensacola demanded that Galvez arrest the rebel and hand him over for proper punishment.

Instead Galvez entered into correspondence with Colonel George Morgan at Fort Pitt, with a view toward joint Spanish-American action against the British on the Gulf coast and along the Mississippi—if and when the time came. Galvez, and Unzaga before him, had always believed that British aggression against Spanish possessions in North America was but a matter of time and opportunity—and who shall say they were not right? Galvez, in fact, believed that a British attack upon New Orleans was more or less imminent and asked for two frigates to protect the city. His talk about British "aggression" seems not to have had too much foundation in fact, but naturally the Americans were enthusiastic about his attitude.

Furthermore, Galvez had managed to communicate his anti-British feeling to Orleanians in general—always supposing that they needed any coercion in that direction. For while Orleanians, most of them, were not pro-Spanish, they were anti-British politically almost to a man, and they clamored for reprisals against the British "aggression." To satisfy them, and himself, Galvez seized all the British vessels at the moment docked on the west bank of the river for purposes of the illicit trade. Eleven vessels were taken and their cargoes sold as contraband, though when the excitement was over it was discovered that two of the ships were really American. As usual, Pollock managed their release. Naturally, the British were incensed and sent naval vessels to New Orleans with demands that the ships and their crews be released. Galvez, according to his own account, met the British with contempt and derision and dared them to do their worst. Probably the British weren't awed overmuch, for New Orleans was in no position to defend itself against a real attack, but at any rate the British withdrew. No doubt they had their orders and the time was not yet ripe, in their judgment, to force the Spanish issue into the open.

In the meantime it was known in New Orleans that British Pensacola was very short of foodstuffs and had considerable sickness. Galvez shipped them one hundred and fifty barrels of flour as a gift, thus relieving their distress, and such generosity on the part of a potential enemy had a salutary effect on British sentiment on the Gulf.

In July 1777 there were deposited at New Orleans two thousand barrels of powder and a quantity of lead and clothing, this supply to be drawn on by Virginia. Of course delivery from New Orleans to wherever the munitions were needed was an acute problem, but it was the problem of the Colonies; Spain had done her part.

Meanwhile Franklin, in Europe, was cementing the ties of Spanish-American friendship more closely, though Charles III was not yet in the mood to declare Spain openly for the Colonies against Britain. Even so the friendship had practical results. The firm of Gardoqui & Son in Bilbao acted for the Spanish government through Arthur Lee, like Pollock an American in Spanish favor, in Havana. During 1778 the Americans secured through this channel thousands of pairs of shoes and stockings, blankets, medical and other supplies. By the end of 1777 Galvez in New Orleans had furnished the western frontiers of the Colonies with munitions to the extent of $74,000, and it was Oliver Pollock who as usual held himself responsible for eventual payment of this obligation. His faith in Virginia and the Colonies, to his ill fortune, was almost unlimited.

In the summer of 1778 a new drain on Pollock's resources and financial ingenuity began. George Rogers Clark and his ragged little army had set out from Fort Pitt to subdue the British posts on the Mississippi and Wabash, and succeeded. When Clark left Williamsburg under orders from Governor Patrick Henry and the Virginia Assembly, he had but £1,200 in depreciated currency to see him through. Governor Henry was shrewd enough to know very well that Clark would need more money if he was to be at all successful, and he told Clark, rather vaguely, that he was to draw on Pollock in New Orleans for what he needed further. Apparently Henry had no specific authority from Pollock in the matter, nor did he mention any limit to Clark.

The good Governor Henry evidently took for granted that Pollock, having helped out before, would be happy to do so again. Further, Henry seems to have had no idea how much even a small force like Clark's would need to spend, and neither had he any way of knowing the extent of Pollock's resources. So giving Henry every credit for patriotic zeal, he was more than a little highhanded in subjecting Pollock, a man he didn't even know, to possible bankruptcy. Probably the real answer is that Henry expected Clark to fail wholly or at least in part, and that there would be little occasion for him to draw on Pollock for any considerable sums. (That is a personal opinion; there is little evidence either way.)

But if Patrick Henry expected Clark to fail he had badly misjudged his man, for fail Clark did not; he hardly knew what the word meant—then. He easily took the British posts on the Mississippi: Kaskaskia, St. Philip, Prairie du Rocher, and Cahokia. It was a bloodless victory, though he had expected opposition. Vincennes on the Wabash also fell to Clark by diplomacy, although he later had to consolidate his hold on it by force, after a winter march and attack that is one of the epics of the Revolution.

All that has been told elsewhere, and this account is concerned with Clark's financing by Pollock in New Orleans. Clark's little store of money was gone within hours of the time he took Kaskaskia early in July 1778, and thereafter he drew on Oliver Pollock. In fact, a draft on Pollock paid the expenses of the priest Father Gibault and Dr. Laffont on their journey to Vincennes to win that post for the Americans.

Thereafter Clark seems to have regarded Pollock as a banker with endless resources and wrote draft after draft on him. Considered from one point of view Clark, like Governor Henry, was taking a great deal for granted. Yet he was driven by circumstances and probably shut his mind against any thought of injustice to Pollock and considered that the end justified the means. Furthermore, he had been instructed by Henry to draw on Pollock and supposed that the latter was in turn being reimbursed by Virginia—or at any rate would be eventually.

Clark did issue some drafts on the Republic of Virginia, but they weren't overly popular in the Illinois country. The credit of Virginia *might* be all right but that of Oliver Pollock of New Orleans was a known quantity. The men who

[81]

sold Clark supplies, on both sides of the Mississippi above and below New Orleans, were the same men who for a decade had been doing business with Pollock. Clark himself was an aggressive and magnetic personality and was well received by the Spanish on the west bank of the Mississippi. De Leyba, lieutenant governor of Upper Louisiana, liked him very much, and there is even an unconfirmed rumor that Clark was in love with De Leyba's young sister. At any rate, De Leyba was in continuous contact with Galvez in New Orleans, Galvez was in close touch with Pollock, and Pollock was honoring Clark's drafts. Thus the situation in the Mississippi Valley was all of a piece.

From the very beginning, and as long as he commanded any resources at all, Pollock backed Clark to the hilt, for he saw what he believed to be the incalculable value of Clark's conquest in the West. And Pollock didn't hesitate to tell Clark how he felt about it at every opportunity.

As time wore on it seemed that Clark's only friend on the outside was the man in New Orleans. He had been gone from Williamsburg for more than a year without hearing a single word from Governor Henry, and the news from Fort Pitt was almost as sparse. But always Clark knew that Pollock was down there at the foot of the river, doing his best for the almost exiled Virginians and Kentuckians.

A list of the goods sent Clark by Pollock and a record of the drafts drawn by Clark for supplies and services purchased on the ground would fill a chapter. Yet Pollock never complained. Late in 1778 he was obligated to the extent of $42,-500 on behalf of the Continental Congress and the $74,000 which Galvez had advanced from the Louisiana treasury. All this aside from his cash outlay and the unknown amount of Clark's outstanding drafts. For Clark's paper did not always reach Pollock soon after it was drawn; in fact, it seldom did. In the Illinois country Pollock's drafts were considered as good or better than any currency and frequently passed from hand to hand for a year or more. So unless Clark informed Pollock of each draft drawn, which he did not and could not, the Orleanian had no way of knowing how much he was in debt on Clark's account. Pollock, instead of complaining, merely wrote Clark that he was straining every nerve and was lucky in that he had friends who were willing to help him.

One has to go a long way down the roster of the Revolution to find a man who had even a fraction of the faith that was Oliver Pollock's.

As month followed month another factor began to influence the financial dealings of the two, and that was currency inflation on a grand scale. News of bad money travels fast, and as the value of Continental currency dropped, prices, even in the West, advanced accordingly. Soon Clark was paying, on paper, $5,000 for supplies that a few months before could be purchased for a tenth of that sum. But that factor was never taken into consideration when Clark drew his drafts on Pollock; to do so would have been utterly impossible in the circumstances. Inflation is inflation and everything must of necessity be touched by the same rot. Of course it was a long time before the extent of these complications was known; in fact, it never was known exactly, and eventually both Pollock and Clark were in so deep that a few thousand dollars one way or another didn't matter in the least.

In the meantime a number of other things had happened on the Lower Mississippi.

James Willing, son of the Thomas Willing of Philadelphia for whom Pollock had acted as land agent, had visited the British settlements and properties in the neighborhood of Natchez and Baton Rouge. And why not? The young gentleman's father was the owner of a good deal of land in the vicinity—what more natural than that the son should visit the property in person? So young James Willing visited and was made heartily welcome by the local British planters and officials. Visitors were few and far between and it was difficult to say with certainty who was Tory and who was not, and of course for his present purposes the visitor was Tory. So Willing visited, went back to New Orleans where he enlisted a band of bravoes, and returned with fire and sword to the British settlements he had lately visited.

In a way it was a futile gesture—the power of England in America was not to be destroyed by raids on isolated settlements of homesick Britishers, who in many cases weren't quite sure themselves whether they were British or American. Willing was censured by many of the Creoles of New Orleans and its environs. He had accepted hospitality and then rudely violated the code of the guest; thus, patriotically inspired or not, he was certainly an undesirable person socially. It appears that Willing didn't much care what New Orleans might think. He was one of the handful of Americans who struck at anything British wherever he happened to find it. And when Clark at Kaskaskia fitted out a gunboat for the winter attack on Vincennes, he mounted on it four swivel guns forwarded upriver by Pollock and named the craft *Willing*—certainly an indication of what he thought of the Philadelphian's actions.

But Willing's social errors were forgotten in the summer of 1779, when Spain formally declared war on Great Britain and Governor Galvez had his wish at last. Again Galvez was convinced that the British intended to attack New Orleans, and this time he may have been right. Ostensibly he began preparations for defending the city, but his real intentions were to attack—he had had such plans in mind for a long time.

Within a few days of beginning his preparations Galvez received a temporary setback in the form of a hurricane, which struck savagely at the city and the river settlements above and below it. Buildings were destroyed, there was much crop damage, and Galvez lost his newly created gunboat flotilla.

Of course Galvez had a Spanish garrison under his command in the city but he doubted it was large enough for a campaign in the field—the force apparently numbered between five and six hundred men, not all of whom were permanently attached to the Spanish military. So Galvez was faced with a problem which has worried many another colonial administrator of a province taken more or less by force: could he count on the aid of the Creoles who were Spanish only because they had little choice in the matter? The Orleanians had tolerated and accepted Spanish rule since O'Reilly's time, but that was no indication that they were willing to fight Spain's enemies for her. But in this case the enemy was British, France had already thrown in her lot with the struggling Colonies, and the Orleanians responded enthusiastically. Something over six hundred men (from the environs of New Orleans as well as the city itself) enrolled in the "defensive" force which was to attack the near-by British posts.

The nondescript and somewhat amateur army left New Orleans late in August, marched up the·east bank of the Mississippi accompanied by a handful of cannon on boats in the river, and attacked the British posts one after the other. And along with Galvez went the always enthusiastic Oliver Pollock, more than pleased with the turn events had taken.

Theoretically, of course, Galvez should have taken the British posts without much trouble. His force outnumbered the strongest British garrison, Baton Rouge, by more than two to one. But Baton Rouge was fortified, had a considerable battery, and its defending force numbered about five hundred men. They might have given Galvez's hastily thrown together army a great deal of trouble, though as a matter of fact they did not. By the first of October the British posts had capitulated, a number of British vessels on the Mississippi, Bayou Manchac, and Lake Pontchartrain had been taken, and Galvez was ready to return to New Orleans, there to prepare an assault against the posts on the Mobile River and as far east as Pensacola.

After his successes on the Mississippi Galvez was re-enforced from Havana and left New Orleans the following February, this time with two thousand men, including most of his original Creole militia. Thereafter delay followed delay, and more than once the doughty Galvez was close to disaster. But his luck held, and though once he was forced to visit Havana personally in search of extra aid, by May 1781 he had taken all of Florida from the British and Spain was in full possession of the Gulf coast from East Florida to Yucatan. The northern boundary, as fixed finally by the Treaty of Versailles, was made the Thirty-First Parallel, running from the Atlantic coast to a point on the Mississippi near the present site of Vicksburg, and Spain's neighbor above that line was the new United States of America. There was to be more than a little trouble over that boundary line in the future, but in the meantime Spain had taken another whack at British territory.

Galvez never returned to New Orleans after the campaign against Pensacola but became captain general of Cuba and eventually went on to succeed his father as Viceroy of Mexico.

By the time the war was over Pollock's financial troubles had begun to pile up on him in earnest. Besides his cash outlays and the amounts he had guaranteed for the Colonies and Virginia, he was involved to the extent of about $50,000 in the matter of Clark's drafts. He had taken for granted that when the war was concluded he would be reimbursed without question, and his creditors had supposed likewise, but both he and they were to get a rude jolt when Pollock actually attempted to collect.

In the first place, Congress was deluged with claims from every side, the national treasury was almost non-existent, and Congress didn't like to pay past debts anyway, no matter how just or how long past due. Again, Virginia was in the process of transferring the Northwest Territory, the area generally agreed to have been conquered by Clark in the name of Virginia, to the Federal government, and in return Virginia expected Congress to assume the debts she, Virginia, had incurred in acquiring the territory—in other words, the drafts by Clark on Pollock. Over and beyond that, most of Clark's vouchers had been lost (curiously enough they were found only a few years ago in the basement of the old capitol of Williamsburg, where presumably they had been stored by some careless clerk), and Virginia was maintaining that many of the claims against Clark, including Pollock's, were invalid because there were no vouchers to support them. There were, in fact, open accusations that many of these claims were completely fraudulent and should not be paid by anyone. Pollock was of course not the only one affected by this situation. Most of the men in the Illinois country who had backed Clark, and Clark himself, were utterly ruined financially. For years these claimants, either personally or through agents, besieged Congress for a hearing and fair accounting. Wherever and whenever Congress assembled the petitioners were there, at first confident, later almost literally on their knees. There were frauds among them, naturally, but certainly they were in the minority. Some of them were paid in part after much haggling, some not at all, and other claims were settled as long as fifty years after the deaths of the original claimants.

In the end Pollock was forced to leave New Orleans in an attempt to collect from Congress in person. His business in the Crescent City had long since vanished. He had neither money nor credit, and it was utterly impossible for him to start afresh. In time some, but not all, of Pollock's claims were recognized, but only after he had given up trying to collect his main balance and was merely trying to salvage something, almost anything, from the wreckage, but he did not figure again in the affairs of New Orleans.

The Revolution was over and New Orleans, in a sort of offstage way, had had its small share in the activities, though of course it had made no difference in her political status. But curiously enough, the newly gained freedom of the Colonies seemed to create no desire for something of the same among Orleanians. One wonders a little—why? When revolution flared in France only a few years later, many Orleanians were more than a little sympathetic toward the republic; not all of them, of course, but a great many of them. In fact, public display of such sympathy had to be frowned on by the Spanish authorities. But apparently the sympathy was for almost anything French, good, bad, or indifferent, and not for the spirit of freedom itself.

Perhaps the most enervating climate on the continent was again a factor.

CHAPTER VII

Spanish Interlude

WHILE Galvez was engaged in his prolonged Gulf campaign and thus absent from New Orleans, the city was governed by the cabildo, or common council; but at the close of the Revolution, in 1785, Colonel Don Esteban Miro, who had served under Galvez, was appointed governor and took up residence in New Orleans.

The Americans north of the new boundary had little love for Miro, though of course their evaluation of him was governed entirely by his attitude toward them. Much of the history of New Orleans during this period has been written from that point of view. That, considered in the light of future events, may have a certain validity, but it is hardly the way to present an objective picture of New Orleans during the last twenty years of the Spanish regime. As a matter of fact Spain, after the close of the Revolution, came to be regarded more and more as a usurper in the domain of the United States. In the light of so-called manifest destiny, perhaps this view, too, was later validated; but at the close of the Revolution Spain controlled vastly more North American territory than did the fledgling United States, and certainly had as much right to it. During the Revolution that right was fully recognized by the Americans; indeed they were glad of it, because most men on the Atlantic seaboard didn't believe they could control the country between the Alleghenies and the Mississippi, much less that vast and unknown domain beyond the great river. Be that as it may, much New Orleans history has been written as though the Spanish never enjoyed more than squatters' rights, that they were merely allowed to use New Orleans and Louisiana until such time as the Americans were ready to exercise their just rights.

Spain had campaigned in the Gulf during the Revolution, it is true, but it had been *against* England rather than *for* the Colonies. And why not? Except as a matter of political expediency, why should a power such as Spain take sides with an upstart republic which was avowedly in opposition to everything Spain had stood for and was? Of course there was only one answer: Spain had fought for what she deemed her rights. The war over, she went ahead with her affairs as before, regarding the United States as having no more claim on her generosity than any other national neighbor.

From Governor Miro New Orleans received little but good. In fact, New Orleans had a succession of Spanish governors with whom it is impossible to find much fault. They had their defects, of course, as what human being has not, but they were a long way from fitting the popular conception of the cruel and tyrannous Spanish colonial governor.

As an example of the reverse of the medal there was the treatment given the Capuchin monk Antonio de Sedella by Governor Miro. Sedella arrived in New Orleans in the spring of 1789, and soon afterward informed Miro that he, Sedella, had been appointed Commissary of the Inquisition for New Orleans. He intended to carry on the Inquisition in the city to the best of his ability and told Miro that he expected to use the garrison in order to discover and properly punish heretics. (Certainly New Orleans would have been a fertile field!) But Miro, instead of playing the part of the cruel Spanish governor and entering wholeheartedly into the scheme, was shocked and horrified. He furnished Sedella with soldiers, but only to put him under arrest and hustle him aboard a ship which the following day sailed for Cadiz and took the American Inquisition with it. And Miro hadn't dallied. In fact, he acted within hours of the time he was first certain of the priest's real intentions, and his action seems to speak well enough for itself. A century and a half later it was maintained that Sedella's intentions had been misunderstood, but that was not Miro's feeling in the matter at the time and his action in so summarily ousting a representative of the Inquisition— if Sedella actually was—required more than a little moral courage.

Father Antoine later returned to New Orleans and attained a considerable reputation for a number of things, though not as a representative of the Inquisition. That, however, belongs to another phase of New Orleans' story and has nothing to do with Governor Miro.

Immediately after the Revolution trade in New Orleans again flourished and the population increased faster than ever before. Twenty-two hundred persons came to New Orleans within five years and at times there were as many as forty ships—sea-going vessels, not upcountry flatboats—moored at the river wharves—certainly no mean number for a town of New Orleans' stature.

Again the historical attitude of the United States toward New Orleans comes into question. According to the British-American treaty ending the Revolution, the citizens of *both* nations were to have free access to the Mississippi "from its source to the ocean." Which was all very well except that neither party apparently had any real right—except that of force—to make such an agreement. The British no longer claimed any territory which touched on the Mississippi, and the United States held the east bank only as far down as the northern Spanish boundary, approximately the mouth of the Red River. Neither of them claimed a foot of territory at the mouth of the Mississippi or for many miles to the north.

The Port of New Orleans

These things being true, it is hard to see how they expected to allocate themselves rights to the river, though of course there was no harm in the declaration for there was always the chance that Spain might acquiesce. The fact is that Spain did not, and there seems to be no reason why she should have. She had fought a series of wars to control the Gulf and saw no reason why she should, to all practical purposes, give away the control she had shed blood to gain. It would have been almost as reasonable for Spain to demand free access to the St. Lawrence.

There was a reason, of course, but it was one of historical necessity and so not likely to be recognized by any of the interested parties. The Mississippi was one of the great highways of the world and so would be a bone of contention until its future was settled beyond doubt and possibility of change.

Because the American territory east of the Mississippi was denied free access to New Orleans, it has often been assumed that New Orleans suffered thereby. That has been the American point of view, but there is not and never was any basis for it. New Orleans *might* have had more trade had the river been free during this period, but it couldn't have been much more. There were good and sufficient reasons.

For over a thousand miles only a mile of water separated Spanish and American territory, and again it was a matter of money and trade not recognizing boundaries. Americans above the mouth of the Yazoo could not take their produce directly to New Orleans, but they could and did take it across the river to Spanish St. Louis and the other posts scattered the length of the Mississippi's west bank. Of course this extra handling redounded to the benefit of the Spanish, and the Americans didn't like it, but that had nothing to do with the life and prosperity of New Orleans. What couldn't come downstream from the east bank found ready movement from the western shore, and New Orleans prospered accordingly.

Furthermore, there was some direct traffic with New

Orleans in spite of Spanish restrictions. Spanish officials could be bribed by the right people, and were. And at least some of the "bribery" was a part of Spanish policy. Spain had more than a few pensioners (a useful word) among the Americans in the Ohio Valley and so was probably better informed about public opinion in that area than was Congress itself; certainly she paid more attention to it than Congress did. For while Spain felt that she was perfectly within her rights in closing the Mississippi, she was also aware that forcible resentment by the frontier Americans would do her no good, right or no right.

New Orleans in the meantime lived a life of her own, a life more or less aloof and very unlike the rest of the Mississippi Valley. Government was Spanish and New Orleans seemed well enough satisfied with it, but everything else was French. That the Spanish made no attempt to change this—except in minor instances—is another example of their easy tolerance.

The city experienced floods, yellow fever, and malaria as always, and more or less took these visitations for granted. She was prospering, at least that part of the white population which was presumed to have a right to prosper, and forming that especial social organization, with its taboos, liberties, odd contrasts, and language which came to be known as Creole. Life was leisurely, both because of slavery and the climate, and a living easy to get. Relations between men and between men and women were strictly ordered and the proprieties well defined. It was an aloof island at the foot of the great river which was becoming, whether or no, more American every year.

It was not without its troubles as well.

Like any other town anywhere, New Orleans had suffered from fires, but never had the damage to the city as a whole been great. On March 21, 1788, it was to be different. During the past few years the population had grown, so likewise the number of buildings. Following a tendency remarked before, all the new buildings had been erected within the original limits of the town, most of them were built of wood, and the city had no fire protection worth the name.

On this occasion a candle on the altar of a private chapel in Chartres Street, the home of Don Vincente José Nuñez, military treasurer of the province, was overturned and set fire to some draperies. There was a high wind blowing, and as the house of Nuñez was consumed the fire spread with terrible speed. It is a matter of record that it was Good Friday and use of the church bells to sound a general alarm was refused, but it is hard to see what difference that would have made anyway. The wind was high and within five hours between eight and nine hundred buildings were destroyed. Evidently this was an act of God, and even had the general alarm been sounded it would have helped but little. Possibly some additional personal property and mercantile stocks could have been saved; that would have been about all.

Governor Miro did his best in the circumstances. He set up tents in the Place d'Armes to house the homeless who could not find refuge with friends and relatives, furnished them rations, and guarded against looting. In addition he at once sent three ships to Philadelphia after a supply of medicines, provisions, nails, and other immediate necessities, to be paid for with government funds. Miro's report to Madrid represents the loss of government property and records as being negligible, but he made a distinction between property belonging expressly to the Spanish authority and that of New Orleans and the province. The parish church, the municipal building—meeting place of the cabildo and repository of the parish records—the Capuchin presbytère, and the jail were all destroyed, as were some of the military barracks.

The losses, as soon afterward inventoried by Miro, reached a total of $2,595,561, a staggering sum considering New Orleans' size at the time.

Staggering as the loss was financially, in another way it was not great. It was generally agreed that in the New Orleans of the eighteenth century there was, architecturally speaking, not one thing worth preserving. It was an ill-built town of nondescript wooden hovels, their only virtue the fact that they provided shelter. Thus the fire may have been a blessing in disguise, though the loss was hard to bear at the moment.

In other places such devastating fires have provided the inspiration for new cities nobler in proportions, more pleasing to the eye, and more convenient for the traveler-about-town. Not so with New Orleans. Ready and willing to rebuild their city Orleanians were; but they rebuilt it almost exactly as it had been before, with the same narrow streets, unimproved, the only open space the block-square Place d'Armes. They hadn't yet learned their lesson and wooden buildings were replaced by wooden buildings, and thatched roofs were not uncommon in the poorer parts of the city.

The private burdens were heavy and there was little or no money for the rebuilding of semi-public structures. Again it was Don Andreas Almonaster y Roxas who came forward with his large purse open. Again is the proper word, for when in 1779 the hurricane which sank Galvez's embryo navy also destroyed the Charity Hospital, Almonaster had volunteered to rebuild that structure. The new and far finer structure—its cost was $114,000—was built during the years 1784–86. A year later, in 1787, Almonaster built a stuccoed brick chapel at the Convent of the Ursulines. So now, after the conflagration of 1788, he volunteered to build St. Louis Cathedral, facing the Place d'Armes on the site of the old parish church. The cathedral is reputed to have cost $50,000. In addition he erected, just above the church on Chartres Street, a new municipal building, now called the Cabildo after the name of the governing body which used it, and around the corner on St. Peter Street he provided a new jail. All this was undertaken at Almonaster's personal expense, his only apparent reward a perpetual weekly mass to be said for the repose of his soul by the priests of the church.

Through his influence, but not entirely at his expense, the town erected the *halles de boucheries,* the old French Market, on Levee Street, where the homesick settlers of the German Coast had first brought their produce. Solid stone, and solid Spanish architecture, the Market stood as it had been built until the 1930s, when the PWA wrought what is supposed to be an improvement upon it.

In 1791–92 Miro was succeeded by Colonel François Louis Hector, Baron de Carondelet, and the latter took what he thought were steps to prevent another disaster such as 1788. He divided the town into four districts, organized a volunteer fire department of sorts, and reorganized the police, all with a view to controlling future fires.

But his preparations were not good enough. In December 1794 some children playing in a Royal Street patio started a fire in the face of a strong north wind, and again it was soon out of control. This fire lasted only three hours but in that time managed to destroy two hundred and twelve buildings in a town not yet fully recovered from the last holocaust. The number of buildings lost was less but the financial loss greater than in 1788, for this time the flames concentrated more on the city's wholesale and retail establishments. Only two stores were left standing, and this time the customhouse was destroyed, but fortunately Almonaster's new structures on the Place d'Armes escaped. Again Almonaster was angel and provided a new customhouse.

In spite of these two disasters only a few years apart, little more was done about providing a better fire-fighting organization, but the city had learned its lessons in other ways. The wooden buildings disappeared, to be replaced by stone, brick, or stuccoed brick structures in the Spanish style, and original French New Orleans began to acquire the general appearance it has even now.

And that is a curious thing. The original French city is known as the French Quarter the world over, and visitors who know no better—as after all why should they?—assume that the architecture is also French; it seems that it should be.

St. Louis Cathedral and Jackson Square in New Orleans. Built
in 1794, St. Louis Cathedral is one of the most famous churches
in North America.

Spanish Interlude

But it is Spanish; that plus certain variations which are strictly New Orleans and nothing else—such, for example, as building some of the older houses on pillars in order to keep out flood-waters, and slave quarters built across the rear of the lots. The inner patios or courtyards, the iron balconies above the narrow streets, shuttered doors and windows, stuccoed walls, and general style are as Spanish as the mantilla and fandango.

Because the social order was so predominantly French the result might easily have been otherwise, for the citizenry could be pretty obstinate about matters it considered to be strictly within its own sphere. But there were a number of reasons for the Spanish effect. The first was of course the government, which naturally followed the home style in its buildings. Another was the influence of Almonaster, who, since he was paying for so much building, presumably dictated what style was to be used. And the final reason was that the architecture was exactly suited to the New Orleans climate, whereas the original structures probably never had been. Shutters provided at once needed ventilation and privacy—shaded patios were cool oases in the wilting summer heat—while high ceilings and thick brick walls contributed to the same effect.

After 1794 the first buildings of more than one story made their appearance, though it was some years before buildings of three and four stories were built. Of course not all the new structures were two-storied by any means, and even now there are whole blocks of one-storied wooden houses in the remoter corners of the French Quarter, houses which are neither French nor Spanish but wholly "New Orleans."

But, French or Spanish, New Orleans was, and indeed the old city still remains, one of the few cities in the Mississippi Valley to be erected with any sort of architectural harmony in mind. It is this effect of Old World harmony in its physical appearance which has caused New Orleans to be called picturesque, charming, enchanting, quaint, and what not. And since this atmosphere is a distinct asset in connection with the tourist trade, New Orleans authority has seen to it that the French Quarter retains it.

Though they cheerfully rebuilt their town so solidly that much of it still stands, Orleanians steadfastly refused to do anything about the streets and the sewerage system—or lack of the latter. Nobody saw any connection between the town's general bad health and the fact that the streets resembled cesspools. As for street improvement, there was an almost universal belief that any sort of paving would soon sink out of sight in the mud. Nobody had ever tried it; they simply took it for granted and let it go at that.

In her trials by fire New Orleans had suffered heavy financial losses, but even as she lost money she was in the process of getting it back with interest. For during this period events which would have an important influence on her future commerce and prosperity were in the making.

Forty years earlier the Jesuits had raised sugar cane on their New Orleans plantation but had failed in their efforts to produce commercial sugar. A few years later one Debreuil, who had experimented unsuccessfully with a cotton gin, took up the sugar problem. He did a little better than the Jesuits but his sugar also was far from being a commercial success. Then in 1791 came the black revolt in San Domingo and a number of French refugees, who had successfully produced sugar in the island, found their way to New Orleans, but for some reason their efforts here were not successful either—it may have been a difference in the type of cane. Two Spaniards, Mendez and Solis, made rum and syrup but seem not to have tried sugar. Louisiana in general despaired of producing the sweet stuff commercially.

Entered then Etienne de Boré. He had lived in France until he was thirty-four, when he married a woman with property near New Orleans (it is now within the limits of the city), and returned to operate the plantation. When, for a number of reasons, it was no longer possible to raise indigo, Boré determined, against the advice of his family and friends, to try sugar. He secured canes from Mendez and Solis, planted a crop, harvested it, and made sugar—$12,000 worth the first year!

The result was agricultural revolution and within a few years Louisiana, with New Orleans its center as usual, was to become the sugar bowl of America.

Within the same period, too, use of Whitney's cotton gin was to become widespread and cotton likewise added to the prosperity of New Orleans and the Delta.

All this, the fires and the financial hardship they caused, the revolution in sugar and cotton production, were primarily civilian commercial concerns, and outwardly the city was becoming a real commercial center. But these purely civilian commercial affairs had an opposite side, and the city was also fast becoming the hottest bed of political intrigue in the Western Hemisphere, the Mecca of those who would far rather scheme in complications than get a living by any simple, direct means.

The tale is long and complicated and probably has a hundred sub-plots which now are lost and forgotten, but there were certain themes and figures which stand out clearly.

The first of these from the North was General James Wilkinson, scoundrel of parts. Wilkinson was one of those not-uncommon figures in the American scene who seem to achieve their greatest rewards by violating every rule of public and private morals. Without much good reason he had been made a brigadier general in the Continental Army, where in time he engaged in the Conway Cabal against Washington and was one of the later intimates of Benedict Arnold. Being suspect in the East, Wilkinson left the army and came to Louisville in 1784, ostensibly as a plain citizen having a look at the new country with a view toward settlement. But public affairs, worthy or otherwise, drew Wilkinson like a magnet, and before long, probably by virtue of his previous military position, he had attained considerable influence over the Kentucky

militia, supposed to have been the only organized body of
opinion in that part of the new territory. This put him in opposition to George Rogers Clark, who despite his numerous
failures after Vincennes was still the dominant military figure
in the West. Wilkinson promptly set about discrediting
Clark, as he had tried to do Washington, and even went so far
as to forge letters to prove a case against Clark. It is true that
Clark was not entirely innocent in the matter of anti-Spanish
intrigue, but what he did was done openly and for reasons
which, if mistaken in the light of future events, were easily
understood. Wilkinson played both ends against the middle
solely for his personal benefit, the middle being the New West
between the Mississippi and the Alleghenies, the ends Congress and the new states on the one hand and Spanish Louisiana
on the other. He tried to incite the Westerners against the
East, then in turn tried to incite them against Spain in order to
sell information of the plan to Miro at New Orleans.

In 1787 Wilkinson went down the big river with a flat-
boatload of Kentucky produce for New Orleans, his plans
well laid in advance. He was stopped at Natchez as a matter
of course but allowed to proceed when he bribed the Spanish
authority there. At New Orleans his cargo was again seized,
but one of Wilkinson's agents—it was probably Daniel Clark
—told Miro that Wilkinson *wanted* his property confiscated
in order to provide an excuse for an attack on Spanish possessions by the Kentuckians. Whether or not Miro believed his
informant—he had other sources of information in the Ohio
Valley—he allowed Wilkinson to sell his cargo and gave him
a personal audience. Thereupon Wilkinson assured him that
the West was ripe for secession from the seaboard area and
ready to fall into the arms of Spain. This was not *quite* true
but there was enough truth in it to make the story plausible.
Whereupon Miro and Wilkinson made a deal. Wilkinson was
to receive secret trading concessions at New Orleans and two
thousand dollars per year, in return for which he was to act
as Spain's agent with a view toward eventually attaching the

West to Spain. At the same time Wilkinson was trying to create the impression in the East that what secessionist sentiment existed was fostered by George Rogers Clark. Thus Wilkinson was guilty of double treachery, for pay, and was known in the Spanish diplomatic correspondence—rather melodramatically—as Number Thirteen.

How far Wilkinson was trusted by Miro and his successors is conjectural, but probably they judged his character as they would that of any man who would sell his country for such a paltry sum and acted toward him accordingly. If Wilkinson had been merely a backwoods agent in the pay of Spain, whose intrigues eventually came to nothing, he would not be worth the space already given him here. But he was a great deal more than that and, given a certain missing element in his make-up, might well have changed the future map of the United States. Not so many years after he formed his Spanish connection he was reinstated in the United States Army as a lieutenant colonel in the Western Department, which was just about the only department of the army at the time. In 1792 he was promoted to brigadier general and when Mad Anthony Wayne was killed at Fallen Timbers in 1796 Wilkinson was made commander in chief of the midget United States Army—again an example of Wilkinson's faculty of thriving best on his misdeeds, for during this time, in fact until 1800, he remained in the pay of Spain as a secret agent. It has been said that after 1791, when Carondelet succeeded Miro as governor and Wilkinson's plans had come to nothing, Wilkinson's status became that of a mere spy. But it is doubtful that Wilkinson ever had any real plans except those which would best serve himself.

There was secessionist sentiment in the West, it is true, but it was in no way co-ordinated. It consisted mainly of resentment toward Congress because of real or fancied neglect, and while this resentment of Congress was almost universal the feeling about Spain was sharply divided. One faction talked of leaving the United States and seeking the protection of Spain, whereas the other party—of which George Rogers Clark was a member—wanted to attack Louisiana and West Florida and annex them to a new republic to be set up in the West. Certainly the two views were radically opposed and, possibly to the good fortune of both sides, there was no one in the West capable of reconciling them.

Neither was Wilkinson's New Orleans trading concession as valuable as he had expected it to be. He shared this concession with backers in Kentucky and the New Orleans arrangement was not an open one. That is, Miro and his successors had no authority to grant such concessions and so for appearance' sake had to confiscate a certain amount of Wilkinson's goods, enough anyway to make his profits no more than ordinary. For Spanish authority in New Orleans was in turn spied upon by agents from Madrid, and a governor never knew what reports about *him* might be filtering across the Atlantic.

But out of Wilkinson's dealings in commerce came one significant thing. In 1788 his flatboats took the first load of trade goods *up* the river to the Kentucky market. Of course other goods had gone before, but always it had been for the Indian trade or had been munitions and supplies for the American frontier troops. This was pure commerce between white men, the forerunner of what the next two decades would bring to the great valley.

In spite of its growing commercial importance and metropolitan atmosphere New Orleans was still a small town, and at this distance one wonders a little how such a small place could contain so much of human activity. Refugees from San Domingo had been welcomed in the city and it was a group of these who set up the first theater in New Orleans, in St. Peter Street between Royal and Chartres. (Was there any significance in the fact that it was almost directly across the street from the new jail?) And the first newspaper, *La Moniteur de la Louisiane*, was published in French by a San Domingan under the patronage of Carondelet.

Spanish Interlude

In the meantime, during the early 1790s, the first reverberations of the French Revolution echoed in New Orleans, and shortly thereafter Spain was again at war with France. In New Orleans the situation was both delicate and confused, the French population torn between conflicting loyalties. Just where *should* their sympathies lie? The war with Spain—or with France if you will—made a choice even more difficult.

But in the French theater "La Marseillaise" was heard for the first time in America and the actors insisted on interpolating all sorts of revolutionary propaganda—they, who were themselves refugees from another kind of revolution. Carondelet closed the theater and—delicate touch—forbade the further importation of Yankee-made clocks decorated with the Goddess of Liberty. In the dives and pothouses—and there were swarms of them—the proletariat sang ditties concerned with hanging the aristocrats, in New Orleans presumably meaning both French and Spanish, to lampposts, though as a matter of fact there wasn't a lamppost in the city and wouldn't be for several years.

Carondelet was frankly worried, and accordingly rebuilt the city's puny fortifications. There were bastions at the upper and lower river corners, and three lesser structures along the line of the present Rampart Street. The chain of forts and stockades was connected with an earthen parapet, and the whole surrounded by a moat forty feet wide. It was this moat on the upriver side which eventually became Canal Street, one of the world's great thoroughfares. To the Orleanians Carondelet explained that the fortifications were for protection from the rampant Kentuckians, and there was some truth in the statement. To Madrid he explained that the forts would serve equally well in the event of an insurrection —which might occur at any time.

Whatever their faults, the lot of a Spanish governor of New Orleans was never a happy one for long at a time.

Although the Westerners had been driven almost to extremes by the Federal government's lack of sympathy with their problems, the government had not entirely ignored their needs. It was slow and acted for reasons other than those advanced by the Westerners, but it did act in time. In 1795 Thomas Pinckney and Godoy of Spain signed a treaty whereby free navigation of the Mississippi was assured for three years, with the provision that the treaty would be extended by negotiation at the end of that period. American produce for transshipment through New Orleans was to be duty free, subject only to reasonable warehouse rentals.

Thus at one stroke the cause of most of the Western unrest was removed. They had no real sympathy with the Spanish and never had had. All they wanted was the free use of the great valley's natural outlet and now they had it—at least for the next three years, and much could happen in that time.

By and large New Orleans didn't care. The treaty merely meant that business should be even better than before, and though Carondelet had been afraid of revolt, his fears had been groundless.

CHAPTER VIII

Enter the Americans

THE DOWN-RIVER FLATBOAT trade got its real start in the three years from 1795 to 1798, and New Orleans got its first close-up of the frontier Americans en masse. Frankly there was only one thing about the new race that the Orleanians liked: the increased traffic it brought to the port.

Of course New Orleans had seen other Americans, many of them—Oliver Pollock, James Willing; Captain Robert George, Daniel Clark, Wilkinson, a host of sea captains and lesser seamen. And while these certainly did not fit exactly into the New Orleans social fabric, they were sufficiently self-possessed and worldly to know their way around and were not offensive to the Orleanians in a social sense—the lesser seamen excepted.

This new breed of frontier American was quite another matter. Frontier America of the late eighteenth and early nineteenth centuries was a hard place and bred a hard race, and when New Orleans became the outlet for their produce it became also the outlet for their pent-up animal spirits. It was the end of the long, hard trek down the river—let no one suppose that because these flatboats *floated* downstream there was no labor involved—the place where they received perhaps the first real money they had seen in a year. The time they spent in New Orleans was, for very many of them, the one carefree interlude in a year of toil, hardship, and frontier loneliness. For this short space they were removed from the restraining influences of wives and families, the criticism of neighbors, and the admonitions of the circuit-riding preacher of the backwoods. Most of them took the fullest advantage of this temporary spell of complete freedom from care and responsibility. All this, of course, is written about those Westerners who flatboated their own produce, perhaps together with that of a neighbor, not the professional boatmen who came later. This latter group came soon enough and created a special havoc of their own, but they were not the first Americans to come down the river regularly. They were, rather, an outgrowth of this earlier traffic.

Of course there was a certain stratum in New Orleans which welcomed this first rush of wild Americans with open arms, ready and willing to provide any and all kinds of entertainment—for a price. For the most part, they had hitherto catered to sailors, and these howling Americans who apparently wanted to crowd a year's drinking, fighting, and general hell-raising into a few days or a week were a new experience. As has been said often in these pages, New Orleans had had a first-rate underworld, considering the size of the town, for years, but it preferred its sin on the quieter side, a knife under the ribs in the darkness rather than open warfare with fists, feet, teeth, and the throwing of furniture. But if that was what the Americans wanted, and apparently it was, New Orleans would be glad to oblige. It required some years to turn the town into the sink of wholesale iniquity it later became, but here was an auspicious beginning.

All of which seems to be a considerable digression from the statement that Orleanians didn't like the Americans, but of course the brothel keepers and liquor dealers were in the minority and in no way represented the bulk of the population. The French Orleanians were disdainful alike of the

Americans and their own lower social strata, but still they never made the slightest effort to do anything practical about the city's sins. Again it appears that the respectable element simply didn't care. They felt above such things as regulating what was in the main petty crime—at least it was petty crime in the beginning—and the morals of people of no social consequence.

In spite of its cosmopolitan character New Orleans differed in many ways from similar cities along the Eastern seaboard. New Orleans, for example, had practically no taverns—meaning accommodations for traveling strangers—whereas in the North and East the taverns were likely to be centers of general social activity. The reason for this was not hard to find. The French were a gregarious and social people among themselves. The plantations radiated outward from New Orleans and there were few plantation folk who did not have both relatives and friends in the city, and country friends and relatives were accommodated as a matter of course, indeed as a social obligation that dare not be refused. Negroes and other servants were taken care of in the same way. Public eating and drinking, except of course among the lower classes, while not exactly frowned upon, were regarded as unnecessary. With New Orleans still not entirely filling up its eleven-by-six squares, there was scarcely a broker, merchant, or businessman who could not reach his home in ten minutes or less from any part of the town—and the siesta, a Spanish innovation, was popular as well. The time would come, and that not far off, when half the business of New Orleans would be done in the coffeehouses, saloons, and restaurants, but that was not so now.

Orleanians in general had such business contacts with the ruffian Americans as were necessary, but otherwise left them to the tender mercies of those who could stand them. It was almost unthinkable that ordinary Americans be admitted to the company of Creole ladies, or indeed to any kind of Creole "society," no matter what their social standing might be at home. It was a prejudice which would require more than a generation of Creole-American government and business association to overcome, and for long after that the coalition was far from complete.

The three years of free deposit at New Orleans passed quickly but it was taken for granted, by Americans and Orleanians alike, that the treaty would be extended. Orleanians might not care for Americans personally, but they liked the business they fostered. As a matter of fact, when the treaty expired it was not formally extended, but neither did Spain close the river as it had before. Instead, relations between Spain and the United States, so far as the Mississippi was concerned, remained in a state of suspension. In New Orleans Spanish officials occasionally haled a luckless trader into the courts, but this was a matter of exercising the local police power rather than national policy.

To Orleanians this was satisfactory enough, but it did not suit the turbulent Americans. They wanted a showdown and were determined to have it. The West had had a phenomenal growth and expected even more, and to the West it was intolerable that the great river should be continually subject to Spain's unexplained whims. This time the feeling was grim and businesslike, almost without bombast, and this time even the East believed the West was in earnest; it believed it so strongly that President John Adams issued orders for an invading force to be made ready on the Ohio. Adams' term was drawing to a close and he was to have no more to do with the New Orleans problem, but now, at least, the East was fully aware of its importance.

In the end the fate of New Orleans was to be determined in Europe, even as it had always been, and it was the meteoric Napoleon who was to be the deciding factor.

New Orleans had watched the first consul with interest since the beginning of his rise, and feeling about him was considerably confused. Because Bonaparte was French, in action at least, Orleanians were elated whenever he achieved a new

Oak Alley. One of the old Mississippi plantations situated not far from New Orleans.

triumph. But, on the other hand, some of his republicanisms distressed them terribly—as, for instance, when he said to the San Domingans: "Whatever your color or your origin, you are free." To the Orleanian whose world was built on Negro slavery, these were indeed ominous words. Orleanians, and a great many other people as well, were yet to learn that the first consul was as fancy a double-dealer as the century was likely to see.

The series of events which were to settle the future of New Orleans began when Spain, in the treaty of San Ildefonso, retroceded Louisiana to France. At the moment Napoleon really wanted Louisiana, seeing in it the opportunity of re-building an overseas empire which would rival England's. But this treaty, like so many before and after it, was "secret." That is, it was consummated in 1800, but Spain continued to rule in Louisiana and France made no effort to take it over. It was the situation of 1763–66 all over again except with the national positions reversed. When news of the treaty leaked out, as it was bound to do, Napoleon publicly denied that it existed or was even contemplated.

Naturally the news leaked in New Orleans, too, and was heard there with mixed emotions. Always there existed the old dream of reuniting with France—but with which France, the old monarchy of Versailles or this rabid new republic? Opinions were based almost entirely on the holders' personal social status, or how much they stood to gain or lose. And whatever the faults of Spain, she was nearer the old France, politically and religiously, than this unpredictable new republic.

For Mr. Jefferson, successor to John Adams, the problem concerned a great deal more than the mere ownership of New Orleans. Should France reoccupy Louisiana it was probable that the problem of the West would merely have changed nationalities. The United States had lately adjusted her diffi-culties with her ex-ally, France, and Jefferson had no desire to start bickering with her all over again—a circumstance which would almost inevitably ally the United States with

England, an almost equally repugnant thought. One alternative, Jefferson realized, might be hostilities with *both* France and England, which would indeed be catastrophe!

Time would simplify the problem for Mr. Jefferson, time and England's sea power. Napoleon's military genius could not affect the movements of the British navy and it became increasingly evident that sea power was the key to Louisiana —at least as long as it remained separated from contiguous American territory. So for Napoleon the issue was clear: he could not chance a defense of Louisiana at the risk of losing presumably more valuable European territory. Actually, Bonaparte did make one gesture toward occupying Louisiana, but the expeditionary force ran afoul of yellow fever and Toussaint L'Ouverture's black revolt in San Domingo and was completely lost. He was again too deeply involved on the Continent to risk more strength in Louisiana. The question arises, why should he need to conquer what had already been given him? Of course he could have occupied New Orleans with a regiment; the army would have been needed to *hold* it against England—and that England would attack was a foregone conclusion. Yet so long as Louisiana remained ostensibly Spanish, England could not attack territory held by her ally against France.

In 1802 Spain again closed New Orleans, and again the news traveled up the river like wildfire, with the West ready to act. (Actually the river had been closed by the personal orders of Morales, Spanish intendant at New Orleans, and was not directed by Madrid, but the Americans were not inclined to split hairs.) But this time the news went on to Jefferson, and he was Westerner enough to realize that this was the moment that counted. There must be action *now* or the West would be lost, and by now the East was beginning to see, though vaguely, to be sure, what such a loss would mean.

It was fortunate for everyone—except perhaps England— that Mr. Jefferson's decision to act coincided almost exactly with Napoleon's decision to be rid of a territory which could bring him little more than trouble. The decisions having been made on both sides, the remainder of the negotiations was largely detail. James Monroe was sent to France to arrange these details, though his appointment appears to have been largely a gesture to impress the impatient West. Robert Livingston was already resident minister in France and could have handled the deal at less expense. Be that as it may, the deal was finally arranged by Monroe and Livingston together and the resultant treaty dated April 30, 1803.

It has been said that Jefferson, and thus Monroe and Livingston, had no intention of acquiring anything except New Orleans and its island, which would have given the United States complete control of the Mississippi's east bank, that it was Napoleon who insisted it be all or nothing. It may be so. Yet Jefferson should have known that without New Orleans the rest of Louisiana wasn't worth much to anyone, and to a lesser extent the reverse was also true; Bonaparte realized that if no one else did. It is probable that Jefferson did intend to acquire more than New Orleans alone but refused to admit to himself how much more. Perhaps he relied on the negotiations in France to settle that. If that seems vague it must be remembered that knowledge of Louisiana as a whole was equally vague, so Jefferson was in a way justified in his feeling. Everyone concerned knew where Louisiana began; no man had the slightest idea where it ended. Since no one professed to know where the western and northern boundaries lay, none had ever been specified in any treaty. Nor were they now. The province was transferred "fully and in the same manner as France received it from Spain in the treaty of San Ildefonso . . . with the same extent it now has in the hands of Spain, and that it had when France [previously] possessed it; and such as it should be after the treaties subsequently entered into between Spain and other States." Vague it was, and certainly it put Napoleon safely outside any future boundary disputes; but the terms could hardly have been more specific anyway. The cash involved, as every school history dutifully

records, was sixty million francs, $11,250,000 at the then rate
of exchange, plus the assumption of certain claims against
France held by American citizens.

Thus Napoleon, for needed cash, did the United States a
service of enormous consequence, though undoubtedly he
viewed the deal more as a blow to British desires. (England,
however, seems not to have been as much concerned with the
transfer as might have been expected.) While Jefferson contemplated his deliberate rashness with growing apprehension
—he firmly believed he had no constitutional right to make the
purchase—the future of the great river was settled and the
West, never apt to worry over such minor details as uncon-
stitutionality if the end was desirable, rejoiced and prepared
to reap the expected benefits.

In New Orleans itself the story was somewhat different.
There the same old drama of duplicity and intrigue was
played out to the end, with the reasons thereof still impossible
of ordinary understanding.

As in 1763–66 New Orleans had heard all sorts of rumors
concerning the negotiations, even from the time of San Ildefonso, but no direct and official information. If Spanish officialdom had such information they didn't make it public. Orleanians, out of previous experience, waited to see what sort
of truth would emerge from the welter of rumors.

There were no doubts on the part of the Americans who
set out for New Orleans in the style of a latter-day gold rush.

M. Pierre Clement de Laussat, French Colonial prefect, arrived in New Orleans late in March 1803 with the air of a
man preparing for a long stay. Recalling the republican attitude toward slavery and the republican anti-Catholicism,
Orleanians and the neighboring planters didn't know whether
to rejoice or despair, but outwardly they were dutifully grateful for their presumed deliverance and final return to the
mother country; and nothing Laussat said or did officially
caused them to believe otherwise than that France had taken

over for good. In fact, Laussat allayed their fears by assuring them that any change in the existing order would only be undertaken slowly and in the light of experience.

It is true that Laussat arrived in New Orleans about a month before the Louisiana Purchase was finally consummated, but he must have been aware of his peculiar status. One of his professed objectives was to prepare for the coming of a large French military force, and while he made little effort in that direction it provided an excuse for not taking over the government from the Spanish, with whom, incidentally, he was on the best of terms. The official news of the American transfer reached New Orleans in July—actually about the same time it was first known on the Eastern seaboard —but still the government remained Spanish and the Spanish apparently made no preparations for departure. No wonder Orleanians, in spite of official statements, were as puzzled as they had been during the Spanish dallying in the 1760s.

Though Laussat continued to talk of an expected French army, naturally none arrived, and on November 30 Governor Salcedo officially handed over the province to Laussat; and the Marquis Casa Calvo declared the people of Louisiana absolved from their allegiance to Spain. The crowd in the Place d'Armes, listening to the hollow ceremonies, must have been struck by the ridiculous hypocrisy of the whole business. In New Orleans "allegiance" to any government had been for forty years hardly more than a word, and a word usually spoken in irony. How could Orleanians be expected to view it in any other light now?

In the meantime the city was again without a government except in the person of Laussat. The latter apparently did not know exactly when to expect the American commissioners and gladly accepted the offer of Daniel Clark, former agent of Wilkinson and now American consul, to form a temporary police force from among Americans already in the city and those Creoles who wished a hand in preserving order. Armed sections of this volunteer force patrolled the streets night and day, until the arrival of United States troops under the command of none other than General James Wilkinson.

The American Commissioners were but a few days away. They arrived in New Orleans to take over from Laussat on December 30, 1803, a short three weeks after the official Spanish-French transfer.

William Charles Cole Claiborne was twenty-eight years old, a native of Virginia, and a career man in American politics. He had early been befriended by Thomas Jefferson when the latter was Secretary of State, and by John—"Nolichucky Jack"—Sevier, delegate from the new territory below the Ohio River. At their suggestion he studied law for a brief time, then emigrated to Tennessee, where his friend Sevier was a power in politics. When Blount of Tennessee was expelled from the Senate and Andrew Jackson took his seat, young Claiborne was given Jackson's old place in the House. He wasn't of legal age for such service but the House didn't seem to mind. In the contested presidential election of 1801 he controlled the vote of the Tennessee bloc and, as was expected, cast it solidly for his friend Jefferson. As reward he was appointed governor of Mississippi Territory and was serving in that capacity when he was named one of the Commissioners to accept Louisiana on behalf of the United States. He joined General Wilkinson at Fort Adams in December and they traveled the rest of the way together.

Of what followed let a better hand tell it:

. . . The time fixed for the entrance into the city was Tuesday the twentieth. Early on that day the American troops, with the bands playing the airs of France and the United States, moved in order of battle to the city gates. There the *Spanish* troops [italics author's] in like order received and then escorted them to the Cabildo on the Place d'Armes, where the Commissioners exhibited their credentials to Laussat.

When the credentials of the American Commissioners, the treaty, and the powers of the French Commissioners to transfer Louisiana had been read to the crowd that filled the Cabildo, the delivery of the Province to the United States was proclaimed, the keys of the city were handed to Claiborne, and the subjects of France absolved by Laussat from allegiance to the First Consul. Claiborne then bade them welcome as citizens of the United States. They were assured that their liberty, their property, their religion, were safe; that their commerce should flourish, that their agriculture should be protected, and that they should never again be transferred.

The speech made, the Commissioners passed out into one of the balconies that looked down on the Place d'Armes crowded with men of six nationalities, where the tricolor which for twenty days had floated over the city was slowly lowered and the stars and stripes slowly raised till they met midway of the staff and were saluted. The flag of the United States was then raised, while that of France was drawn down and delivered into the hands of a French officer. As he marched off toward the barracks with the flag wrapped about his waist, the Commissioners went back to the hall of the Cabildo and to a fine dinner made ready for them by the order of Laussat.*

Claiborne has been assailed from almost every possible angle, from his extreme youth to the fact that he was not versed in the ways of the Creoles and so could not hope to gain their confidence; and he has been accused of all possible inefficiency and blundering. In almost every case his critics can muster the facts, and yet in their speculations none of them have suggested a man better suited to the place—and who might have accepted it. Claiborne was young, yes, but that was a day of young men in American government, and certainly he had had considerable experience. His legal training, while not extensive, was as good as most lawyers of the day. He had served a short time on the Tennessee Supreme Court of Law and Equity, had spent four years as a member of the House, about a year as territorial governor, and, perhaps as important a consideration as any, had the confidence of the national government as represented by Jefferson. Admit-

*A History of the People of the United States, by John Bach McMaster. New York, 1892.

tedly he might have had *more* experience, but certainly he was not a novice in government and had had more actual experience than did Lincoln when the latter campaigned for his first national office. As for a man who could sympathize with and understand Creole New Orleans, speak its two languages fluently, and at the same time govern it brilliantly—where was such a paragon to be found in the United States of 1803?

In the meantime New Orleans was again in turmoil, its citizenry once more confused, apathetic, and doubtful of all avowed good intention. In the first place, Claiborne's appointment had been made hurriedly and, since Congress had not had time to provide a specific governmental organization, Claiborne of necessity worked by rule of thumb. American now, the city in its everyday affairs still had to be regulated by the old Spanish laws—an integral part of the freedom-loving United States being governed by the code of the most reactionary government in Europe. The situation was not without its humor, but few Orleanians appreciated it then.

There was another thing—the continued presence of Spanish troops, government officials, and military officers. Because Daniel Clark had organized a body of home guards immediately after the Spanish cession, it would naturally be assumed that the Spanish had pulled up stakes and departed. Relinquish authority they did, thus the home guards, but leave they emphatically did not. They stayed right where they were and even refused to evacuate the barracks for use of the American troops.

Actually the Spanish had been given three months in which to leave the territory, so for the time being they were within their rights so far as their mere presence was concerned. But as ordinary military courtesy, if nothing else, it seems they should have handed over the military property to the dominant military authority, or at least have shared it with them. Instead American troops were quartered in the rat-ridden old fortifications or in tents in the swamps outside the city (during the worst part of the winter), and the United States paid high rents for buildings in which to store baggage, provisions, munitions, and hospital stores. Moreover, Spanish troops mounted guard daily as they had for years, and Spanish officers, from colonels to the lowliest lieutenants, haunted the coffeehouses and taverns, telling all who cared to listen that New Orleans would again be Spanish, and that soon.

To further complicate matters, the French Commissioner Laussat, with some influence because of his nationality if nothing else, also stayed on and did his bit to worry Claiborne. In the face of all this, who and what were Orleanians expected to believe?

Why, then, did not Wilkinson, with American troops at his back, assume his rightful position? Well, why indeed? Probably the best answer is that the Spanish had obstinate reasons of their own for staying, and that Wilkinson, more than vulnerable to Spanish pressure, was afraid to move openly against the power he had served for more than a decade. Had Spanish officialdom made public certain diplomatic records and correspondence, Wilkinson could have been turned overnight into the most contemptible figure in America. Even Laussat, who probably knew far less about him than the Spanish, represented him as being flighty, ignorant, rattlebrained, frequently drunk, and guilty of all sorts of other follies.

Why, also, did not Claiborne, who was supposedly the territory's chief magistrate, insist that Wilkinson act? The answer to that is obscure also, but certain reasons may be deduced. While Claiborne was Wilkinson's superior, it was also true that the latter had been specifically named military commandant by Jefferson. In addition Wilkinson was also commander in chief of the United States Army, a position not to be lightly defied even though one might believe the incumbent guilty of a great many misdeeds. And Wilkinson was a past master of explanation and excuse. Laussat might think him a fool, but he was cunning enough never to be caught openly in his misdeeds.

The following April the first contingent of Spanish troops,

some three hundred men, departed, and the barracks were handed over, but not until July were the general magazine and other military premises evacuated. Even then the Spanish commissioner, Casa Calvo, his assistant, and many other officers lingered on.

Claiborne was having troubles of his own with his one-man government, and though he tried to place the blame on the stubborn Orleanians, there was a great deal to be said on their side.

In the first place, in all the many times they had been abruptly ordered to change their national allegiance, Orleanians themselves had not once been consulted—the American occupation had provided no exception. In fact, the Americans had not even given them the consideration they had professed to show some Indian tribes. (Vocal American minorities have denounced contemporary annexations—such as Russia's taking of Estonia and Latvia—on purely humanitarian grounds, but it is difficult to see where the difference between that and the Louisiana incident lies. Time and circumstances differ, yes; morally it was the same thing.) But that aside, Orleanians had plenty of other just complaints. Part of the Louisiana Purchase terms was the stipulation that Orleanians were to enjoy the full benefits of the American system and be freely admitted to the Union as soon as practicable. It was easy for Mr. Jefferson, the Great Democrat, to agree to that. The trouble was that the United States was apparently making no effort to carry out the agreement. It was not only the larger principles of free government which were neglected, but the minor governmental drudgeries as well which are seldom thought of until they cease to function.

New Orleans was the first *seaboard* territory to be added to the original Colonies, and as such it required certain special legislation. But there were no customs regulations or men to administer them, no means of registering and licensing shipping, and no courts for administering United States laws. Pilot service in the long stretch of Mississippi from New Orleans

to the Gulf had been established as part of Spanish governmental administration, and now that also stopped functioning.
And because of all this a lot of business was going to the dogs,
whereas it should have been booming. It isn't reasonable to
blame Claiborne for all of this; he couldn't possibly manage
everything himself.

There was, too, a long and bitter Congressional battle over
the whole business of the Louisiana Purchase, but that is only
incidentally important to this chronicle and Orleanians were
only mildly interested. Congress might split hairs forever but
in the meantime Orleanians had to struggle with everyday
reality, and now when one spoke of Orleanians he meant not
only the Creoles but the new influx of respectable American
businessmen as well.

While Orleanians fretted and Claiborne struggled as best he
could, Congress was preparing a bill dealing with Louisiana.
Actually, the delay was not great and, all things considered, it
was hardly possible to move any faster. In general, the government planned for Louisiana was bad—but it might have
been a great deal worse. First, the bill divided the new territory into two parts, the lower portion to be called the Territory of Orleans. The governor was to be appointed by the
President for a term of three years. Under him was to be a
secretary appointed for four years, and a legislative council
of thirteen members. There was to be one superior court and
such inferior courts as the council should determine. In addition trial by jury was to be limited to criminal cases and civil
suits involving more than one hundred dollars.

Orleanians couldn't see a shadow of self-government in
the bill, as indeed there wasn't. In fact it was hardly different
from the old Spanish form. For all officers, including the
Legislative Council (a neat term), were to be appointed by
the President, with the Senate having no right of approval.
The council was to have no regular sessions and no powers
whatever except those allowed it by the governor. It could
neither introduce laws nor reject them, could not even hold

a session without the express consent of the governor. In short, the whole thing was a perfect blueprint for a despotism, and, strangely enough, Jefferson and Madison not only approved it but were supposed themselves to have framed it.

But if the bill touched off a bombshell in New Orleans, it did more in Congress, and the fight over it was bitter. Opponents of the bill not only showed that it violated the terms of the Purchase treaty but every concept of free government in the United States as well. The bill was passed, but only after modifications and compromises that removed a few of its worst features. Trial by jury was provided in all cases, and the House tried to get the Legislative Council elected by the people after the first year. The Senate would not agree to this last provision, but as a compromise the life of the entire bill was limited to one year. The argument was a good example of the cleavage which existed between the directly elected House and a Senate more remote from the people.

The government organization was to take place October 1, 1804, and Jefferson duly appointed the officers, including the council. But when it came time to organize, five of the appointees, Boré, Bellechasse, Cantrelle, Evan Jones, and Daniel Clark, refused to serve. They gave as reason their belief that the United States did not intend to keep the province, and that if and when it was again taken over by France or Spain they would suffer for having served in the American government. At this distance their fears seem a bit fantastic—but it is worth noting that two of those refusing service, Jones and Clark, were Americans; Clark, of course, having served as American consul before the Louisiana Purchase.

It was two months before a quorum could be obtained in the council, and in the meantime a petition of protest against the entire arrangement had been laid before Congress. The three men who carried the petition to Washington were Pierre Sauvé, Pierre Derbigny, and Jean Noel Destréhan. One wonders if they remembered a similar petition carried to Versailles by Jean Milhet in 1765. This later petition set forth the trials and tribulations of the Orleanians at great length, and in equal detail stated what should be done about them. On the whole, they were more successful than Milhet had been.

The eventual result was that Congress gave to the territory of Orleans, February 7, 1805, a government similar to that of adjacent Mississippi Territory, with the further proviso that it would be admitted as a state when its free population reached sixty thousand.

Offhand it appeared that the petitioners from New Orleans had done rather well, all things, including time, considered, for Louisiana had been part of the United States for less than fourteen months. Congress could debate longer than that over a misplaced comma. But the Orleanians were far from satisfied. They didn't object to being a part of the United States, but they insisted that they should have been admitted as a state immediately, that such was the only honest interpretation of the treaty terms. That other territories had not been so admitted had no bearing on the matter as far as the Creoles were concerned.

Up to the time the bill was actually passed, the Orleanians had stuck strictly to business, but as soon as it was law, and they had voiced their opinion of it, they had struck up friendships with the British and French ministers and, of all people, Aaron Burr! They swore publicly that the law would not be tolerated and that if they couldn't get satisfaction in Washington they would find it elsewhere—in Europe, if necessary. They stated further that from what they had seen in Washington they had no high opinion of the Union anyway. It is fair to assume that Sauvé, Destréhan, and Derbigny were fairly representative of the strongest and most vocal part of the New Orleans population, and certainly *they* were anything but co-operative. Orleanians appeared willing to compromise so long as all the compromise was done by the other side. With a whole population like that, is it any wonder that Claiborne couldn't govern to everyone's satisfaction?

The fact was that Washington, having heard and seen some

of its most prominent citizens, didn't think much of New Orleans either. They gave some basis for the reasons set forth by Jefferson, Madison, and John Randolph for giving New Orleans its original form of American government. They argued, first, that some injustice must be expected in any radical shift in government, and that, further, the United States had never before been called upon to provide a government for such a strange assortment of peoples. So much was manifestly true, whether or not the inferences drawn from it were correct. In New Orleans and its immediate environs there were Frenchmen, Spaniards, Creoles, Americans, Acadians, Germans, Irishmen, American Indians, Englishmen, odd people from Malaga, the Canaries, and all the other Caribbean islands, and Negroes of every shade and condition of servitude. There they were, side by side, in company with their almost innumerable beliefs, customs, religions, racial prejudices, and taboos. It is doubtful that any other city on earth sheltered a more motley population, certainly no other city as small as New Orleans did.

What sort of miracle in government, Mr. Jefferson asked, did the Orleanians expect?

Business was good and, once political differences were straightened out, was destined to get better. Congress passed an act governing tonnage and import duties in the territory, and in it included regulations covering banking, circulation of money, the mint, ports of entry and delivery, and customs districts. In addition New Orleans, under the terms of the Purchase treaty, enjoyed certain advantages in the French and Spanish import traffic. On the Eastern seaboard cargoes in other than American bottoms paid a tonnage duty of fifty cents per ton. At New Orleans the tonnage rate for French, Spanish, *and* American vessels was a mere six cents. The seaboard cities raged at this discrimination, but adherents of the Purchase treaty got around this on the ground that the "discrimination" clause in the Constitution was applicable only to "ports of one state as against those of another." Louisiana was not a state and therefore the discrimination argument didn't apply. It was very fine hairsplitting, of course, but the import trade was growing year by year and New Orleans was on the long end of the argument.

In both 1802 and 1803 the export and import trade of the city, in spite of political turmoil, exceeded $5,000,000. In the years immediately following both tonnage and cargo value was to double and triple with a rapidity that would have been amazing had not the potentialities of the great valley been taken into consideration.

And now the physical shape of the city was changing almost as rapidly. Because the Americans were not welcomed in the old French city, they had early begun to set up one of their own. It lay along the river above the old Tchoupitoulas Gate, across the moat which became Canal Street, and was known as the Fauborg St. Mary, or St. Marie. In 1801 there were only five houses in that area, but after that it grew rapidly and was known as the American quarter. It was along the river here that most of the flatboats from upriver docked —ocean shipping mostly used the Quay before the old city— and it was here that the first dives for the accommodation of the rivermen were established.

Elsewhere, too, the city was spreading out. Ten years before Governor Carondelet had impressed slaves from their town and country owners and dug the Old Basin Canal, extending Bayou St. John and bringing it clear up to the boundary of the old city. The canal at once provided better drainage and a means for the increasing traffic on Lake Pontchartrain to reach the city. Once this had all been plantation land and later became an area of small gardening tracts. Now it was becoming the fashionable Fauborg St. Jean and boasting homes far more elegant than anything in the city itself.

Tradition has it that when the Americans—including under that head also Britishers and Irishmen—moved in they almost immediately took over the commercial affairs of the city. Pushing and ambitious they were, yes, but it must be remembered that the Creoles were doing very well commercially long before 1803, and they continued to hold their ground. The newcomers thrived because there was plenty of business for all, not necessarily because they were better managers. And one advantage the Creole had and maintained for generations: he was landlord to the city and prospered accordingly. Dives such as the Sure Enuf Hotel and the House for Weary Boatmen, on Girod Street in the vice area known as "the Swamp," might be operated by some of the toughest customers outside of jails, but the ground rents were paid to the gentlefolk in the oldest sections of the French city.

The population when Claiborne took over has been put at from eight to ten thousand, but in reality no one knew exactly what the figure was, no matter how official. It was impossible to know, for the population both grew and changed almost overnight.

But one fact was paramount above all others: for the first time in fifty years the Mississippi lay within the boundaries of one nation, a nation, furthermore, which ranged from the Atlantic seaboard to—to where no man would know until Lewis and Clark came back from the mouth of the faraway Columbia. It was a comforting thought, and a significant one.

CHAPTER IX

Growing Pains

CONSIDERING that the Burr Conspiracy was a complete failure from start to finish, and that the failure extended even to the efforts to punish the conspirators for their intentions, a vast amount of wordage has already been wasted on it. Yet because of its cast of characters, and because it was intimately concerned with the city, some account of it necessarily belongs in any record of New Orleans' past.

The intricate personality of Aaron Burr is a fascinating subject for speculation, but the speculations are already numbered in the hundreds and here an account of the main facts will have to serve.

Vice-President of the United States under Jefferson, public figure for a generation before that, Burr must have planned his treason long before the morning of July 11, 1804, when in a duel at Weehawken Heights he shot Alexander Hamilton. Perhaps before that the plans for treason were no more than idle dreams and speculations; at any rate, the death of Hamilton, an astute but not-too-popular politician before his death but a martyred public hero afterward, provided the impetus which changed the dreams into deliberate plans.

Burr's mind was undoubtedly one of the best of its time, at least until after the Hamilton affair, but even that did not help him foresee the, to him, devastating results of Hamilton's death. Almost overnight he dropped his role as a very popular Vice-President of the United States and assumed that of a fugitive wanted for murder in the state of New York. That was the fact which forced Burr to put his plans into action at once or forget them entirely.

Probably no one today would presume to state categorically what Burr's real objective was. Probably he himself was never certain. He planned revolt in the Mississippi Valley, yes, and in Mexico as well. What would happen after that was on the knees of the gods. If Spain backed him against the United States, events would take a certain course. If England backed him against either or both the United States and Spain, then the road would lead elsewhere. In any case, New Orleans was, as always, the key to everything else, the first point to be mastered and held. Other things would develop from that.

For the best part of a year Burr ranged the Ohio and Mississippi valleys and from Washington to Georgia, planning, scheming, talking, laying the groundwork for the future. He saw or communicated with everyone of importance and many who were not—the French and Spanish ministers in Washington, the protesting New Orleans Commissioners to Washington, Senators, Representatives, and territorial delegates from and in the West, Andrew Jackson, old Colonel George Morgan, General James Wilkinson, a host of others. In some very fertile ground he unbosomed himself completely, taking his listeners (apparently) into his innermost confidence. When his tentative overtures met with quick hostility and vehement loyalty to the Union, he lapsed into his role of gentleman having a leisurely look at the country—Wilkinson's old role all over again. Everywhere he went he was received with the honor and respect due an ex-Vice-President, and out there the fact that he had killed Hamilton wasn't held against him in the least. The West considered shooting a Federalist no crime —rather the reverse.

It was Wilkinson, as commander in chief of the army, upon

whom almost everything depended. Burr spent four days with the general at Fort Massac near the mouth of the Ohio, and when he left for New Orleans Wilkinson furnished him with a military escort. The evidence seems to show that the two were in perfect agreement. They even agreed upon a secret cipher in which to correspond. And why not? Was this not merely a revival of what Wilkinson had claimed to have planned years before? It would be interesting to know how much Burr knew of Wilkinson's old designs—or how much, if any, the general unburdened himself now.

On June 26, 1805, just about a year after the Hamilton mess, Burr arrived in New Orleans. Governor Claiborne dutifully communicated the news to Madison: "Colonel Burr arrived in the city this morning." Among other letters of introduction Burr carried one from Wilkinson to the ever-faithful Daniel Clark, in which the general stated that Burr would confide a number of things which it were better not to put in writing. No doubt he did.

Colonel Burr, as befitted his station, was wined and dined by Governor Claiborne and also, through the good offices of the Creole gentlemen he had met in Washington, by others as well. The colonel was in the best of humors. The army's chief was behind him and his long journey had somehow convinced him, no doubt because he so wanted to be convinced, that the West was ready to follow him as one man. Here in New Orleans evidence of unrest was all too plain— or so he thought. Though in New Orleans it was easy for a man to hear whatever pleased his ears and probably at least a few followers could have been found to colonize Hades. The conversation at certain Creole dinner tables must have been fascinating, for all that it must also have had an air of unreality about it. Something like: "My dear Colonel Burr, of course you are in earnest, and believe me, so am I—but we'll both feel better by noon tomorrow."

Burr spent two weeks in New Orleans and then, highly pleased with the situation there, set out for St. Louis where he had a date with General Wilkinson, assuring his New Orleans friends that he would return in October.

It is impossible to know how many Orleanians pledged their aid to Burr. Daniel Clark was in the scheme, though through Wilkinson rather than Burr, the three New Orleans Commissioners to Washington, and undoubtedly a considerable number of others. Lost in a world of conquest and empire which existed only in his own mind, Burr had a lot to learn about the Creoles. They would follow him, *if*— No people were readier to rush into the most fantastic intrigues and few less temperamentally able to bring them to any conclusion.

But Burr did not return in October, nor yet for many more months thereafter. He found trouble in plenty waiting for him, both with Wilkinson in St. Louis and later with the stupid and clumsy courts of Kentucky.

Through the autumn and winter he stood the endless rounds of newspaper publicity and court hearings, smiling his suave and supercilious, forgive-them-they-know-not-what-they-do smile, denying very little, always standing squarely on his legal rights as an American citizen, and letting the courts confuse themselves. He bore with them, almost apologetic when they failed utterly to convict him of even disturbing the peace. Henry Clay acted as his counsel in Kentucky and Andrew Jackson was almost ashamed that he had ever suspected evil of Colonel Burr.

Meanwhile boats for the filibustering expedition were building on the Ohio and Cumberland, and recruiting of man power, under various guises, went on as before.

There was something Hitlerian in Burr's conduct. Probably there wasn't a man between Pittsburgh and Natchez who didn't believe Burr was up to something—but what was it? To this man he had promised one thing, to that man something entirely different, and when matters were brought into court the evidence, what there was of it, was always so contradictory that no conclusions could be reached. And then there was the very enormity of Burr's professed plans. They were so all-inclusive that men disbelieved in them even while swearing loyalty to Burr. Men *wanted* it all to be true but just couldn't convince themselves that it was possible.

It was late in the year 1806 before Burr was ready to act. Slowness of communications and other difficulties had made quicker action impossible.

In the latter part of July Burr had dispatched a concluding letter to Wilkinson, supposedly then in St. Louis. The letter was carried by Ogden and Swartout, two civilian Burr henchmen of long standing. Following the trail of Wilkinson, they learned he had gone into the Red River country, where he was engaging in one of the ever-recurrent boundary disputes with a Spanish force. It was October 8 when Swartout reached Wilkinson at Natchitoches, Ogden meanwhile having gone on to New Orleans.

That letter to Wilkinson was one of the most lying Burr ever composed. In it he stated that everything was in readiness: that sufficient troops had been enlisted; that England had engaged to furnish the needed naval force and that Commodore Truxton of the U.S. Navy was going to Jamaica to arrange with the British admiral there; that five hundred troops under his, Burr's, command would leave the Falls of the Ohio November 15, and that Wilkinson was to join them at Natchez for the final advance against New Orleans.

To Wilkinson this was both good and bad news. He had long since decided to betray Burr, though he fully intended to do it in his own devious way. On the other hand, some of what Burr wrote might be true—Wilkinson could not be absolutely sure it was not—in which case Wilkinson's own forces might be overwhelmed. For the sake of the record Wilkinson confided the contents of Burr's letter to the colonel commanding the troops at Natchitoches, explaining that the news must be communicated to Jefferson at once and that they should make haste to protect New Orleans. Presumably he didn't find it necessary to explain why the Burr letter was in cipher and why, above all, this stupendous news should be so conveniently supplied *him* in advance.

Wilkinson was faced with the problem of acting against Burr and at the same time keeping himself in the clear. In spite of his professed consternation it was twelve days before he wrote Jefferson and then he told him that the expedition was aimed at Vera Cruz, not New Orleans. Further, he made no effort to warn the military at Fort Adams, Chickasaw Bluffs, or Fort Massac, all of which Burr would have to pass on his way to the South. It seems probable that Wilkinson believed he would fare best by dealing with Burr in person—and in private.

Toward the first of November Wilkinson arranged a temporary truce with the Spanish and then left for New Orleans. Swartout had gone there two weeks earlier.

In the meantime the news, or rather rumors, had reached New Orleans. Some of Wilkinson's troops arrived in the city somewhat ahead of the general, and the city was on edge. Claiborne, too, had heard the news, and he must have had the sensation of sitting on a volcano about to erupt. Rumor had it that thousands of Orleanians were involved in the plot, and while to Claiborne that seemed unlikely, he couldn't be sure. Actually, Claiborne must have long known that something was afoot, though he was too wise to believe everything he heard. But Jefferson, too, had let him down, for the President had been well aware of Burr's intentions for at least six months.

And Claiborne had something more to worry about. The acting governor of Mississippi, Cowles Mead, had written him concerning the situation, and he was a good judge of Wilkinson's character. He told Claiborne that if the revolt actually took place the outcome would rest, not on Burr, but on what Wilkinson did. He suggested further that Wilkinson's attitude might be determined by the number of men Burr was finally able to muster; but that in any event he, Claiborne, was to consider Wilkinson a traitor and act toward him, or at least think about him, accordingly. Claiborne had already had considerable experience with the general, and probably had his own opinion of him, but certainly this intelligence didn't make him feel any more secure.

The stage set to his liking, Wilkinson entered New Orleans in person, his timing calculated exactly. The first thing he did was demand that Claiborne declare martial law—to the military mind the first thing to be done in any emergency; to the judicial civilian mind the best way to make a bad situation worse. Claiborne assured the general that he had every confidence in his good intentions, but that he did not believe the situation called for such drastic action. (It is worth surmise that Claiborne did believe martial law was warranted, but if much of what he had heard was true then martial law with Wilkinson was worse than simple anarchy without it.) Wilkinson stormed; Claiborne was courteous but obdurate. Together they saw the New Orleans chamber of commerce, explained the situation as they saw it—Wilkinson playing his part superbly—and described the need for co-operation. The merchants promptly subscribed to a defense fund and a temporary shipping embargo was agreed upon—this last in order to procure sailors for the gunboats and other naval craft then lying in the harbor—though why these vessels, already in the active service of the U.S. Navy, needed extra manning is one of those things which are beyond knowing.

Wilkinson did not get his martial law, at least he did not get it with Claiborne's acquiescence, but the turmoil in New Orleans would not be stilled and to many Orleanians Wilkinson was the man of the hour.

Sunday in New Orleans was not a day of peace and quiet as it usually was in cities of the East. In New Orleans the folk attended early mass, then turned out en masse to enjoy themselves in every possible way. The streets, saloons, cockpits, coffeehouses, and beer gardens were thronged and did their best business of the week, and it was on such a day that rumors traveling from mouth to mouth made their best speed.

Thus on a Sunday, December 14, Wilkinson arrested Dr. Julius Erich Bollman, one of Burr's numerous henchmen, and lodged him in jail. The arrest was of course illegal, since Bollman was a civilian and there was no martial law, but that didn't stop Wilkinson for a moment. Swartout and Ogden, on their way to join Burr, had been taken near Fort Adams and brought back to New Orleans, where they were already confined on a naval vessel in the harbor.

Burr adherents in the city promptly obtained writs of *habeas corpus* from Judge Workman of the Orleans District Court and an attempt was made to release the prisoners. Legend has it that two days elapsed before the court's officer could find a boat which would take him out to the prison vessel, though this seems utterly preposterous. The riverbank of New Orleans was then as packed with boats of all kinds as its streets are now with automobiles. At any rate, the officer got there eventually, to find that only Ogden remained. Swartout had mysteriously disappeared, was, in fact, already at sea on his way North.

Ogden was released, but along with one Alexander was rearrested the next day, and this time Wilkinson saw to it that the ensuing writ of *habeas corpus* was ignored. The court issued a writ of attachment against Wilkinson, but that, too, was obviously worthless. Judge Workman appealed to Claiborne, but the latter confessed himself unable to do anything. Whereupon Workman resigned and to all intents and purposes the civil authority ceased to exist and Wilkinson was supreme in New Orleans.

With Wilkinson rushing hither and yon, the militia under arms, and fresh contingents of United States troops everywhere, the city was naturally in a dither. No one seemed to know when it would all end. Burr and his attacking force were long overdue and no one in New Orleans knew when they would arrive, though on January 14 another of Burr's aides, a General Adair, arrived and announced that Colonel Burr, alone, would arrive within a few days. It appears that

Adair didn't know what he was talking about, but nevertheless Wilkinson arrested him, and along with him Judge Workman.

But it was all smoke and no fire. Burr was indeed on his way down the Mississippi, but he was also two months behind schedule, and the West showed a singular reluctance to spring to arms behind him. The dream evaporated as he came closer to New Orleans. Instead of five hundred men already enlisted at the Falls of the Ohio, he was unable to muster a hundred between Louisville and Natchez—and even this little band did not reach Bayou Pierre, above Natchez, until late in January.

It is impossible to say exactly when Burr became certain of Wilkinson's reversal, but whenever it was Burr knew from that moment that everything was finished. The whole thing, supposing it ever had any real life, died silently. Burr was arrested by the Mississippi militia, taken to Natchez, and released under bond, which he promptly skipped.

In the finale Natchez was as near as Burr got to New Orleans. His lesser followers went unmolested and those who did not return home settled in Orleans and Mississippi territories and set about the business of getting a living.

The conspiracy had a lively aftermath when Burr was tried before the United States Supreme Court, Marshall presiding, in one of the strangest legal trials in American history; but for New Orleans the drama ended when, in May, Wilkinson departed for Virginia to appear at the trial. Burr, for want of the required evidence—which existed but was not presented at the trial—was found not guilty *according to the evidence submitted*. Wilkinson continued in the army without change in his position and Swartout, as punishment for his sins, in time became Collector of the Port of New York, where he managed to steal a fortune.

Much has been written about the rigid social barriers set up by the Creoles, especially against the Americans, and in theory much of it is true. But there never was a barrier of that kind which was not breached again and again, so that generalities can never be completely trusted. Many Spanish officials, for example, married into Creole families and remained in New Orleans or its environs. The same thing was true of the immigrant Americans; not all of them, obviously, but enough to demonstrate that Americans were not considered complete pariahs. Governor Claiborne, when his first wife died of yellow fever, married one Clarissa Duralde; and at her death he married Suzette Bosque. These marriages did much to put Claiborne on a friendlier footing with the Creoles, and other Creole-American alliances helped in the same cause. There were die-hards who steadfastly refused to have anything to do with anything American, simply because it was American, just as years later there were other Southerners who professed to believe anyone born and reared above the Mason and Dixon's line was automatically equipped with horns, tail, and an urgent desire to wreck everything Southern, but they were in the minority.

Contrary to popular belief, however, New Orleans did not overflow with Americans immediately after the Louisiana Purchase. Emigrate to New Orleans they most certainly did, and those who arrived were both aggressive and vocal, but it was years before they constituted any great part of the population. By 1810 the city had more than doubled in population and in the city and its environs there were perhaps 25,000 people. Of these perhaps as many as 3,000 were Americans who might be considered a permanent part of New Orleans. Of course those who came by way of the river and stayed a few days or at most a couple of weeks were numbered in the uncounted thousands, just how many no one ever knew, and while they contributed immeasurably to New Orleans' prosperity and made an indelible impression on some phases of its character, they were no more—or less—important than the seamen who came in from the other direction. These transients, however, did not pay taxes, own property, or vote, and to that extent were not a part of the city's inner life.

Growing Pains

New Orleans greatest increase in population during the first American decade came from the West Indies, and by and large they were a sorry lot of new citizens. They came from Cuba, from San Domingo, Guadeloupe, and every other Caribbean island. During one period of two months in 1809 (so wrote George Cable), fifty-eight hundred persons—whites, free blacks and mulattoes, and slaves—arrived from Cuba alone. After 1808 the importation of slaves was forbidden, yet these, and more, came in. There were just not enough American officials to handle this tide of immigration—and to determine who was slave and who was not was an impossible task. Altogether this influx from the islands has been estimated at ten thousand, and that within a very short period.

A common religion and common language made these newcomers welcome on their individual social levels. Yet the vast majority of them were illiterate, poverty-stricken, lazy, and unmoral rather than immoral. And with them they brought an astounding amount of tuberculosis and syphilis. A city with a much larger original population could have absorbed such a tidal wave—nationality and slavery aside—without upsetting its social equilibrium too much. New Orleans, with its county seat population of 10,000, could not. Claiborne even made a plea to American consuls in Havana and other Cuban ports, urging them to help hold back this tide of undesirables, but without much luck.

Claiborne was never without his troubles. He himself was finally forced to fight a duel with Daniel Clark because of a quarrel concerning Clark's old friend Wilkinson, and Micajah Lewis, Claiborne's brother-in-law and private secretary, was killed in a duel caused by a dispute in which he defended the governor. Until the Civil War the duel was by far the commonest way of settling personal arguments—if they can be said to be settled that way—and there was hardly a man in public life who had not fought at least one duel. And not infrequently duels were fought for nothing except the excitement involved. For years Exchange Alley, a short, narrow street between Royal and Chartres, was given over almost exclusively to fencing establishments, and no young Creole's education was complete without a thorough knowledge of the Code of Honor. And while dueling as a *pastime* was probably confined to the Creoles, the Americans had their full share in it as a means of satisfying honor.

Another source of annoyance to Claiborne was the Capuchin priest, Father Antoine Sedella, the one-time agent of the Inquisition who returned to New Orleans only a few years after he had been so summarily deported by the Spanish Governor Miro. The Inquisition was never again a matter of concern, but otherwise the priest seems to have been continually involved in some kind of public dispute. As curé of St. Louis Cathedral he was a devotedly religious man and the Catholic portion of the community, which meant everyone who professed any religion at all, swore by him, and women especially were his strong supporters. Aside from this Sedella was continually at odds with his ecclesiastical superiors, usually publicly, and, though there is little evidence to support the charge, he was widely supposed to be deeply involved in political intrigue. (Even if that had been true it probably wouldn't have prejudiced the Creoles against him.) Claiborne at least was suspicious enough of his intentions to write his dossier for the benefit of the Secretary of War, and once called him to account in person. In 1805 he was suspended from duty by the vicar general of the diocese, Father Patrick Walsh, but the protest of the Orleanians was so great that Sedella's reinstatement was forced. He was also one of the intimates of the Marquis of Casa Calvo until Claiborne succeeded in ousting the Spaniard from the territory. He lived to be eighty-one and one of the best-liked men in New Orleans, and it seems probable that some of the friction he caused came from the fact that he was a Spaniard named Sedella, whereas some of his superiors were men with Irish names like Walsh.

Meanwhile the vice section of the American Quarter grew

like a weed and almost nothing was done to regulate it. In fact, the few law-enforcement agencies of the city practically ignored it. Their attitude was that if men were fools enough to visit the place they must be prepared to take the consequences. Never a day but what saw street brawls and fights which, when nationalities were involved, sometimes became bloody riots—one could start a fight almost anywhere by shouting for or against Napoleon. In the French Quarter vice was almost equally widespread but on the quieter, more genteel side, and St. Anthony Square, the open space behind St. Louis Cathedral on Royal Street—now the cathedral garden— was a favorite and convenient dueling site.

In September of 1807 the town was rocked by the near pitched battles known as the Batture Riots. When the flatboaters first came down the river and rendezvoused at Tchoupitoulas Street, that street was almost directly on the riverbank. But as years passed the Mississippi steadily built up new land here until today the street is more than six blocks from the river. Of course no such amount of land was formed by 1807, but enough to be worth claiming had been formed— especially since this was both American commercial and vice area and ground rents high. On behalf of certain clients Edward Livingston attempted to take over this new ground, and his right to do so was several times upheld by the courts. But legal decisions made little impression on the inhabitants of the Swamp and they fought, literally, for what they considered their rights.

This Edward Livingston was a man of considerable parts. He was a brother of the more famous Chancellor (Robert R.) Livingston of New York. He had held numerous offices there and, through negligence rather than dishonesty, became a defaulter. Making over his property to a trustee, he came to New Orleans about the time of the Louisiana Purchase and hung out his shingle as a lawyer. It was he who drafted the petition carried to Washington by Sauvé, Derbigny, and Destréhan, and he soon became the most prominent

The Port of New Orleans

American lawyer in the city. The old French and Spanish laws were notoriously tangled, and with the overlayer of the newer American law became even worse. It was Livingston who made the first intelligent attempt to bring order out of this chaos, and when Louisiana was admitted as a state a few years later much of Livingston's effort became part of the state's basic law. But he is probably best remembered as counsel for the Laffite brothers, Jean and Pierre, who were his most prominent clients.

The Laffites (the correct spelling, incidentally, though not the usual one) are probably New Orleans' best-known romantic figures, and no less a personage than Mr. Cecil B. De Mille has seen fit to build a moving picture around some of their more genteel exploits. New Orleans nowadays thinks of the Laffites both fondly and proudly, as indeed it did in 1810, but as a matter of sober fact their moral relation to the city was about the same as that of the Capone gang to Chicago—except that most people nowadays would consider the illegal liquor trade less reprehensible than slave-running, illegal or otherwise.

The origin of the Laffites is obscure, though it is generally agreed that they came originally from the vicinity of Bordeaux and that Pierre had served in the French navy. They appeared in New Orleans sometime in 1806 and are said to have operated a mercantile establishment in Royal Street and a blacksmith shop at the corner of St. Philip and Bourbon streets, although there is little beyond hearsay to show that they ran the smithy. But operate the store they did, and stocked it almost entirely with smuggled merchandise which they sold at bargain prices. It was an open secret in New Orleans that the Laffites dealt in contraband, but smuggling, in the view of most Orleanians, was no crime—in fact, it had been a recognized occupation since the time of the first Spanish regime.

Never was any city in the United States more nicely situated for the business of smuggling. Between New Orleans and the Gulf there lay a vast area of swamp and semi-swamp, crossed and recrossed by greater and lesser waterways almost beyond counting. The bayous and lakes are to the Delta country as the Thousand Islands are to the Great Lakes. From Barataria Bay or Breton Sound an experienced boatman could make a hundred round trips to New Orleans and never use the same route twice. And almost any route from either place to the city is shorter by half than by way of the Mississippi, though of course the great majority of these routes are navigable only by boats of the shallowest draft. All this country was a liquid wilderness then and has changed as little as any wilderness in America. There are Orleanians who will tell you that no one ever thought of improving the roads south of New Orleans until Prohibition made it necessary to haul liquor up from the Gulf by truck.

For year this Gulf coast had been the refuge of smugglers and pirates disguised as smugglers, and it was for these that the Laffites acted as New Orleans agents. Most of these smugglers gave themselves a veneer of legality by operating as privateers under the authority of the then republic of Cartagena. Since Cartagena was theoretically at war with Spain, these privateers theoretically were supposed to attack only vessels under the Spanish flag, though in practice they took whatever they could get their hands on. Thus the goods sold by the Laffites, and by many another New Orleans merchant as well until the brothers managed to get a monopoly, were not only smuggled through the United States customs but stolen in the first place.

For two years the Laffites prospered exceedingly and were in a fair way to become solid and respected citizens. But with the year 1808 two things happened which changed the course of their ambitions. One was that Claiborne was becoming increasingly angered over the steady customs violations, and the other was that henceforth the importation of slaves into the United States was forbidden. This latter law coincided almost exactly with the rush of the cotton- and sugar-producing boom in Louisiana and the value of slaves, and the demand for them, tripled and quadrupled overnight. Slaves had been a standard item of commerce for a century, but now they had become really valuable.

It was at this point that the Laffites expanded and began to show their real organizing ability.

Learning that certain of the smuggling groups were at odds because of stealing from each other and cutting prices, the Laffites stepped in at the opportune moment, stopped the internal strife, and welded the scattered gangs into one efficient organization. In modern terms, the Laffites simply muscled in and took over.

The two islands Grand Terre and Grand Isle, which form a sort of barrier between the Gulf and Barataria Bay, became Laffite headquarters and in time a large establishment was erected. The younger brother Jean, with his principal lieutenants Béluche and Dominique You, superintended operations here while Pierre continued to look after the New Orleans end of the business. Jean insisted, in the beginning at least, that none but Spanish ships should be taken, thus keeping the sea-going traffic on the semilegal side. The forces of the United States, specifically the forces available to Claiborne, he did not consider worth bothering about. It was almost a certainty that no court in Orleans Territory would convict them even if they were caught.

Jean completely rebuilt the establishment on Grand Terre and in time it became the showplace of the Gulf coast—and in more ways than one. Besides a considerable mansion for his own use he erected extensive slave quarters, huge warehouses, and homes for his men, and bordellos, cafés, and gambling rooms for the use of customers as well as his own crews. It became common for ladies and gentlemen from New Orleans and its neighboring plantations to visit Grand Terre and Grand Isle on periodic shopping tours, the Laffites arranging everything from transportation to entertainment and accommodations on the islands, and the visits became pleasant excursions to look forward to. Entertainment was lavish and the selection of choice merchandise as extensive as any in New Orleans, with prices much lower.

Naturally the cost of maintaining such an organization was large, but so were the profits. Some idea of the money involved can be seen from the fact that sometimes, after an especially good haul, three to four hundred Negroes were disposed of in one day, and at that time in Louisiana prime field hands were worth from eight hundred to a thousand dollars, delivered—and the Laffites guaranteed safe delivery.

Of course Claiborne was aware of all this but he could only make token efforts to stop it. A few raids were made on the establishment at Grand Terre, but their results were usually humorous rather than effective. Between Barataria Bay and New Orleans lay the honeycomb of swamps and bayous, and when it was necessary the Baratarians simply vanished, to reappear when the raiders had gone. And once, in the best romantic tradition, a raiding party was captured intact, lavishly entertained, and its leader offered a place in the organization.

The Laffites enjoyed their greatest prosperity between 1808 and 1813, and while their depredations would be stopped eventually the time was not yet.

In the meantime Orleans Territory had long since passed the population mark of 60,000 required for full admission to the Union; in fact, in 1812 her population was nearer 75,000. The quality of the populace was beside the point; the original bargain had contained no qualifications in that respect. The Congressional row over the question of admitting her to the Union was as bitter as that concerning the original Louisiana Purchase, but in the end the champions of statehood won and the territory of Orleans became the state of Louisiana on April 30, 1812, with Claiborne as its duly-elected first governor—proof enough that while he might have been disliked he was most certainly trusted.

CHAPTER X

New Orleans and General Jackson

IT IS AN ODD COINCIDENCE that Louisiana's coming of age should occur in the same year as the beginning of the second war with England. The war itself was brought on by Jefferson's embargo and the resultant prostration of American commerce on the Atlantic seaboard, but New Orleans hadn't been affected in the least by the East's troubles. In fact, business not only went on as usual but continued to get better. The war was very remote as far as she was concerned. A few of her sons, ready for action in anybody's war, went off to join one of the armed services; there were a few shifts in the personnel of the permanent garrison; otherwise it was almost a year and a half before New Orleans felt any of the war's impact.

It seems that any attempt to guess England's strategy, no matter how elemental, would have taken into account the possibility of a determined effort against New Orleans. Besides being the key to the great valley and rapidly becoming rich, New Orleans was still one of Britain's lost but not forgotten loves. Perhaps the probability of an attack on the city was taken into consideration whenever American authority had time to worry over anything outside the problems of the moment, which wasn't often. For the United States had managed to get badly involved in a war it wasn't prepared to fight and which almost no one had really wanted. Rich and unprotected prize that she was, New Orleans would have to wait until the fires on the Great Lakes and the seaboard were extinguished. If that was too late—well, then it was too late. It was difficult for the East to worry about the Crescent City when Washington was actually in flames.

Trading on the luck of fools and angels, New Orleans didn't worry either. And her good luck was remarkable, for from the outbreak of the war in June 1812 until late autumn of 1814 there was no time when almost any sort of British force could not have taken New Orleans with ease. Yet during this period the city went her tranquil way, unworried by as much as a hostile rumor.

Britain took her time but she would get around to the matter of New Orleans eventually.

The Battle of New Orleans, in December of 1814 still to be fought, is almost always included in any list of "great," "decisive," or "important" battles of the world, though actually it belongs in none of these categories. It is included in such lists mainly because of the terrible contrasts in the casualties of the two armies and looms importantly in American history because it was such a decisive victory—of its kind—over the old enemy, Britain. It was also the event which in time elevated Jackson, the "Hero of New Orleans," to the Presidency, but that is another story.

And not the least amusing part of the Battle of New Orleans is the fact that any complete account of it must go back to the local campaign Governor Claiborne was waging, somewhat unsuccessfully, against the brothers Laffite.

Well liked as they were, the Laffites could go too far. In time their business in smuggled and stolen goods, mostly of the luxury class, became so extensive that it was having a real effect on the legitimate trade of New Orleans, and naturally that could not be allowed. In July 1814 a grand jury indicted the Laffites and Pierre, along with Dominique You, who happened to be in town, was promptly lodged in the calaboose.

Thus matters stood when Jean, at Barataria, received what must have been the surprise of his colorful life. The surprise came in the form of a visit from one Captain Lockyer of the British navy, who had lately been on active service with the forces opposing General Jackson in the Floridas, where both parties had been running wild over what was supposed to be Spanish territory. Lockyer prefaced his Barataria visit by shelling a vessel, probably one of the Laffites', and running her aground. Thereupon Lockyer and two other officers went ashore with Jean, who had put out to meet them, and delivered to him certain letters.

The letters were typically British. One contained a manifesto addressed to the people of Kentucky and Louisiana by Major Edward Nicholls, calling upon them to rise and throw off the tyrannical yoke of the United States and accept the protection of His Majesty's Government; one was an address to the Baratarians as a whole, stating that if they did not join the British in their just war against the United States and leave off attacking Spanish vessels, the British would destroy them as punishment for their previous attacks on British shipping; one was to Jean Laffite personally, offering him a captaincy in the British navy and protection for his property in return for his aid in a coming attack upon New Orleans. (There are accounts which say that Laffite was also offered thirty thousand dollars with the other conditions, but this seems to belong in the same category with the statements that he personally helped Jackson plan the Battle of New Orleans—New Orleans' habit of gilding the lily.) A fourth and last letter gave Laffite instructions in the event he decided to come in with the British.

Jean pondered the proposition overnight, then asked for two weeks in which to make up his mind. Lockyer consented —there was plenty of time—and agreed to return in a fortnight for an answer.

Thereupon Jean got busy. He sent the letters to Edward Livingston in New Orleans and in return for the information they contained asked for Pierre's release. Just how Pierre did get out of jail no one now knows, but on the day following the arrival of the letters in New Orleans he was missing. It may have been merely coincidence, for Claiborne immediately posted a thousand-dollar reward for the return of the missing man.

Pierre now being free, Jean made another overture through Livingston. He advised that the three British vessels still hovered off Barataria and that he, Laffite, in spite of his alleged crimes, wished to remain loyal to the United States. Should he therefore apply to the United States for relief from the indictments against him? Claiborne, properly, didn't bother to answer officially. As governor of Louisiana it wasn't his business to advise a man under indictment by that same state. But he pondered all this at length, wondering how much of it might be true. A somewhat similar offer had been made once before—and Claiborne was in no mood again to be made a fool of by the Laffites. In the previous year the governor had put a price of five hundred dollars on Jean's head, whereupon Jean promptly plastered New Orleans with bills offering five *thousand* dollars for the governor. It was humor Orleanians could appreciate but it did Claiborne's dignity no good.

Yet neither did Claiborne care to make a bad mistake, so he asked the advice of General Villeré of the New Orleans militia, Colonel George T. Ross of the army, and Commander Daniel T. Patterson of the navy. Should he or should he not enter into negotiations with the pirates? Villeré voted "Yes" but Ross and Patterson voted an absolute "No"—for at the very moment they were preparing to finish the Laffites, this time for good and all. Claiborne agreed to abide by the vote.

A few days later Patterson dropped down the river with three bargeloads of troops and at South Pass was joined by an armed schooner and six gunboats. By sundown of September 16 Patterson had taken seven Laffite cruisers and three armed schooners and spent another week utterly destroying everything on Grand Isle and Grand Terre. There were prisoners galore, but Jean and Pierre Laffite were not among them.

In the meantime Jackson, late in September, had been advised by President Monroe that the British had an expedition against New Orleans under way and charged Jackson with the city's defense. The expedition was supposed to have left Ireland early in September. Monroe had ordered five thousand additional troops raised in Tennessee and sent to join Jackson's present force.

The troops from Tennessee arrived just in time to take part in a foray which had nothing to do with the orders to defend New Orleans: they marched against Pensacola and Fort Barrancas. These objectives taken with ease, Jackson left twelve hundred men at Mobile, sent a thousand after British and Indians on the Escambia River, and ordered another two thousand to Baton Rouge. One wonders how long Old Hickory calculated it would require a fleet to sail from Ireland to the Gulf.

One regiment he did send to New Orleans, and he himself followed slowly—he was really very ill—arriving in the city on December 2.

Meanwhile the Laffite-Claiborne letters, along with the British disclosures, had been published in New Orleans, and Livingston took it upon himself to do something about it. He called a public meeting in one of the coffeehouses and stated that he hadn't the slightest doubt that the British letters were genuine and that Laffite had told the truth. Thereupon a committee of defense was formed and some useless resolutions passed, but nothing else came of the meeting. Claiborne called a special session of the Legislature and asked for troops, money, and a defense council. The Legislature listened politely—then adjourned.

New Orleans and General Jackson

Providence has indeed watched over Americans whenever they have come to grips with the British.

Even as the Legislature adjourned the British fleet was off Cuba—and a formidable fleet it was. In it were fifty of the best vessels the best navy in the world could muster, and they carried enough guns to level New Orleans with the ground. The troops were veterans from almost every British field of victory in America and on the Continent, and not a few of them had assisted in the sack of Washington. The naval force was commanded by Admiral Cochrane, with the entire expedition under Sir Edward Pakenham, brother-in-law of the Duke of Wellington, and both men had long since proved themselves in Europe. Things military and naval considered, New Orleans should have been no more than a light engagement for such a force. The British thought so too. They had even brought along a set of civilian officials, and many officers had their wives aboard.

Pakenham and Cochrane had the choice of two approaches: one straight up the river to New Orleans; the other by way of shallow Lake Borgne to take the city in the flank and rear. They chose the latter and so prepared the way for one of the worst British defeats on record.

A good but not airtight case can be made for not choosing the river route, though the reasons usually given for so doing are not the best. It has been said that the British were afraid they could not run the fire of Fort St. Philip, about twenty miles above Head of Passes, but that is surely nonsense. The British had their blind spots but they well knew what their guns could do—and the guns of Cochrane's flagship alone should have made hash of Fort St. Philip within half an hour, and at New Orleans there were no fortifications worth mentioning. No, the chief objections were that devilish stretch of water between the Gulf and New Orleans and the season. For a sailing vessel that piece of river was bad enough at any time, but in December the prevailing winds were from every direction except south and the fleet might well have lain in the river for weeks before raising New Orleans. It would have been far better for the British had they done so—for even if they were becalmed, what possible harm could have befallen them? At worst it would have meant only a little more delay. But they were in a hurry and so chose the other approach—and defeat utter and complete.

Thus the mighty British fleet entered Lake Borgne—really a shallow arm of the Gulf—came so far, and stopped, the larger ships, and the great weight of guns, unable to move farther in. Troops were transferred to such lighter vessels as could move in the shallow water. This was on December 10. Shortly afterward six of Patterson's gunboats were sighted, Captain Lockyer gave chase in a fleet of barges, and by noon of December 14 captured or destroyed all six. News of this occurrence was the first intelligence New Orleans had that the enemy was almost at its back door. As the crow flies this point on Lake Borgne is about fifteen miles from the heart of New Orleans, and while by no means even a large part of the fleet had come that close, they were all near enough. How such a force could so approach an old Indian fighter like Jackson without detection is a nice mystery, but there they were.

Even with the British so close the Legislature dallied, but Jackson, all credit to him, did not. Illness or no, he was instantly the Jackson of furious and unhesitating action. He sent orders that in case of invasion by way of the river Fort St. Philip was to be held as long as a gun remained to be served. General Coffee was ordered down from Baton Rouge and told to move night and day. Without hesitation he declared martial law and issued a proclamation ordering that every able-bodied man in New Orleans either prepare to fight or take the consequences—and he promised that the consequences would be harsh. Spurred to action by such a leader as Jackson could be, Orleanians shook off their lethargy and responded enthusiastically. It was then that the Laffites reap-

peared suddenly in the midst of the excitement and offered
their services in the emergency, and Jackson, who had had
his turn at damning them in no uncertain terms, accepted.
The Baratarians were experienced gunners and he had need
of such. Presumably the Laffites themselves did service somewhere, though on the pay roll of the artillery company composed of Baratarians it is Dominique You who appears as
captain, with Béluche as his lieutenant, and the names of Jean
and Pierre are not on that list.

All this, of course, required time, but the British, never
noted for their speed in military matters, were allowing
Jackson the time he needed.

A large portion of the British land force was put ashore on
the Isle au Poix. This small island is at the Lake Borgne end
of the Rigolets, the waterway which connects Lakes Borgne
and Pontchartrain. While this was being done, and a week
was spent in the operation, two British officers entered Bayou
Bienvenue, where they were welcomed by friendly Spanish
fishermen who had a small village at the mouth of the bayou.
These fishermen guided the two officers up Bayou Bienvenue
to one of its branches, Bayou Mazant, and thence to a drainage
canal which took them to the heart of the Villeré plantation,
on the Mississippi just six miles below New Orleans. There
the two Britishers examined the ground with a view toward
the placement of troops and returned to the Isle au Poix in
their own good time. Two days after their departure an
American sergeant and eight men arrived at the fishing village
to serve as outpost. Jackson had waited seven or eight days
before placing this small picket between him and the advancing British.

Even then the picket was worthless, for on the morning of
December 23 seventeen hundred men moved across the lake,
surprised and captured the picket, and moved forward along
the same route the two officers had used. At the plantation
the Villeré family was made prisoner but young Major Villeré
managed to escape and carry the alarm to Jackson in New

Orleans. There wasn't an armed force of any kind between them and New Orleans, and if it had not been for Villeré's fortunate escape the British might well have marched up the levee to the Suburb Marigny without being challenged.

The order for mobilization went out immediately, and within a half-hour some of the regular troops were in motion. The fourteen-gun *Carolina*, one of Patterson's vessels, dropped down the river with orders to shell the British positions. By nightfall Jackson had three columns in contact with the British. Fog made any kind of accurate shooting impossible and the British retired slowly, with Coffee's men pressing them as best they could. A certain amount of British re-enforcements arrived and the entire British force found shelter from the frontal fire behind an old abandoned levee, with the new levee protecting them somewhat from the blind firing of the *Carolina*.

On the morning of the twenty-fourth, oddly enough, neither side renewed the attack. Pakenham was busy pouring new troops onto the field and Jackson's men, aided by a huge force of drafted slaves, were feverishly throwing up an earthwork on a line which began at the Mississippi levee and eventually vanished in the cypress swamps on Jackson's left—the British right.

What happened after that is the old story of British delay and hesitation. By Christmas morning Pakenham had around six thousand seasoned men on the field, and yet he refused to attack until the gunboats—the *Carolina* had been joined by the *Louisiana*—were put out of action. Naturally this needed guns which had not yet had time to get up—moving heavy guns along those narrow bayous was no light task. Two days elapsed, during which Jackson's men built furiously, before nine fieldpieces, two howitzers, and a mortar were in place, but once there they quickly sank the *Carolina* and damaged the *Louisiana* so badly she was forced to withdraw. On the twenty-eighth Pakenham again advanced, only to halt abruptly when he came in sight of Jackson's fresh earthworks.

New Orleans and General Jackson

Here again is something of a mystery—for how could even a blind British general have been so close to the Americans for three days and remain so totally unaware of what Jackson was up to? But Pakenham could and did. Faced with this barrier, he decided against assault—for the time being. He fell back, put his men in camp, and ordered up more artillery to soften the American position. British soldiers and sailors worked like mules, and by New Year's morning they had thirty more heavy guns in position. By eight that morning the fog had lifted and the batteries opened fire on Jackson's fortified line. The Americans returned the fire—Jackson also had a small amount of artillery in position by now—and so accurately that by noon the British batteries were silenced, either the guns wrecked or the gunners driven off by small-arms fire, though it appears that the casualties on both sides were small.

The terrific cannonading did little damage to the American fortifications. It is popularly supposed that the breastwork was constructed largely from cotton bales, but such was decidedly not the case. Where could they have gotten, on such short notice, enough cotton bales to erect a useful line more than a mile long? Actually the earthwork was just what its name implies, wet Louisiana earth at that, and just about the best possible protection from the artillery fire of the time. British shells would have smashed stone, masonry, or timber barriers to bits; in the wet Louisiana earth they merely buried themselves harmlessly. (Modern engineers, attempting to blast earthen levees with high explosive during flood emergencies, have had the same experience. Sometimes it has taken days to blast a hole in a levee large enough to let any appreciable quantity of water through.)

His batteries out of action, temporarily at least, Pakenham spent another full week bringing up more reserves, until he finally had something over eight thousand men almost within sight of the Jackson line.

In the meantime Patterson, after the sinking of the *Carolina*,

[151]

had retired to the west bank of the river and there erected a battery of his own. Apparently it either gave the British a great deal of trouble or they expected it to, for they went to elaborate lengths to silence it. The Villeré drainage canal ended a considerable distance from the Mississippi levee; so Pakenham decided to extend the canal—by hand—as far as the levee, then drag his troop barges along the extended canal, over the levee, and thence cross the river for the attack on Patterson's battery. It was a terrible chore—but considered worth the effort because Pakenham intended to send over considerably more than merely enough men to handle the battery. The plan was discovered by the Americans, however, and a detachment of Kentuckians was sent hurriedly to New Orleans, ferried across to Algiers, and moved down the west bank on foot to join Colonel Morgan and his Louisiana militia at the battery.

Colonel Thornton's contact with the defenders of this battery was to be the signal for Pakenham's frontal attack along Jackson's entire line.

The morning of January 8 arrived, cold, damp, and foggy as usual—and what transpired thereafter has been told and retold a thousand times.

In the first place, Colonel Thornton and his men, through no fault of their own, got away to a bad start. They were feverishly at work hours before dawn, but the hoisting of the heavy troop barges out of the improvised canal and over the levee, by hand, was a herculean task which in itself almost finished them. And embarking twelve hundred men in barges from a slippery, muddy, sloping riverbank in darkness and thick fog is in itself a formidable chore. Once afloat, they found that the brown current was far swifter than they had supposed, and though they fought the heavy sweeps the best they could manage was a landing some three miles below Patterson's position. And there the disembarking process was as bad as the embarking had been.

This is at least one writer who believes that most of the

real heroes of the Battle of New Orleans were in that dogged British detachment of Thornton's.

On the Plain of Chalmette Pakenham paced nervously, watched the slowly lightening sky, and strained his ears for the sound of firing on the west bank of the Mississippi. No such sound came.

The British lines were formed and waiting impatiently; dawn had come; the fog was lifting. Still no sound came from over the river, but Pakenham could wait no longer. He gave the signal to advance.

Jackson's earthwork sprawled behind a shallow ditch called the Rodriguez Canal—and, incidentally, it was a straight line, the hardest kind to defend and the kind no competent strategist would deliberately choose. The main British attack force was formed behind another shallow ditch which paralleled Jackson's line at a distance of about four hundred yards. Thus the British advance had to cross almost a quarter mile of open plain before reaching the American line. And just to keep everything in the proper British tradition the ranks, despite the fact that they had been in camp near by, went into action carrying not only full packs and equipment but armloads of sugar cane to be used in filling the ditch just in front of them. The heaviest attacking force was on the British right, facing the point where Jackson's earthwork dwindled away into the cypress swamp. The line here was held by Coffee's Tennesseans, standing knee-deep in water. The Creole militia, companies of San Domingans, free Negroes, the New Orleans Rifles, and the Baratarians were at that end of the line nearest the levee, with the available artillery distributed as evenly as possible.

Every schoolboy knows that the British were cut down like ripe wheat before the scythe. And what else might have been expected? The scarlet lines reeled, staggered, threw away superfluous equipment, re-formed, and came again and again. General Gibbs, leading the attack on the American left, was killed, but not until he had reached a point only twenty yards from the parapet and the galling rifle fire. Pakenham rode into the melee, attempting to rally the men, and was struck down by a cannon ball. Command passed to General Lambert, and he immediately ordered a withdrawal along the entire line.

Meanwhile, Thornton had at last gone into action, although when the main assault against Jackson began only about half of Thornton's force had reached the west bank of the river. There he struck savagely at Morgan's defending force and routed it completely. Thornton himself fell, badly wounded, but his men surged on, smashed Patterson's battery, and spiked the guns, their mission successfully completed. From there they pushed on up the river to a point about a mile behind Jackson's rear. If they could have recrossed the river behind Jackson; if Pakenham's frontal attack had not failed so dismally; if—— But General Lambert recalled them that night.

In the assault against Patterson's position Thornton's men had inflicted one hundred and twenty-seven casualties, or about ten times the number inflicted by the British on the east bank.

The British countersign for the day had been "Beauty and Booty," and though there was plenty of both in New Orleans none of the British ever saw it for himself. Generals Pakenham and Gibbs were dead and General Kean mortally wounded before eight o'clock in the morning. The official time of the action was two hours and five minutes and in that period the British suffered some two thousand casualties —2,017 to be exact—and a loss of five hundred prisoners. The seven hundred dead included three generals, seven colonels, and about seventy-five officers of lower rank.

Jackson reported his losses in the main assault as six killed and seven wounded—a truly astonishing figure and the reason the Battle of New Orleans is listed among the world's greatest!

At noon a truce was arranged and all that afternoon and by torchlight that night the British busied themselves with burying their dead and caring for the wounded, and on the following day they were still at their gruesome task.

The British withdrawal, partially because of the heavy toll of wounded, was terribly difficult. To effect it they remained in more or less their original positions for another ten days, maintaining a harmless artillery fire. The boats they had managed to get through the narrow bayous and the Villeré canal were now needed for the guns, equipment, and wounded, and the whole men had to return to the shore of Lake Borgne on foot. The only foot routes through the swamps lay along the wet margins of the bayous and now these, with so much traffic, soon became quagmires. Bundles of reeds were used to build a footing, but on the night of January 18, when a final withdrawal was made, the advance soon trampled the reeds into shreds and the going was worse than ever. Even on that last march the British lost many another good man.

Jackson at no time made any attempt to assault the British in turn. Officially, he stated that he was charged with the defense of New Orleans, and defend it successfully he most certainly had. On the other hand, he was never one to avoid a fight, even against odds, but he knew very well that turning his enthusiastic but ill-assorted soldiery against the British and their still superior artillery was by no means the same thing as standing off the British from behind a safe earthwork. Then, too, despite the terrible British losses, Jackson was still too much outnumbered to think of attacking. He had been outnumbered throughout the action, though the exact figures are hard to arrive at and are unimportant anyway.

Of course the Battle of New Orleans has been considered a great American victory, though from the evidence it would appear to be more nearly a British defeat. If that is too subtle a distinction then put it that the Americans, and Jackson, were wonderfully lucky. If the factors involved in the Battle of New Orleans—perhaps, but not necessarily, leaving out the human element—had been strung together as an abstract problem in strategy, no military authority on earth would have given Jackson a chance. Jackson in Pakenham's place probably would have succeeded. But these are old bones and best left lying.

For years afterward the south wind carried the stench of shallowly buried British dead into the streets of New Orleans, perhaps reminding the city of what it had escaped; and even now the moss-draped oaks under which Pakenham's body lay until the sand of battle had run out are known as the Pakenham Oaks. Since that day the Plain of Chalmette has served no useful human purpose—unless it be as a reminder.

But the most ironical touch of all was the news eventually received in New Orleans: the Treaty of Ghent, concluding the war, had been signed on Christmas Eve, 1814.

But for the moment victory was victory and that was all that mattered. Jackson was the hero of not only New Orleans but the entire country as well. The carping critics would come later, and in the meantime New Orleans would not be cheated of its right to rejoice.

When the army at last returned to the city it was greeted in a manner befitting conquering heroes. There were triumphal arches in the Place d'Armes, parades of troops through the narrow streets lined with crowds who cheered themselves hoarse, the celebrating thunder of artillery fire, solemn ceremonies of thanksgiving at St. Louis Cathedral, and as a fitting climax a Grand Victory Ball in honor of General Jackson and his lieutenants.

Claiborne and certain other sober-minded men saw in the victory something more than a successful defense of New Orleans. They knew that comradeship in arms can be a powerful force in uniting divergent opinions and hoped and believed that this victory would go far toward joining Creoles and Americans. It was a help, certainly, but battles are sometimes soon forgotten while the small frictions of everyday endure.

The Battle of New Orleans had scarcely ceased to echo

when the Laffite lawyers started suit for recovery of the vessels confiscated in Patterson's Grand Terre raid, and about the same time several people of prominence suggested to Claiborne that he quash the indictments pending against the Baratarians. Claiborne would not do that—it is more likely that he could not; such action on his part would seem to have been of doubtful legality, even had the Laffite charges been State instead of Federal. But the Laffites were not in custody and both Claiborne and Jackson had advised the President of the Baratarians' meritorious action during the emergency. In his report of January 21, 1815, Jackson has been thus quoted:

Captains Dominique [You] and Béluche, lately commanding privateers at Barataria, with part of their former crews and many brave citizens of New Orleans, were stationed at Batteries Three and Four. The general cannot avoid giving his warm approbation of the manner in which these gentlemen have uniformly conducted themselves while under his command, and of the gallantry with which they redeemed the pledge they gave at the opening of the campaign to defend the country. The brothers Laffite have exhibited the same courage and fidelity, and the general promises that the government shall be duly apprised of their conduct. . . .

On February 6, 1815, Madison gave a full pardon to every Baratarian who could produce a statement from Claiborne that he had taken part in the Chalmette battle.

Shortly after the mass pardoning the government offered the captured Laffite vessels at public auction, and they were bought by a man named Sauvinet, previously an occasional backer of the Laffites. Whereupon Jean and Pierre immediately got the former gang together and prepared to go back into business—though possibly they did not intend to reestablish themselves on United States territory.

The new project did not fare so well, and within a few weeks Jean's chief lieutenants had left him. Dominique You came back to New Orleans and turned honest citizen, though he did go in for small-time politics. Chigizola, another Laffite aide, went into the Venezuelan navy, and Vincent Gambi turned out-and-out pirate on his own and was killed some few years later.

Thereafter the Laffites operated from Gulf ports outside the jurisdiction of the States, and though they still supplied much of the New Orleans contraband trade in both slaves and goods, they themselves were no more familiar figures in the city. What was probably their last appearance in the city had to do with the misdeeds of one of their crews. The brothers had in 1819 purchased a new schooner in New Orleans, and a crew of sixteen commanded by Robert Johnson and Jean Desfargues was sent to bring the vessel to Galveston, then Laffite headquarters. But the boys couldn't resist temptation and off the mouths of the Mississippi promptly attacked a Spanish vessel. While they were looting the prize they were surprised by the United States revenue cutter *Alabama*, which captured the lot of them after a short fight. The eighteen prisoners and the captured schooner were taken to New Orleans, where the United States District Court promptly found all eighteen guilty of piracy and sentenced them to hang. Pierre was already in the city, and Jean rushed there as soon as he heard the news. They fought with every possible means to free their followers, but the best they could do was a pardon for one and temporary reprieves for the others. When the reprieves expired Johnson, Desfargues, and the remaining fifteen were publicly hanged in the Place d'Armes.

New Orleans knew the brothers Laffite no more.

CHAPTER XI

Flatboats, Packets, and Prosperity

IN MOST OF THE RECORDS, and there are a great many of them bearing on the point, the name of the first steamboat on Western waters is given as the *New Orleans—* in some instances *Orleans*. The weight of evidence seems to be with *New Orleans*, though it could have been plain *Orleans*, a shorter version of New Orleans widely used in the West of the period. Unquestionably this was the first steamboat actually to operate in the West, and thus her story belongs here, but before going into that there is an earlier attempt which is worth recording.

Elsewhere in this book there is brief mention of a Spanish Intendant-Commissary named Morales. It was he who in October of 1802 closed the Mississippi to Americans for the last time, but he should be remembered in New Orleans history for something else. In this same year Morales, or at least someone in his department, issued a permit for the construction of a *steamboat*, the American gadget which was to revolutionize river commerce in the great valley. The permit was issued to one James McKeever, sometime captain in the United States Navy, and doubtless Morales supposed him to be a harmless lunatic. Fulton's successful *Clermont* was still five years away and there is every reason to suppose that

Morales had never heard of such a thing as a steamboat, though at the time there were perhaps two or three steam *engines* operating in New Orleans. The boat, if successful, was intended for service between New Orleans and Natchez, and the hull, eighty feet in length by eighteen feet beam, was built on the Ohio sometime in 1803. Floated down to New Orleans, she probably appeared very much like any one of hundreds of powerless craft on the Mississippi. McKeever was joined in the enterprise by an Orleanian, M. Louis Valcour, and an engine purchased from Oliver Evans of Philadelphia, the Evans who conceived and constructed the amazing Orukter Amphibolos.

It would be pleasant to record that McKeever and Valcour launched their vessel successfully, but such was not the case. The river dropped unexpectedly after the engine was installed and the boat left high and dry. Their capital exhausted, the partners removed the engine and rented it to one William Donaldson, who operated a hand sawmill. As mill power the engine was successful; too much so in fact. The engine naturally displaced a number of hand sawyers and, angered at losing their jobs, they are supposed to have set fire to the mill. Incendiary or not, the fire completely destroyed both mill and engine and McKeever and Valcour were out of the steamboat business.

The foremost steamboat proprietors in the United States were Robert Fulton and Robert Livingston, and, to a somewhat lesser degree, Nicholas J. Roosevelt. Fulton had visualized his boats primarily as river craft, and it was but natural that his thoughts should turn to the Mississippi system, the greatest of them all, after the *Clermont* was an assured success. But Fulton knew very little about the Mississippi, and in 1809 he sent Roosevelt from Pittsburgh to New Orleans on a long journey of inspection. Roosevelt made soundings, checked possible channels and current speeds, made notes on fuel supplies and commercial possibilities. In New Orleans he smoked the best Havana cigars, listened to the enthusiastic talk in the coffeehouses, and watched the teeming commercial life of the water front. Then he returned to New York by sea and assured Fulton that steamboat service on the Western rivers was not only possible but would be highly profitable. Thus the first steamboat service in the West was a carefully considered enterprise, not something that just happened.

The project was planned by Livingston, Fulton, and Roosevelt, with the latter in actual charge of operations. The *New Orleans* was built (1810–11) at the mouth of Sukes Run, on the Monongahela at Pittsburgh, by mechanics brought from New York. She was three hundred tons, one hundred thirty-eight feet in length by twenty feet beam, was stern-wheeled, carried two sails, and cost $40,000, about half of which she earned during her first year of operation. Her lines followed those of the ocean vessel rather than those of the duck-bottomed packets which were to come later, when the needs of the rivers were better understood. Her engine was placed in her hold, which was of considerable capacity, and she was deep-keeled—in general, the worst possible design for shallow river water. This was reflected in the fact that though she was finished in March 1811 it was not until the following October that the Monongahela water was able to float her. She then made the Pittsburgh–Louisville passage, seven hundred miles, in seventy hours. Low water again held her at Louisville and vicinity until December, when she set out for Natchez, and on the way she weathered the worst earthquake ever known in the Mississippi Valley. At Natchez she took on some freight and a few passengers for New Orleans, where she arrived on January 10, 1812. A committee of prominent citizens was invited to inspect her and on the following Sunday Roosevelt ran a successful excursion to English Turn and back at three dollars per person.

Against the Mississippi current the *New Orleans* didn't do quite as well as had been expected, but even so she was far superior to any other mode of upstream transportation. After her arrival at New Orleans she went into the New Orleans–

Natchez trade and operated there until July 1814, when a sudden drop in the river at Baton Rouge plunged a snag through her hull and sank her.

A month after the completion of the *New Orleans*, in 1811, Edward Livingston persuaded the Legislature of Orleans Territory to award sole steamboat privileges on the Mississippi to the Fulton-Livingston combination, somewhat as had been done by the state of New York. As long as there were few steamboats on the river this monopoly was more or less enforced. A storm of protest was unleashed in the upstream states, but there was little they could do about it except retaliate in kind; and by the time there were enough boats in operation to make retaliation felt, the United States Supreme Court had ruled the monopoly illegal and declared the rivers open to everyone.

But above all the point had been made, the fact that the river could be navigated by steam-powered vessels had been established, and the Steamboat Era had begun.

The *New Orleans* was of course followed by other steamboats, though in the beginning they did not come with any great rush. They needed time to build and, crude as the early ones were, not every hammer-and-saw boatbuilder could turn them out.

The second steamboat on the lower river was the *Comet*. She made two trips on the New Orleans–Natchez run but she was a midget craft, only twenty-five tons, and could not compete with the larger and more powerful *New Orleans*. Sometime in 1814 she was dismantled and her engine sold for use in a cotton gin.

Followed then the *Vesuvius*, also built for the New Orleans trade. She arrived at the city in the spring of 1814, and in July attempted the return trip to Louisville. She made seven hundred miles up the Mississippi, a gallant try, but there went aground on a sand bar and was marooned for several months. When high water at last floated her off she returned to New

Orleans and went into the Natchez trade. During 1815–16 she ran regularly to Natchez, but in the latter year, on a return trip to New Orleans with Captain Frank Hart commanding, she caught fire, burned, and sank.

Then came the *Enterprise*, built at Brownsville, Kentucky, for Captain Henry Shreve, and she was to make history in a small way. On her maiden trip to New Orleans in December 1814 she carried munitions for General Jackson. After the war she made a number of trips down-river to the Gulf, acting as tow for sailing vessels inbound for New Orleans. Never was such service more sorely needed, but presumably the upriver runs were far more profitable. After one trip up Red River and several to Natchez, she attempted the Louisville run in May 1816—and made it, in twenty-five days, two hours, and forty minutes. It was a transportation landmark. (The *Aetna*, sister boat to the *Vesuvius*, is supposed to have passed Natchez with a cargo for Louisville in November 1815, but apparently she never arrived.) And it was the *Enterprise*, or rather her Captain Shreve, who fought and broke the Fulton-Livingston monopoly. The *Enterprise* had been attached in New Orleans by Edward Livingston, but Shreve carried his case to the Supreme Court and won it.

In the meantime the flatboats continued to float down to New Orleans, the bearded boatmen gazing with wonder and sometimes awe as they passed an occasional steamboat, probably unaware that this smoke-belching contraption would soon deprive many of them of a way of life—though this was not to happen in a year, or even a considerable number of years. It is true that steamboat freight hauls increased enormously from year to year and as more packets came into service, but the amount of freight to be hauled also increased enormously. Yet there never was a time when certain types of freight in small quantities could not be moved to New Orleans by flatboat more cheaply than the packets could or would carry it. A farmer in Kentucky could build a flat from his own timber, load it with grain, lard, hams, staves, etc., and float it to New Orleans in his slack season, his expenses only what food he consumed on the way and a packet deck passage back home when he'd had his fun.

It is common to lump all such floating craft under the heading "flatboat," though actually there were a great variety of types, each of which had a proper name. There were arks, Mackinaws, broad horns, sleds, keelboats, packet boats, real flats, and even ordinary rafts. Most of them, of course, were propelled and managed by heavy sweeps, but there were a few that sported paddle wheels operated by horse- or hand-power, for the principle of the paddle wheel was known long before it was utilized by steamboats. These clumsy affairs carried every conceivable kind of freight, human and otherwise. There was nothing humanly useful which could not be sold in New Orleans, and many of these things were of the simplest kind, the kind of things which could be produced by any man willing to work—stone, hay, hand-hewn lumber, coal, charcoal, barrel staves, lead from the little mines in the Fever River country around Galena; all, including the boat itself, found an eager market in New Orleans.

Probably this is as good a place as any to say that any figures on steamboat and flatboat tonnage and numbers are purely relative. That is, there are as many sets of figures as there are would-be statisticians. Some of them may be right in places, but in which places? since no two of them agree. Many of the figures are useful in making comparisons, but the actual figures must not be taken literally.

For example: En route from Natchez to Louisville the packet *Despatch*, in 1816, reported counting 2,000 floating craft of various kinds in the *daytime only*. Now of course many, perhaps half, of these craft were operating locally, or at least not going to New Orleans. This count was made during one trip, in daylight only, and the *Despatch* could make the run to Louisville in about three and one half weeks. But call it a month, multiply by twelve, and you arrive at the enormous total of 12,000. Another set of figures puts the arrivals of flatboats and barges at New Orleans during 1816 at 1,881. You pay your money and take your choice.

Another instance: A government report gives the total number of steamboats constructed in the West up to 1828 as 314. During this period 133 were lost or decommissioned for one reason or another, thus leaving a total of 181 still in service. Yet without pausing for breath this same report puts steamboat arrivals at New Orleans during 1828 at 698—which is the equivalent of saying that every packet on the rivers made about four annual trips to New Orleans, which is manifestly absurd.

Again, one record states that in 1842 there were 450 steamboats in service in the West; but another says that 705 packets were built *before* 1835. Of course there was always a great gap between the number of packets built and the number actually in service, especially over a period of twenty or thirty years. But these quoted figures are enough to illustrate the vast disagreement over numbers of any kind.

The figures on flatboats vary just as widely. In 1816 New Orleans arrivals are given as six steamboats and 1,881 flats and barges. Five years later the figures were, respectively, 287 and 1,225—apparently a perfectly logical increase in packets and decrease in flats. In 1826, after another five-year interval, steamboat arrivals were 608, flats unknown. The figure for packets seems reasonable enough, and presumably the number of flats decreased accordingly. That was the trend, and it is generally assumed that it continued so until the flatboat count dwindled to nothing. But consider this: In 1845 New Orleans arrivals are given as approximately 2,500 steamboats and 2,700 flats. Thus the confusion only increases.

But perhaps all this is beside the point, for no matter how much the figures varied they all pointed to an enormous increase in tonnage, and that was the important thing.

It is customary to speak of the New Orleans river front as the "harbor," and to some that may have something of an absurd sound, since the city's harbor is that part of the

Mississippi River which lies in front of New Orleans. Webster, however, says that a harbor is "a port or haven for ships"; or "any navigable water where ships may ride in safety," so the Mississippi before New Orleans certainly qualifies. And from 1820 on it is probable that no other harbor in the world could display a greater variety of shipping. To every type of craft which sailed the oceans there were added that typical American thing the steam packet, the peculiar lake and shallow water craft, and the flats and barges in their endless variety. In the beginning vessels of all kinds tied up wherever they could find a convenient place before the quay of the French city, and later the flatboaters showed a preference for the Tchoupitoulas Street sector in the American Quarter above Canal Street. But with the coming of the steamboat regulations were put into effect. In the teens steamboats were ordered docked *only* between the upper side of Canal Street and the lower side of Customhouse Street, a distance of about three blocks. Ocean vessels in general still docked below this area and flatboats above. Areas were also designated for the use of fishermen, shrimpers, oystermen, coasters, and the like; and flatboats were allowed to be broken up for lumber only within certain prescribed limits.

By 1821 the value of exports had jumped to $16,000,000 and growth of all kinds, while it had not begun to reach its eventual rate of increase, was little short of amazing. Population had moved up to around 30,000 and seemed to increase every day—as it actually did. New businesses in endless variety came into being as the need for them arose: ship and steamboat chandlers, steamboat repairmen and mechanics, indeed the whole race of steamboatmen, from stevedore to lordly pilot. In the beginning it had been supposed that steamboats should be manned by seamen, but it didn't take long to discover how fallacious that theory was. There was absolutely nothing in common between the muddy rivers and deep blue water except that they were both wet. Steamboaters had to be created as a race apart, as railroaders were a little later.

Flatboats, Packets, and Prosperity

Lloyds of London discovered New Orleans to be a particularly choice place to do business in America, and sober, thoughtful men believed confidently that New Orleans was destined to be the greatest city in the world. Their reasons for so believing were good, and for that matter are as good now as they were then—for the city is still the natural gateway of the Mississippi Valley and the valley is still "one of the most amazing regions in the world in the extent in which it possesses those qualities which make for habitability in the highest degree of comfort by white men and women." Yes, bigger than London, Paris, New York, or any of the ancient and forgotten capitals of the world. It was never remotely to approach such stature, but it wasn't because the natural ingredients weren't there. Orleanians of the 1830s couldn't foresee how they would fail in the crucial decades that were to follow, how, in fact, they were already sowing the seeds of failure.

In the meantime there was the rushing reality of everyday.

Claiborne, after twelve years as governor of territory and state, was succeeded in 1816 by Jacques Villeré, son of the Joseph Villeré who fifty years before had revolted briefly against the Spanish and died in prison. Claiborne went to the United States Senate but died in less than a year, and his body was brought back to New Orleans and buried in the old St. Louis Cemetery just beyond Rampart Street.

There were no manufactures except those homely and necessary kinds which may be found in any village, and no attempts were made to establish any. The commercial heart of the city was the broad, open levee, its lifeblood the trade which flowed back and forth across it day and night—that and the subsidiaries thereof. Down from the valley came the produce of half a nation, to flow outward to that part of the country which lay beyond the Alleghenies, to Europe, and to the other Americas—stone and coal, flour, corn, wheat, oats, hay, lard, hams and bacon, barreled pork, lumber, hides, beef, stoneware, lead, potatoes, cider, cheese, sugar, rum, molasses, whisky, tallow, salt, and rice.

Back through the gateway, though always in much smaller volume, came silks and broadcloth and linen, French wines and brandies, British cutlery, tools, chinaware, manufactured cotton goods. From Cuba and the islands came more sugar and rum—Louisiana never produced more than half the nation's needs in these. From Central and South America came coffee and tropical fruits, mahogany and rosewood for fine furniture. From Mexico came silver, cochineal, and pimento. The great valley was insatiable; it never left off crying for more.

The newer sections of the city resembled gold-rush camps more than anything else, and almost anyone with a little capital, or even a personality to take the place of capital, could prosper. And everywhere the confusion and waste were appalling. Foresight and economy were words which simply did not exist.

On the wharves, which were nothing except the broad, flat tops of the levees, cargo piled up in small mountains, and frequently it stayed there for weeks. There were twenty-odd years of activity on the wharves before any real effort at protection was made. Perishable goods lay unprotected in blistering sun and pouring rain and losses from these causes were enormous. It has been estimated that the tobacco trade alone suffered an annual shrinkage in value of $100,000 on the New Orleans wharves. Losses in baled cotton and other commodities were comparable. In New England such losses would have been considered nothing short of criminal madness; Orleanians merely shrugged and laughed them off. If insurance didn't cover the losses, you simply wrote them off and moved on to the next deal. In time congestion on the wharves became so bad that ordinances were passed which forbade owners to leave cargo on the wharves for longer than one week. After that it was picked up and deposited in the municipal warehouse, where the owners were fined before being allowed to reclaim it. But the owners didn't mind in the least; in fact, they heartily approved, for it was cheaper to pay the fine then to provide transportation and storage space of their own.

There were half-hearted efforts at improvement, but like most municipal attempts of the period they came to nothing. The First Municipality decided to build wharf sheds from Esplanade Avenue to Canal Street—the limits of the French city—but deciding to build was as far as the project got.

Practically all business was handled on a personal basis and there were no public warehouses or auction rooms. Sea captains coming in with unconsigned cargoes had to hunt their own buyers because there was no central market. Of course many consignors had their own connections, most of them in fact, and the demand for everything was so great that there was never any difficulty in disposing of any goods. But the prices received, for the lack of a central marketing system, was something else. In 1836 the firm of Forstall & De Lizardi began building a warehouse and auction room 400 by 400 feet, to hold 25,000 hogsheads of tobacco, and there were other minor efforts along the same line; but there were no public auction rooms or exchanges until the 1840s.

City transportation was another knotty problem, and one which was not quite all the fault of the commercial interests. As has been pointed out before, the flatboat landing had originally been along Tchoupitoulas Street, and the earliest American warehouses had been built there. But as the Mississippi created more "made" ground, or *batture*, the vital river moved farther away from Tchoupitoulas Street and stevedores were no longer able to move cargo directly from vessels to warehouses because the warehouses weren't there. Instead, mules and drays were required to haul cargo from wharf to warehouse, and more drays and mules and men to haul outgoing cargo from warehouses to outgoing ocean vessels, most of which were docked before the First Municipality. By the 1830s some 1,300 vehicles were in this service alone and the narrow streets—the streets in the newer American Quarter had for the most part not been made wider than those in the old French city—were indescribable quagmires. Gravier Street, second above Canal, leading away from the river, was the first to be paved. Orleanians looked at the cobblestones and laid bets about how soon they would sink out of sight. But they didn't sink—and presently Creole landlords were paving streets in all directions and thus increasing the rental value of their property.

Stone for pavements—and for other building purposes as well—was in such demand that vessels coming otherwise empty could make a profit from their stone ballast. One wonders in passing why shell—crushed oyster shell—was not used as a surface for New Orleans streets before cobblestones. Bayou Road, running from the French city to Lake Pontchartrain and paralleling the Old Basin Canal and Bayou St. John, was satisfactorily surfaced with shell; so was the road along the New Basin Canal when it was dug to connect the heart of the new American city with Pontchartrain. Shell had certain drawbacks—when it was very dry it gave off a stifling dust but one easily settled by a very little moisture —but it was a good surface otherwise, at least on a par with gravel, and it was both cheap and plentiful. It wasn't used in the city, though it seems that almost anything would have been better than the horrible New Orleans mud.

Steam as power became increasingly important. In 1820 a steam ferry to the river's west bank was established by Pierre Derbigny, S. Henderson, and A. L. Duncan, and in 1941 steam ferries still carry the same East-West traffic across the Mississippi—for in two hundred and twenty-four years of existence New Orleans has not yet gotten around to bridging the Mississippi River. Behind the levee and shipping of the Faubourg Marigny below the French city stood the Levee Steam Cotton Press, built in 1832 at a cost of a half million dollars. In 1835 the Orleans Cotton Press, costing three quarters of a million and of comparatively larger capacity, was erected in the American city. These two presses, together with the smaller ones already in existence, had a capacity of half a million bales annually.

Cotton! At first it had been cotton and sugar and all the other produce of the great valley. Then cotton and sugar had moved to the fore, and in the end cotton was supreme. Sugar cane could be produced in only a limited area; the other produce of the valley might be consumed or moved elsewhere; but cotton was the Deep South's own. It could be grown in every Gulf state and far up into Tennessee, Arkansas, and southern Missouri. Around that primary fact grew much, if not most, of the South's economy and much of her political thought and action. It was around cotton that most of the South's credit system revolved, and New Orleans was the heart of that system.

Along the Mississippi, above and below New Orleans, though mostly above, as far as Natchez and beyond, were created the almost legendary plantations which the South liked to think of as typical of all of it. Many of these establishments were really fabulous. They represented gracious living, in some of its aspects at least, at its very best; they were the window dressing of a certain type of American civilization. And to the poor planter in northern Mississippi, living in a log house and raising cotton with six mules and as many niggers, these beautiful places and the life that revolved about them represented the supreme pinnacle of human achievement. It was a wonderful dream—but a very great deal of this luxury was managed on credit. Not all of it, of course, but a very great deal. That is not to say or imply that the luxury was achieved simply by borrowing the money to finance; it was nothing as simple as that. It began when all a man needed for growing cotton was a piece of Delta land—the banks would see that he got everything else.

And in time debt became a familiar part of the cotton economy. The planters, except for the fortunate few, did not pay their loans, and, with the increased demand for cotton and corresponding rise in prices, the bankers did not want them paid. Idle bank deposits produced no interest. Flooded crops and crop failures for other reasons from time to time added to the debt which still went unpaid, and there were aristocratic planters who were never actually solvent. It was the banks of New Orleans which furnished this planter credit. New Orleans was full of banks and the banks full of money—or at least notes; these same notes, which frequently were never paid, merely extended from year to year, often with the unpaid interest added. Having financed the growing of the cotton, to finance it further, through all the processes of ginning, shipping, pressing, and shipping again, was but a natural step.

There was a time when New Orleans boasted that she owned or controlled half the available capital of the United States, though this was no more than an idle boast. No one at the time could say positively what the capital resources of the United States were. And yet in various ways this Southern financial illusion persisted until after the Civil War. At the beginning of that conflict the South believed confidently that the North would be broke within six months, whereas the South's cotton would sustain her indefinitely. It might have —had the cotton economy not been already insolvent. The result was that the South progressed more rapidly toward open bankruptcy, whereas the North, after vastly more actual spending than the South, emerged from the conflict financially stronger than she had been before.

Of course this is an oversimplification of the financial status of both New Orleans and the South as a whole. But the important point is that from its earliest days of prosperity the city did a great deal of its business on credit, which was loose if not completely unwarranted. There was nothing new or strange about that and it was to happen again and again everywhere in America. All this is merely to record that it also happened to New Orleans—and in New Orleans' usual big way.

But in the New Orleans of the 1820s and 1830s there was

no shadow of financial doubt—there seldom is. A man could borrow money from any bank on a cargo or crop of cotton, either actual or potential, on the strength of his or his grandfather's name, or just on his face. Even the Orleans Theater Company was licensed to do banking and insurance business.

In the meantime Liverpool and Havre cried for cotton and more cotton and New Orleans could see nothing ahead but long years of prosperity. And in those easy years ahead Orleanians would get around to those problems they had no time for now. They were problems which cried aloud for solution, and the fact that they went unsolved was what caused the dream of being the world's greatest remain just that, a vague dream and no more.

Already there were tiny clouds on the horizon, and some of them were very close.

One of them was the bar across the mouths of the Mississippi. It had always been a problem, and the Spanish sixty years before had provided regular pilot service and considered it a part of government. But as the bar grew worse with the years, ships became larger and drew more and more water. And as New Orleans advanced to the position of one of the world's greatest ports, the approach to it grew more dangerous and difficult. It has been written that the bar pilot service, independent of government after the Americans took over, became almost criminally careless and undependable, and perhaps that was true. Even so it is begging the question. The pilots neither selected the site of New Orleans nor created the bar of the Mississippi.

The fact remains that by 1830 the bar had become of such proportions that the newest, largest, and fastest ocean vessels, those which would naturally have carried the vast and valuable cargo of New Orleans, were actually unable to reach the city. New Orleans' ocean cargo was being carried in bottoms that were second and third class in capacity and speed.

There were times when ships lay grounded on the bar for

days and even weeks, sometimes preventing other vessels from entering or leaving, and it is impossible even to estimate how many millions of dollars were lost on that great pile of Mississippi mud. The problem became so acute that ship-builders in the East—there were never any of consequence in New Orleans—tried to find a solution in the very construction of their vessels. The New Orleans trade was that important to seamen everywhere. Thus came into being the vessel known as the "New Orleans packet." Hitherto it had been supposed that to be fast a ship had to have a considerable dead rise, that is—for the benefit of landsmen—it drew considerably more water, sometimes as much as two feet, aft than forward. But that type of vessel was also designed for the maximum amount of trouble at the Mississippi bar, and thus the New Orleans packet was designed with a perfectly straight bottom and drew exactly the same amount of water fore and aft. It turned out that this design in itself did not reduce a vessel's speed; on the contrary, with certain other alterations in design it actually increased it, but that had nothing to do with the problem of the Mississippi.

Of course New Orleans shippers were aware of this—the fact probably haunted them. What did they do about it? To all intents and purposes, nothing. A feeble attempt was made to deepen the water at the bar by agitating the surface of the bar in the hope that the current would carry away the loosened mud and thus deepen the channel, but the best that could be said for that was that it didn't make the bar any worse. In 1836–37 there was talk of building jetties, as Pauger had advocated a hundred years earlier, and the Chamber of Commerce petitioned the Federal government to spend $300,000 for improvement—*any* kind of improvement—of the river mouths. That also came to nothing.

Now at the time the responsibility of the Federal government in regard to river and harbor control had not been fully determined, so its responsibility for the Mississippi bar can't be determined here. The point is this: The value of New

Orleans' exports for 1836 was $43,500,000. This value was increasing every year and in 1846 it had jumped to $77,000,000 and was soon to pass the hundred million mark. Yet New Orleans wanted the Federal government to spend a paltry $300,000—apparently on the ground that the city couldn't possibly afford it, even to preserve her very life, for the problem of the bar was growing rapidly more acute. It is quite true that the sum suggested was utterly inadequate to the task—fifty years later Eads' jetties in South Pass cost $5,350,000 to build. But what if the job would have required $10,000,000, or even twice that? What was that when set against the New Orleans business which just before the Civil War reached the tremendous total of $324,000,000, practically all of which was connected in some way with the harbor?

Whatever it was it was too much for the imagination of Orleanians. Of course they were human, they couldn't foresee everything—but it was they also who predicted New Orleans would one day be the greatest in the world. This refusal to spend a dollar to gain a thousand was a poor start.

Far away to the north, beyond the ken of most Orleanians, there was another cloud on the horizon and its name was Erie Canal, the second cloud of many to come. In 1835 the Erie carried from Ohio to New York 86,000 barrels of flour and 98,000 bushels of wheat. It was a tiny drop in the bucket and New Orleans didn't miss it, but ten years earlier that produce would have passed through New Orleans. It was an omen of the future.

There were other things. New Orleans was rapidly becoming one of the world's great ports, yet there was not a single line of ocean vessels owned or controlled by the city's shippers. There were ships available, of course, or at least they were available most of the time; but they were not New Orleans vessels and Orleanians did not and could not regulate either freight rates or the availability of needed vessels. Eastern fleet owners were naturally co-operative—they were in shipping to haul cargo wherever it was to be had;

but there was always the difference between owning and renting. Orleanians knew that, too, but again they were to do nothing about it. In the 1830s they subscribed $258,000 to create the Ocean Steam Navigation Company—which never hauled a cargo in a bottom of its own.

New Orleans business firms grew wealthy and powerful, and yet it has been estimated that seven eighths of them were connected with like firms on the Eastern seaboard. This connection was not merely a matter of reciprocal relations, for the benefits were almost all on the side of the Easterners. When a New Orleans broker sold five thousand bales of cotton to a Manchester manufacturer, the sale was apt to be handled in New York, Boston, or Philadelphia. When a New Orleans merchant bought a cargo of hardware somewhere in Sheffield, chances are his order passed through the hands of someone in New York. All this was utterly unnecessary. Nevertheless, that was the way it was done, and to that extent Orleanians shared both their profits and independence.

And yet the city prospered beyond all imagining and in spite of these things. Perhaps the examination of these dark economic patches has nothing to do with the essence of New Orleans and belongs at least partially in the realm of speculation. But these things do help explain what New Orleans was and what she became.

CHAPTER XII

The Place and the People

ASIDE from its almost fantastic commerce, what manner of city was this?

To begin with, it was not one city but several. Claiborne's belief that the Creoles and Americans would be drawn together by their comradeship in arms was premature, to say the least. In fact, they continued to disagree to such an extent that it was necessary for the Legislature to authorize the creation of separate city governments—which was equivalent to dividing the city according to race and class.

There were three of these municipal units in the beginning: The First Municipality was the original French city, corresponding almost (but not quite) exactly with the French Quarter of present New Orleans. Here the original Orleanians had their homes and businesses, along with those French, Spanish, and Island émigrés who gravitated naturally to this Creole society and were welcomed by it. Here was the citadel of Creole conservatism—perhaps reaction would be a better word, for the Creoles were conservative only in the sense that they violently resented change of any kind.

The Second Municipality comprised the American town which grew up above Canal Street, and it was violently— the word is chosen deliberately—American.

The Port of New Orleans

The Third Municipality was the area below the French city and had many of the characteristics of the other two. Originally it had been the plantation of the Marigny family, and it is generally believed that Bernard Marigny, an inveterate but unlucky gambler, was forced to subdivide the plantation in order to pay his gambling debts. It was known first as the Suburb Marigny, then as the Faubourg Marigny, and finally as the Third Municipality. It was perhaps symbolical that the three parts of the city weren't even numbered according to their geographical arrangement.

At the head of these three units there was one mayor, but each of the three elected its own municipal council and otherwise conducted its own municipal affairs, though the First Municipality was for many years the seat of both the mayor and the state government and to some extent was the most influential of the three politically.

The result of this separation was about what might have been expected—utter confusion and cross-purposes. Even so New Orleans for many years preferred the confusion to unification and co-operation.

In 1813 two young and zealous representatives of the Massachusetts and Connecticut Missionary societies, John F. Schermerhorn and Samuel J. Mills, toured the valleys of the Ohio and Mississippi in the interest of churchly morals. Everywhere they found the state of both public and private morals very low indeed, but New Orleans was the last word. They could not imagine, they said, a city more completely given over to sin, and when New Orleans changed it was only to get worse.

Now this writer is one who believes that organized religion in the Western world has never, except in rare cases—Salt Lake City, for example—been a dominant force in shaping the character of any city. It has been a factor, yes, but never the dominant one which by its very nature one supposes it ought to be. The Church has maintained the fiction that it has been a powerful moral force, but proof of that is hard to find.

The Place and the People

Put in figures it might be something like this: It is relatively easy to show that at a given time in New Orleans there were, say, three hundred brothels; yet the Church cannot reasonably argue that but for its influence there would have been five hundred or four hundred and twenty.

Nevertheless, the religion of a city is a part of its history, if only in a negative sense, and as such is worth examination. For more than a hundred years New Orleans was Catholic; it had no Protestant church at all until a decade after the American occupation; and even then the Catholic Church remained vastly superior in numbers and influence. So if the shortcomings of the Catholic Church appear to get more attention here than those of the Protestant, it is only because the Catholic Church was and is so superior numerically.

From the very beginning the Catholic Church in New Orleans concerned itself more with superficial religious observations than with the extension of moral principles into the everyday life of its people. That is, it remained aloof from the public life of the city, apparently content as long as the people paid lip service to the faith. The Church married, baptized, and buried its parishioners and to a certain extent instructed them in the generalities of the faith. In between times what the folk did was their own business. Having labored over the individual, the Church assumed that the folk would behave themselves collectively. There is, of course, a great deal to be said for that religious theory—the trouble was that in New Orleans it didn't work. There were, naturally, numberless other places where the theory didn't work either, but New Orleans was always an outstanding example of the failure.

The sins of omission of the Church in general in New Orleans are so many that a fat volume couldn't contain them all. From its actions one can only assume that the Church took Negro slavery for granted, and while it did not condone prostitution it certainly made no organized public effort against it. There is not the slightest doubt that the priesthood castigated the individual for his or her sins of commission, and yet since prostitution and other vices flourished as they did one can only conclude that these exhortations did no practical good. And certainly it is true that crooks, brothel keepers, liquor dealers, gamblers, corrupt politicians, and plain prostitutes made up part of the Catholic—and later Protestant—congregations. The population at large compared with the avowed number of communicants in the churches leaves no doubt about that. There is a difference between the two figures, of course, but it would be absurd to suppose that everyone profiting from one kind of vice or another belonged only to that stratum of the population which was outside the Church.

It would be equally absurd to suggest that the Church as such contributed to the vice of New Orleans, but it did little to combat it and in at least some instances it came perilously close to being allied with it. The Church, for example, operated lotteries in open competition with those privately run, and the excuse that the profits were used for the work of the Church didn't alter the fact that the ultimate effect on the gambler was exactly the same in either case. And, much later, one of the chief considerations of the monopoly granted the Louisiana Lottery Company was that it make an annual payment of forty thousand dollars to Charity Hospital, which in turn was administered by the Ursulines. Furthermore, a large amount of the money which went into the building and ornamentation of many of New Orleans' churches came from the profits of vice. Sufficient proof of that lies in the very fact that the money was so readily available. The Church has a ready answer for that, too, but it has never helped in the reduction of vice.

Illiteracy is not in itself an indication of vice, far from it, but, given certain other factors, it is a big help and New Orleans had, even in the 1830s, several times its reasonable quota. Schools were half-hearted affairs at best and a great proportion of the foreign population had no intention of becoming literate in any language. So, too, 95 per cent of the blacks—though not partial blacks and free Negroes—were denied any access to the printed word. Neither did the Creole population at large believe in excessive formal education. It was all right for priests and notaries and the like, but the ordinary gentleman considered it a useless appendage, a waste of time better spent at the café or the gaming table.

New Orleans loved to gamble, had done so since Bienville's time, and still does. The tide of organized gambling ebbed and flowed, but it was always there. There were times when the only public gaming houses were dingy dumps in side streets, and times when such establishments as St. Cyr's, Toussaint's, and Hewlett's on Chartres Street, and John Davis' place at the corner of Orleans and Royal streets, paid a license fee of seventy-five hundred dollars per year and admitted none but the most respectable or responsible citizens—they were not necessarily the same thing. Reform movements also ebbed and flowed, but it was hard to reform a people who would rather gamble than do anything else on earth. The amount of money which changed hands through gambling was enormous and beyond computation, and the stakes included not only money but steamboats, ship cargoes, thousands of acres of land, and crops not yet harvested. The custom of these more prominent gambling establishments was drawn from the ranks of the most prominent citizens—merchants, planters, professional men of stature, and members of government. And with most of them gambling was not an occasional indulgence but an avocation. Since most of these higher-bracket gamblers were men who normally would have taken the lead in civic affairs, it was no wonder that garbage piled up in the streets and the harbor went to the dogs.

With less than a third of its present population of half a million there was a time when the city supported no less than five hundred gaming establishments of one kind and another, and in its heyday the Louisiana Lottery Company's drawings amounted to almost fifty millions of dollars annually—which makes the Irish Sweepstakes look like a country church raffle. It was in New Orleans, too, that the policy game, so dear to the heart of the Negro, got its start.

It naturally followed that every other form of vice flourished equally well. Prostitution was more prevalent in the American city, but the French Quarter had its share and was due for more. In 1836, when the population was recorded as 60,000, there were 543 saloons, cabarets, taverns, barrel houses, etc., one for each 110 persons, paying an annual liquor license of $200. Heaven only knows how many more operated without licenses of any kind except the protection paid the police and politicians. There may have been cities which had a greater per capita consumption of liquor, but they were hard to find. New Orleans is still a doughty champion in this respect. It is said that during the late unlamented Prohibition Era there were New Orleans saloons which never closed for as long as a single day, and since Repeal many a saloon has long since thrown away its door keys. What use are keys to places which never close?

Five hundred gambling houses, between five and six hundred places selling liquor, perhaps almost as many brothels —this may be too high a figure, since they did not run that high proportionately when the figure was known with some accuracy—is it any wonder that almost every form of crime did equally well? Pickpockets, footpads, burglars, greater and smaller thieves of all sorts, confidence men, every sort of grifter down to the thugs who rolled helpless drunks were commonplace. And since the police had long since given up trying to cope with the criminal element—even if they made arrests the courts usually turned the culprits loose unless they happened to be Negroes—it naturally followed that they should go into business with it. So they went into the business, and stayed there. Officials of the city government went into the business and stayed there. As far as I know there are no available figures on the comparative corruption of officials in various American cities, but if there were New Orleans would certainly be far up in the van. Proof of that statement can be found in any New Orleans newspaper file of the last hundred years—and for the most part the papers only recorded those instances where the grafters were publicly charged. Thus when the tactics of the Long machine in the New Orleans of the 1930s became so rough that they made national headlines, the rest of the country was shocked, amused, surprised, or interested, according to the individual point of view. Orleanians may have been interested or amused but they were neither shocked nor surprised. They knew the Long machine was merely carrying on a time-honored tradition and not doing nearly so well at it as many of its predecessors had.

There was many an honest cop in the older New Orleans, just as there are now, but they were not representatives of the force as a whole. It is probable, however, that the corruption of the police in these modern times finds its outlet in general inefficiency and in sadistic minor persecutions—especially in regard to the Negro population—rather than in graft involving any great amount of personal profit. It is only fair to say that New Orleans is not unusual in this respect—the same statement would apply to some degree in any city of the South.

So, too, both the Catholic and Protestant churches in New Orleans had their heroes and heroines as individuals. In times of flood and fire and pestilence the clergy has displayed a public devotion and disregard of personal sacrifice as great as any to be found anywhere in the world.

Flood and pestilence were factors which had a tremendous influence on civic virtue and civic conscience.

As opposed to floodwaters pestilence has been by far the city's worst enemy. Flood damage since the city's founding has been enormous and has only been eliminated during the last few decades. (One hesitates to write "entirely eliminated," for surely no man can say that the Mississippi is entirely conquered. From Cairo to Head of Passes the folk *believe* that it is, but——) Loss of life was never great because there was always ample warning of approaching floods and Orleanians early learned to prepare for them. When the Mississippi was rising rivermen could predict almost to the hour when it would go over the top of the levee. Then, too, the building of levees has only lately ceased to be a continuous process that went on for more than two hundred years. And floods in the city, while common, were never violent affairs. Sometimes floods approached from the direction opposite the river and levee, that is from Lake Pontchartrain. Occasionally a strong north wind lasting for days would slowly move the shallow waters of the lake into the bayous and canals until they overflowed into the city; and at other times, when the Mississippi broke through the levee far above the city, the river would surge across country into Lake Pontchartrain and again approach the city from the rear. Thus the recurring floods were nuisances and property destroyers, but they were not often deadly.

But disease! That, indeed, was another matter!

Malaria was common and always had been, but it was also common throughout the great valley. But malaria, too, was more of a nuisance than anything else, and it was possible in time to become immune to it.

Yellow fever, smallpox, and cholera were other matters altogether, and the first two had been frequent visitors in New Orleans for more than a century. Their visitations were always bad enough, though some were naturally worse than others. In 1832 an epidemic of yellow fever had almost prostrated the city but was slowly dying out, when cholera struck. It had come by way of Europe, struck the Eastern seaboard first, and arrived in New Orleans late in October. How many persons died from one disease or the other in the period which immediately followed cannot be determined exactly, though it is known that six thousand died within one period of twenty days and that the count for some days reached five hundred. Even in the most modern cities the bureaus of vital statistics would have trouble coping with a death rate of that kind.

It was at this time that the New Basin Canal was being constructed, largely with immigrant Irish hand labor—the Irish were always the pick-and-shovel champions of America—and many an Irishman was buried, or rather left to lie, in the muck of the canal where he collapsed over his shovel. The cemeteries could not begin to accommodate the waves of dead; priests and ministers worked day and night at hurried burial ceremonies; and how many bodies were simply dumped into the current of the river can only be guessed at. Because water was invariably struck a foot or so below the ground level it has long been, and still is, a New Orleans custom to make all burials—except those of Jews—aboveground. Almost everyone has seen or read of the slightly gruesome tombs, or "ovens," of stone and brick which really give New Orleans cemeteries the appearance of cities of the dead. But now this method of burial was abandoned for the first time. Tombs of even the simplest kind could not possibly be built fast enough and trenches, rather than graves, were dug and bodies by the cartful dumped into them without ceremony.

There are a great many accounts of these recurring epidemics, and for the most part they are written with a singular detachment unusual in any writing of the nineteenth century, even though the writers themselves had suffered grievous personal losses. Perhaps it was the same sort of detachment which seems to come to the survivors of a modern city which is repeatedly bombed. Violent and ugly death becomes so commonplace that the senses are dulled and cannot react in the ordinary way.

Of course every epidemic of this character caused an exodus from the city. Those who could leave did, returning when the disease had run its course. How many carried the disease even as they left, and died elsewhere, can never be known either, but they must have been legion.

It is true that modern methods of public-health protection

were largely unknown, but even so there were medical men
in New Orleans who knew—or guessed—that the foul condition of the city as a whole was partially responsible for these
scourges. Even in its healthiest years the death rate in New
Orleans was far higher than any other comparable city in
the country, despite the denials of the city's publicists. For
one thing, there was the stubborn refusal of the commercial
interests to consent to immediate wholesale quarantine the
moment one of these diseases made its appearance; it would
"be bad for business!" Doctors were known to attribute yellow-fever deaths to other causes and newspapers deliberately
refrained from printing the cause of death if it happened to
be one of the communicable diseases. Everywhere in the city
the streets were littered with garbage and all manner of
human refuse. Stagnant waters bred mosquitoes by the millions. (The mosquitoes in the city were so vicious that they
had created a style. Men in New Orleans, in order to protect
sensitive calves and ankles, wore long trousers a generation
before they were common elsewhere.) Where the streets
had been paved there were still no underground sewers and
the refuse was dumped into the stone gutters at the edges of
the pavement. Sometimes rain washed this refuse away, but
even then it was only to deposit it somewhere else. Gangs
of Negroes from the city prisons were also used to clean up
some of this refuse, but one can imagine that they didn't
break their backs over what was always a hopeless task.

It is easy enough to recount the shortcomings of Orleanians
and even to work up a reasonable indignation over their
failures to make the most of their obvious opportunities. And
yet was there ever another city in America so beset by natural
difficulties? If there was a vast amount of vice, and there
was, some of the tolerance toward it was accounted for by
a certain prevalence of the "tomorrow-we-may-die" feeling.
There was also the widespread belief that a great amount of
New Orleans' woe was inevitable in the very nature of things,
that to do anything about it was beyond human capability.

The Place and the People

It was not, of course, and in time these obvious difficulties were overcome, some of them in the most ingenious ways. Yet this feeling of inevitability was held by men who otherwise were not fools at all. As a comparison consider the fact that it is generally agreed that one of the curses of the modern city is the vast cacophony of unnecessary noise it generates. Yet who in New York and Chicago has done more than nibble at the edges of the problem?

It was a strange city of strange contrasts, and beside the vast sea of degradation and vice and human greed there were oases of dignity and grace and beauty. If the streets were quagmires underfoot they were also channels of moving, living color that could be matched nowhere else in America. The multicolored stucco and brick walls of the French Quarter were weathered into the loveliest of pastel tints; the doorways and fanlights were models of wooden grace; the handwrought ironwork of grilles and balconies and street lamps has hardly been matched elsewhere in the United States. If the land on which the city stood was marshy it was also fertile almost beyond belief and everywhere, practically the year round, there was a riot of foliage and flowers. Even now there is hardly another city in America which so clothes its nakedness with natural beauty, where streetcars and taxis roar past under balconies festooned with carefully tended greenery. And nowhere on the Gulf coast is there another city whose streets are so shaded by trees which have grown to a natural old age in their own earth.

There were graceful houses where the very best in the physical aspects of existence were taken for granted and such luxuries as the time afforded were commonplace. Houses were dressed with the finest in silver, china, glassware, and furniture that the world's best craftsmen could produce, and life moved with a liquid rhythm that was as perfect as any until then designed in the New World. Many a gape-mouthed country lad had returned to the semi-frontier of the upper valleys with at least a glimpse of the good things the world held for those who could get them. The lanky young Abe Lincoln, who saw New Orleans first in the summer of 1828, was only one of many. A glimpse of the private grandeur of the Rue Royale and Faubourg St. Jean was all such as these were likely to get—but it was something the imagination could embroider.

And there were other queer islands of endeavor. In a city which to a large extent was built on a slave economy, where almost every household of consequence had its slave or slaves, a white typographical union—in 1810—not only bluntly stated its demands but got them!

Again, in a city which could at times be exceedingly hard on its black human property, there were some nine hundred "free people of color" who were paying taxes on property conservatively valued at $2,500,000, and who themselves in turn owned more than six hundred slaves. And this was only a part of the so-called free people of color; there were many more not included in this group.

The clashing of a dozen tongues could be heard in New Orleans' streets and along her wharves, and yet the French tradition, in spite of the fact that New Orleans had not been French in more than lip service for seventy years, remained so strong that all laws, ordinances, and public notices were published in English *and* French for another generation at least. In fact, the French tradition so gripped the Creole mind that the aristocracy still thought of France as the mother country—and a very close mother. The city mourned Napoleon's death to a degree second only to Paris itself, and Orleanians who would not dream of visiting New York or Washington knew Paris as well as they knew their own Vieux Carré. They sent their sons and daughters there to be educated as a matter of course, and in most cases even their slaves were more articulate in French than English.

Somewhat apropos of that—in the North and East the hordes of immigrants were for the most part Americanized rapidly, and if in some places the process was slower, the newcomers at least had little influence on the older residents. On the whole, the newcomers came ready to accept certain American things which had attracted them in the first place, but, oddly enough, in New Orleans the process was being reversed as far as the Americans were concerned. From the beginning the Creoles had resented having an American pattern forced upon them, and they had fought it as best they knew how. In the end they changed the Americans more than the Americans changed them. The influences of climate, food, manners, architecture, and language worked to make the Americans more Creole than the Creoles. It was a slow process, an almost imperceptible change, but it was there. It was simply the old case of the convert to a way of life becoming more enthusiastic about it than the originators themselves. Even the architecture of the American section copied that of the French; it was not identical but it was nearer to that of the French than anything else.

New Orleans had learned that she lived in the heart of one of the world's great food-producing areas, and her cooks were beginning to master the art of cookery that would soon make them famous the world over.

The city was early aware of the new thing called the railroad, and as usual was ready to have a try at it. By 1830 the New Orleans & Pontchartrain Railroad was hauling passengers and goods from Decatur Street in the French Quarter to the shore of Lake Pontchartrain at Milneburg. The trains were horse drawn and the passenger fare was thirty-seven and one half cents. By 1835 the New Orleans & Carrollton Railroad was carrying passengers up the river shore from the American city to the suburb known as Carrollton, long since a part of New Orleans, at a fare of twenty-five cents. Some writers have made the distinction that the N.O.&C. was a street railway, while the N.O.&P. was a railroad, but in any case they were early examples of their genre in the United States and New Orleans is entitled to whatever honor that may be. These transportation systems were successful within their limited ranges, and when the greater railroad craze swept the country a few years later New Orleans was ready —or thought it was. A railroad project called the Charleston & Cincinnati was planned to tap the Ohio Valley market for the seaboard, and in answer to that challenge a charter was secured for the construction of the New Orleans & Nashville Railroad in 1835. Its promoters even got as far as importing a shipment of rails from England, but in the end nothing came of the project. The national financial collapse of 1837 put a temporary stop to all railroad construction, and when the crisis was past the New Orleans & Nashville was forgotten. With New Orleans it was the old story of procrastination, and it was to be many a year before she was to have a rail connection of consequence.

Nor was the city backward in other things. Sometime in the early 1820s James H. Caldwell made his appearance in New Orleans. He was an actor and actor-producer, and opened the first theater to be operated as such in the American city, in competition with John Davis' much more pretentious Theatre d'Orleans on Orleans Street in the French Quarter. Caldwell's theater was on Camp Street a short distance above Canal, and the swampland around it was so wet that Caldwell was almost running a showboat—in fact, on occasion he furnished boots in order that his patrons might reach his foyer with dry feet. But Caldwell had ambitions to be something more than an actor-manager, and he had ideas. From England—he was himself an Englishman—he imported the first gas machine in the South, at first merely with the idea of lighting his theater with the device. But it was so popular that before long he decided to branch out. After a series of false starts, of company organizations and reorganizations, he at last, in 1835, had the New Orleans Gas Light & *Banking* Company under way. The plant was located in the square bounded by Gravier, Perdido, Magnolia, and Robertson streets, and equipped with much more pretentious machinery, imported from England as the theater equipment had been. And weird-looking stuff that machinery was too. The first principal main was some two miles long, ran down Camp Street, across Canal, and thence along Chartres Street in the French Quarter. From this point Caldwell went on to become New Orleans' first utility tycoon.

Incidentally, this gas plant of Caldwell's was a good example of the New Orleans industrial establishment using slave labor. All manual labor was slave, whites being employed only in supervisory capacities, and the Negroes and their families lived in quarters inside the walls of the plant. In 1860, when Caldwell died, the company carried on its books "live assets" of $53,000. The following excerpt from a contemporary newspaper account of Caldwell's funeral is a good example of the sort of thing indulged in by the newspapers—ask a simple question and as answer you would get a platform lecture on the history, moral virtues, and future prospects of Negro slavery in the South. The papers seldom missed an opportunity to open up in this vein:

A striking feature of the funeral ceremonies was the presence of a large number of slaves of the gas company, who, dressed in their neat attire, and bearing themselves with the greatest propriety, marched in the procession even in advance of many of the white friends of the deceased. When the religious rites were concluded, the grief of the Africans sought relief in loud sobbing and in the most expressive evidences of sincere affection. It is well known that these negroes have always been subjected to a strict discipline but a kind and just treatment, and it attests the admirable working of our social system, as well as the noble qualities of our deceased friend, that such manifestations should be made by those to whom he had stood in the relation of master.

It may have been true—but in any case Caldwell had erected a fifteen-foot brick wall and a first-class set of iron gates to insure the affections of his chattels.

Always and everywhere were the outlandish contrasts between people and manners and customs. Between St. Peter

and St. Anne streets, on Rampart Street but just beyond the
line of the original French city, lay the plot of ground known
as Congo Square. It lay within a stone's throw of that most
modern thing in New Orleans, the line of the Pontchartrain
Railroad, and was known as Circus Square and, after the
Civil War, as Beauregard Square. For some years after the
American occupation the place was used by Gaëtano's Circus,
a one-horse tent outfit which was almost a city institution
until it was put out of business by a drunken crew of rioting
flatboatmen with nothing better to do. In 1817 it was decreed the one place in the city where slaves might gather
and amuse themselves, and then only until sunset on Sundays
and under the supervision of the police. This ruling stood for
about twenty years, but eventually such use of the Square
was limited to the months from May through August, and
then only on Sundays between 4 and 6:30 P.M. For years
the Square was the one New Orleans Negro institution of
importance, and the name "Congo" was the Negro's, not the
white man's.

No Negro missed the Sunday gathering if he could help
it, and if only half the eyewitness accounts of the spectacle
are true it must have been a sight worth seeing. In time it
became such a well-known city institution that few visitors
missed seeing it at least once. There are scores of accounts
of the dances and ceremonies written by white men, some of
them vivid and picturesque, but none of them indicate any
inside knowledge and understanding of what it was all about—
and the Negroes never told. Of course some of the dances
had no more special significance than the Lindy Hop or the
Charleston, and some of them were no more than innocuous
exercises in which even the supervising police took small
parts. But there were other things with a deeper meaning,
meaning which the Negro did not explain, no matter how
much or by whom he was questioned—and when the Negro
decides to be evasive he is a champion. Probably many of
them did not fully understand the symbolism of all their

Spanish arsenal in New Orleans. Erected in 1838 on the site of
the old arsenal originally used by the Louisiana Legion. Now
a part of the Louisiana State Museum.

demonstrations but responded emotionally to them without question, drawn by some urge beyond their immediate experience.

It is said on good authority that in the New Orleans of the 1820s there were a number of Negroes who had been tribal chiefs and medicine men in their native Africa—and it would be strange if that were not true. For the blackbirders took whatever able-bodied Negroes they could lay hands on, and though importation of slaves into the United States was forbidden after 1808, everyone knows that the trade continued for years afterward. It is pointless to attach too much importance to these fragmentary expressions of a tribal culture that was fast being forgotten. Nevertheless, for the New Orleans Negro who was without literature, music, religion, and even language of his own, at least some of these Sunday festivities had a deeper meaning than any white observer ever understood.

In 1835–36 the boom in New Orleans was approaching its crest, as indeed it was everywhere in America. Property values increased—on paper—without rhyme or reason; banks had up to 90 per cent of their real assets loaned; rents increased 50 per cent during 1835–36; no speculation was too visionary. The Panic of 1837, full credit for which is sometimes given to New Orleans' old friend General—later President—Jackson —prostrated New Orleans along with the rest of the country. Banks and speculative ventures and balloon values vanished overnight. And yet at that period in its history the panic was no more than a purgative which the country badly needed. At least that was true of New Orleans. During the actual period of the depression the city was experiencing its triumphs.

In 1837 the first St. Charles Hotel was opened to the public, and no matter what its architectural failures and eccentricities it was by all odds the most imposing structure west of the Alleghenies. During this period the annual carnival later known as Mardi Gras had its beginnings. It was about this time, too, that the New Orleans custom of five-o'clock steamboat departures began to take shape. Five o'clock in the afternoon gradually became the standard hour for upriver departures. It was late enough for a departing passenger to have finished his day's business, late enough for final cargo to be aboard, and early enough for all passengers to be well settled before supper aboard. Promptly at five they backed into the current, black smoke rolling from the towering stacks and open furnace doors throwing a red glare over the sweating black bodies of the firemen, bells jangling orders to engine room and main deck. With waving passengers lining the rails, the pilots jockeyed for position, hunted the easy water nearest the boats still docked along the New Orleans shore, and gradually found their places in the majestic parade line. It was a sight worth coming a long way to see.

For all its chronic and occasional ills New Orleans felt entitled to a certain complacency. In only a few years more than a million bales of cotton would roll across her wharves, and in 1840 her population was officially 102,193—Chicago's was 4,500—and she was fourth ranking city in the United States.

CHAPTER XIII

The End of an Era

NOWHERE IN AMERICA was the Mexican War of 1846 more popular than in New Orleans, and nowhere was the direct profit from that adventure in imperialism greater. By the very nature of its geographical position New Orleans enjoyed a natural trade advantage with both Mexico and Texas. The interior Texas trade by way of the Red River was one of the richest in the Mississippi Valley, especially after the beginning of the steamboat era and the successful destruction of the navigation-obstructing Red River raft by Captain Henry Shreve. The coastwise Gulf trade was also a rich vein running directly into New Orleans and could be worked by vessels of almost any size. There were strong mercantile firms in New Orleans that confined almost all their activities to the Mexican trade—and of course for a long time much of present Texas was automatically included under the heading Mexico.

Offhand it might be supposed that these firms at least would have been opposed to an open conflict with Mexico, but such was not the case. New Orleans was always a hotbed of intrigue directed against this or that regime in one of the Latin-American countries. Most of the time, of course, the internal affairs of these sometimes unhappy countries were absolutely none of New Orleans' business, but with a zest for interference equaled only by its failure to solve its own problems, New Orleans was always ready to ballyhoo for another filibustering expedition. A persuasive man could find followers for almost any harebrained adventure, and when the entire United States undertook a filibustering jaunt on a big scale, New Orleans was naturally enthusiastic. Even those commercially most interested in Mexico, if not openly in favor of the war, were not opposed to it. They couldn't see where or how it would cause them to lose any of the trade they already had, and its successful conclusion might very well improve trade, at least from the American standpoint. Making war seems an odd way to improve relations with one's best customer, but it made sense to a great many Orleanians—as it has to other people before and since.

The city itself supplied a reasonable number of men for actual service in the field, mostly through the mediums of militia units already organized. In that day the local militia unit was not infrequently one of any city's most influential male clubs, and New Orleans was by no means an exception. In fact, most of her militia personnel rated high in the social scale and many a private went off to war in a uniform which resembled a stage admiral's dress suit. Yet New Orleans' contribution in man power was numerically nothing extraordinary. It was not nearly so great proportionately as some of the rural Middle West, for instance. Perhaps it is best to say that she furnished a reasonable number of men and let it go at that.

But the war brought the city a minor wave of additional prosperity. It was the one great American advance base, and into it at one time or another poured almost every American soldier of the Mexican War except those engaged by way of California. From the warehouses of New Orleans came every kind of supplies needed by an invading army except perhaps such things as ammunition and guns. Passing soldiers swelled the incomes of brothels, gambling houses, and saloons.

The End of an Era

Perhaps as many as 80 per cent of the troops used in Mexico saw something of New Orleans. All the regiments from west of the Alleghenies funneled into the city, most of them for the first time, by way of the rivers. And to the country youths of Indiana, Ohio, Illinois, Pennsylvania, and Vermont, New Orleans was a revelation. Few of them had imagined anything like the Crescent City, much less actually seen it, and for not a few of them the city remained a place of bitter memories. Not a few of them carried venereal diseases from New Orleans to Mexico and back home again, and some of them, wasting from wounds and disease picked up in Mexico, came back to New Orleans to discover it was one of the worst places in North America in which to be ill. Troop transports, a great many of them of New Orleans registry, were not only privately owned but privately operated during their period of war service, and some of them were hell-ships indeed.

On the rivers the packets which made steamboat history temporarily left off carrying cotton and its kindred products, including planters and their ladies, and became troop transports. They were packet names to conjure with, the Broadway Limiteds and Zephyrs and Rockets of their day. There was the *J. M. White*, whose time from New Orleans to St. Louis in 1844 was only four hours and fifty-five minutes behind the all-time record set twenty-six years later, in 1870, by the *Robert E. Lee*. And according to no less an authority than Mark Twain, the distance, because of the eternal vagaries of the Mississippi, was about eighty miles farther in 1844 than in 1870. There was many another fine packet temporarily in the transport service—the *Sultana*, the *Eclipse*, the *Belle of the West*, the *Duke of Orleans*, and a host of others that made packet history in their day.

The packets were the best-known and most popular inanimate things in the New Orleans of the forties and fifties—if the packet can justly be called an inanimate thing. Men and boys of all ages conceived a blind devotion to certain

[197]

packets in a way later reserved for the Brooklyn Dodgers and Notre Dame football teams. They made a fetish of knowing their favorite's every eccentricity of performance, knew exactly what her best runs were, and the first names of her officers. Men postponed business journeys in order to ride their favorite boat. Social position was somewhat determined by the prestige of the packet on which a man served, and his opinions on any subject valued accordingly. A black fireman or stevedore off the *A. L. Shotwell* or the *Empress* was not to be considered as remotely in the same class with a similar rating off some egg crate running to Golden Meadow or the Yazoo.

It is an odd but true thing that the river packet, insofar as its mechanical development was concerned, reached its zenith in the late forties and early fifties. Of course there were certain minor refinements made later, safety devices principally, but in general packet design was frozen after 1850. They had reached their peak in speed, luxury, and carrying capacity. In this they were much like the steam locomotives of a half century later, when high-wheeled passenger engines set speed records unbeaten by much-publicized, newfangled, streamlined Diesels forty years later. Many of these packets, like those named above, were the giants of the river, yet loaded to near capacity with cargo and passengers they attained speeds up to eighteen miles per hour *against* the Mississippi current. Over the 1,200-odd miles from New Orleans to St. Louis they averaged up to fourteen miles per hour on that grueling run, not running time, but time from point to point, with no allowance made for stops.

The packets were by far the finest possible kind of craft for navigating the shallow and tricky waters of the Western rivers, and their invention and development could not have occurred at a more providential time in the history of the United States. But when one writes that they reached their peak in the fifties that is not the same thing as saying that they *could not* have been further improved. The fact that their design was frozen meant simply that men chose, for various reasons, to leave it at that and turn to other things. In this instance the other things were the railroads and all their subsidiary appurtenances. If for certain reasons it should become necessary for much of America to return to horse-drawn vehicles—and as this is written in 1942 it appears that we may—does anyone suppose that the buggies and carriages of the 1940s will not be tremendous improvements over those of the 1890s? Of course not. Likewise there was nothing to prevent the further improvement of the steam packet except lack of incentive for those who could have done the job. And of course packet improvement would have included improvement of everything that pertained to them—waterways themselves, terminal facilities, routes and schedules, and regulation of competition. It was really these subsidiary reasons which brought about the downfall of the packets. Packet owners simply could not afford to set up terminal facilities, even in towns and cities of consequence, whereas the railroads could and did build—mostly with other people's money—freight and passenger terminals in every hamlet. Everyone knows what the result was.

The packets and small flatboats were not the only ways in which produce came to New Orleans. Some of the greatest tonnage moved in the shape of coal boats and lumber rafts. Coal boats usually came down in pairs, lashed together, and manned by a crew of fifteen or twenty. Wood rafts, both logs and finished lumber, might be seventy feet wide by three hundred long, and both rafts and coal boats continued to operate as "floaters" long after steam came into general use. They were the juggernauts of the rivers and woe betide any other craft which got in their way! Because these craft were always large and unwieldy they usually waited upstream for what was called a "coal-boat rise," and then let go. Anything which got in their way, unless it happened to be the bank, was simply annihilated—anything floating, that is, until the steam dredge came along. Raftsmen and coal boaters learned to their sorrow that a steam dredge spudded in was about the same thing as Gibraltar. Of course both coal boats and lumber rafts operated mainly in the upper reaches of the rivers, though New Orleans got its full share of them.

By the 1850s steam tugs were in more or less regular service between New Orleans and the Gulf, or rather between the Gulf and New Orleans, for no skipper liked the expense of a tow when it could be avoided and any tub which could float could reach the sea *from* New Orleans without aid. By this period, too, the steam-propelled ocean vessel was no novelty along New Orleans' wharves, and yet it was not a commonplace either. There was a reason. Steam power, from the time it was applied to ocean vessels, was of necessity installed in vessels of considerable size. One consideration was the massive weight of the machinery itself, and another was the fuel-storage capacity needed if any real distance was to be covered. Thus if any room was to be left for cargo there had to be plenty of hull. And hulls of that size simply did not negotiate the Mississippi bar.

A notable exception was the steamer *Illinois*, which in 1826 made the passage from New York to St. Louis, via New Orleans, in twenty-nine and one half days. That, however, was more of a stunt than anything else and was by no means a regular thing. It was a fact, however, that certain enterprising skippers did give New Orleans commercial interests something of a scare with a few of these presumptuous through boats. When steam tugs began towing ocean vessels from the Passes to New Orleans the thought naturally arose—if a tow this far, then why not farther? There was plenty of water at least as far as the mouth of Red River. Some of these passing craft gave New Orleans a bad case of nerves, though nothing much was ever lost through these adventurous skippers. There wasn't enough trade in this extra one-hundred-and-fifty-mile stretch to warrant spending much time or money to get it.

Not the least of the odd sights to be seen in the harbor of New Orleans were the fresh new square-riggers which anchored there without ever having had salt water under their keels or a salt breeze in their rigging. They were Pittsburgh-built and came down by way of the Ohio and Mississippi, to be documented at New Orleans and sent to sea with cotton for Liverpool and Havre. More than a hundred of these vessels went to sea from New Orleans. In their way they seem as queer as the submarines that have been built on the Great Lakes and sent to sea by much the same route. Were someone to announce that he was writing the maritime history of Pittsburgh, Pennsylvania, most laymen would consider that a joke in the tradition of the Swiss navy, yet there would be nothing illogical about it. Someone—it was Leland D. Baldwin, I believe—has told the story of the American skipper who was almost jailed as a fraud in a foreign port because his papers showed that he had cleared from Pittsburgh—and he had! And one way to silence chamber-of-commerce boosters from any American seaport, when they speak of modern tonnage figures and boast of their own port as being "second" or "seventh" or whatnot, is to remind them that in 1940 Pittsburgh could point to having by far the greatest water-borne tonnage in the world!

Now of New Orleans all these things are true; yet it is wise neither to generalize too broadly nor to be too dogmatically exact. For example: while most of the shipping from New Orleans to the Gulf moved under its own power, many of the cotton ships, especially those bound out with the early crop, were towed downstream in the interest of time and literally *dragged* across the bar. The bar tug pilot picked the likeliest spot in the mud barrier and let drive with full power. And often a heavily loaded outbound vessel needed this aid more than one of the same draft coming in light against the current—and the New Orleans trade was always heaviest on the export side. The same qualification must be made to the statement elsewhere that New Orleans shippers owned little tonnage themselves. That was true insofar as New Orleans maintained no shipping *lines* comparable with the early American Black Ball or the British Cunard Line. There were, of course, all sorts of vessels in New Orleans registry. An official government report of 1859 gives New Orleans' tonnage in steam vessels as 75,789, but this includes *both* ocean and river craft, so it isn't enlightening in some ways. It is safe to assume, however, that the great majority of this was river tonnage.

In the decade prior to the Civil War steamboat arrivals in New Orleans were as follows:

1851......2,918		1856......2,956
1852......2,778		1857......2,745
1853......3,252		1858......3,264
1854......3,076		1859......3,259
1855......2,763		1860......3,566

An average of almost ten a day at the peak! Is it any wonder that packets were moored two deep along the New Orleans levee and that the parade of departure at five of an afternoon was an imposing sight?

Of course all, or almost all, of this New Orleans-bound cargo went to sea, and yet it seems reasonable to quote these columns of steamboat figures and omit any comparable list of brigs, schooners, barkentines, clippers, and whatnot. And the reason is that New Orleans was first and foremost a river town. The distinction is a little subtle. The sea trade was and is there, obviously, and as obviously the city owed her very existence to that fact. Furthermore, most of the great natural seaports of the world are also, for elemental reasons of physical geography, at the mouths of rivers. Some of the greatest American ports—Philadelphia, Seattle, Baltimore—are much farther from the actual open sea than New Orleans. It is somewhere in this realm of geography that the difference lies, for New Orleans is neither close to the open sea nor at the *mouth* of the Mississippi. The Mississippi enfolds the city in a great loop and the only time the city knows from experience that the salt sea has a tide is when, at long intervals,

the river drops to a point where water from the Gulf over-
comes the gigantic pressure of the Mississippi and flows out
of New Orleans' household faucets. The sea is a long way off,
but the river is always there, enclosing the city on three sides;
and it is the river which time and again has driven New
Orleans into its upper stories and attics, not the sea. Ask the
man on New Orleans' streets how many times he has been to
the river's mouths and three out of five will be surprised
that they might be expected to have been there at all. Much
of New Orleans is quite well aware of its dependence on
the sea trade but not at all aware of the sea itself. To all
this the average Orleanian asks, "Well, and what of it?" The
fact that he thus puts the question perhaps supplies the reason
why the city became a midget with a prodigious personality
rather than one of the world's great cities.

The city rolled on through the fabulous era of the fifties,
that period of robust national health just before the disease
of civil war set in.

Everywhere there was a state of flux. Even the old Place
d'Armes was changed so that Bienville, Kerlerec, Miro, and
even Claiborne would not have recognized it. The St. Louis
Cathedral of Almonaster came down and in its place was
erected the present structure of that name—said by reliable
witnesses to be by no means an improvement. French mansard
roofs blossomed on the Cabildo and the Presbytère, flanking
the church structure. Facing the square on two of its other
sides were erected the block-long Pontalba Buildings, the
project of old Don Almonaster's daughter Michaela, wife of
Xavier Delfair, Baron de Pontalba. With all this taking place
on three sides of it, the sun-baked Place d'Armes was reno-
vated with trees, flower-bordered shell walks in geometric
patterns, a centerpiece of General Jackson on an excited
horse, and was renamed Jackson Square. Not many years later
General Ben Butler, Union commandant of New Orleans,
finished the statue by having cut into its pedestal Jackson's

own words to a rebellious South Carolina: "The Union must and shall be preserved."

A few blocks from Jackson Square the U.S. Mint was busy with the flood of fresh gold which came by way of Cape Horn. In 1851 the value of the produce which rolled down from the great valley passed the hundred-million-dollar mark and continued to surge upward toward the two- and three-hundred-million line. In the North the railroads and canals were cutting relentlessly into the total trade going to New Orleans, yet the aggregate was so vast that New Orleans never missed it. How could it? More shipping than ever lined the wharves and perhaps 10 per cent of the ocean arrivals were steamships. The St. Charles Hotel burned to the ground but was promptly rebuilt, and in the French Quarter the St. Louis Hotel continued as the Creole social center. Slave auction marts were maintained in both the St. Charles and St. Louis, and the latter was in winter the scene of the principal Mardi Gras balls. There must have been something ironically symbolic in the fact that the city's chief social centers were also its principal slave marts.

Nor was there lack of comic relief. In 1851 P. T. Barnum brought Miss Jenny Lind to the city in the course of her triumphant tour of the States. According to all accounts the otherwise colorless Miss Lind possessed one of the world's greatest voices, but she had neither a sense of humor nor a capacity for glamorizing herself. Someone in the Lind-Barnum entourage—it sounded exactly like Miss Jenny herself—remarked that, "In New Orleans drinking seems to hold its chief abiding place in the New World and drunkenness may be regarded as one of the more prominent features of the lower classes." One wonders if the remarker overlooked the upper classes or if "lower" was supposed to be doubly expressive. At any rate, Mr. Barnum not only echoed the sentiment but donated five hundred dollars to the local temperance fund—New Orleans had one, believe it or not!—and gave one of his celebrated lectures on the evil of drink. Orleanians jammed the hall to hear him, cheered him to the echo, and then probably went out to have a few drinks. They could appreciate a first-rate humbug when they saw one and Barnum, if he had been so of mind, could have made a large permanent place for himself in New Orleans with almost no effort. But the folk also turned out to hear the Swedish Nightingale, and, as it so happened, the party had to stay in town an extra day because Miss Lind refused to travel on the Sabbath. However, she did not refuse to sing on Sunday —always New Orleans' big day of the week—and thus both she and Barnum profited by being able to give *two* farewell concerts instead of the customary one!

At least part of the city's appreciation was on the artistic side. New Orleans liked elegant singing, or at least was willing to support it, and the opera, an institution unfamiliar in most of the United States, had long had a foothold in the city. Grand opera had been brought to New Orleans by Julia Calvé in the depression year of 1837. It was first performed in Davis' Theatre d'Orleans, by now under the direction of John Davis' son Pierre and one Charles Boudousquié, who later married Mlle. Calvé.

During the season there were four operatic performances per week and they soon came to be the socially correct thing—a fashion that was repeated wherever opera was performed in America. In 1859 Boudousquié became manager of the newly finished French Opera House, at the corner of Bourbon and Toulouse streets, and while correct society transferred its affections to the newer house the Theatre d'Orleans continued to present opera for some years. In both establishments some of the presentations were excellent indeed, but some of them were also what show business in these days would call "lahsy." In the Europe of the nineteenth century opera companies were as common as circuses and could be hired on the same basis. It was only natural that New Orleans should import its share of lemons.

Much has been made of the cultural value of the opera in

The Port of New Orleans

New Orleans, though its actual worth is hard to define. About all it proved conclusively was that New Orleans could afford Europe's most spectacular form of polite entertainment. It was first and foremost a species of display, though undoubtedly the music was, most of the time, a cut above that of the Royal Street concert saloons. When the deserted, rat-ridden old building finally burned in 1919—it had but lately become the property of Tulane University—newspaper editorials shed crocodile tears over the passing of a cultural landmark—but its passing was so little regretted that no one ever got around to cleaning up the debris of the fire.

Crime and corruption kept pace with or ran ahead of the city's increase in population and prosperity. From 1840 to the beginning of the Civil War city government was largely a farce, elections hardly more than pitched battles between political factions, all of whom were equally knavish. Taxes were high, and yet the city received nothing for its money but corruption and trouble. In the New Orleans political annals of the forties and fifties will be found the names of men who were later enshrined in the Confederate pantheon—Judah Benjamin, John Slidell, H. C. Warmoth, P. G. T. Beauregard, John T. Monroe, and a host of others. Many a so-called Confederate statesman got his start in the weird politics of Southern state and municipal government. The separate municipal councils were gotten rid of in 1852, and the city government moved from the Cabildo to a new City Hall, on Lafayette Square above Canal Street. There were many who hoped this consolidation would help matters, but of course it did not.

The form of government doesn't necessarily have any influence on corruption. If anything this made matters worse, for power was thus concentrated in the hands of fewer men. New Orleans for years remained the dirtiest and most unhealthful city in North America, and not a little of this can be laid at the door of corrupt government. Back of it all was of course an indifferent public, but it was government which was directly responsible. There have been municipal governments in the United States which stole all they wanted and still managed to provide all the ordinary conveniences of a city—on the ground that they and their families also had to live there if nothing else. Not so New Orleans. Its politicians didn't believe in giving the city *anything* for its money.

Startling as it may seem, there was not a foot of underground sewer in the city until 1880, when the St. Charles Hotel built a private main emptying into the Mississippi. Shortly afterward D. H. Holmes Company, a department store, built another which was also used by a few other business houses. But not until 1892 did the city, then with 250,000 inhabitants, do anything more about sewers—and then it farmed the whole business out to a private corporation! The same sloth prevailed in every other department of city management—police and fire protection, city records and vital statistics, and water supply, this last always an especially acute problem in New Orleans. Most corrupt city machines early learned, for their own good, to let the fire department more or less alone, for fear that they would some morning discover there was no city. But in 1890, when most cities of 25,000 had long since taken fire protection into their own hands, New Orleans was still paying an annual lump sum to a private organization for fire protection—or lack of it.

Crime literally ran wild, and the city served as a regular winter haven for well-known criminals vacationing from colder climates but still keeping busy. But these outlanders were only the froth. New Orleans had home talent that compared favorably with any in the world, and it always did its best to live up to its reputation. If it was short in any field it was that of crimping. Shanghaiing was always a favorite and profitable pastime in most deep-water ports, but for some reason it never caught on in New Orleans. Perhaps it was that after doping, slugging, robbing, and otherwise maltreating seamen and other wayfarers, the dive-keepers couldn't be bothered with the trouble of delivering them on shipboard.

Gallatin Street in the French Quarter, only a few squares removed from the U.S. Mint, was probably the toughest two blocks in America. Nowadays it is an unpretentious midget thoroughfare extraordinarily quiet even in the day-time, given over for the most part to gloomy warehouses. It was fairly quiet during the daylight hours of the 1850s, too, but from sunset to dawn it was hell on wheels. There was not one legitimate business in the street and the police never entered the area except in heavily armed parties during the daylight hours. At night no officer of the law would approach the area. A remark attributed to a denizen of another vice area might well have been applied to Gallatin Street—he said, in effect, that he didn't see what people had to complain about because there were no respectable citizens in the area anyway—a gem of understatement. There was no law or order whatever in Gallatin Street until Union troops took a hand during the Civil War. Not that they attempted to es-tablish any law or order; they didn't. But they did not hesi-tate to put Gallatin Street in its place whenever Union soldiers ran afoul of it.

Ordinary citizens went armed as commonly as they wore their hats, though statistics indicate that most of them were notoriously bad shots. The great majority of all crime went unpunished unless its perpetrators happened to be caught in the act by the police, which wasn't often. Even then the courts seemed to act on the assumption that all criminals were victims of persecution and entitled to nothing but the best at the hands of the authorities. Should the criminal by some chance be convicted, he found that the parish prison was run by criminals for criminals, and that his stay there would be made as comfortable, even as luxurious as possible. If even then he found his stay irksome the current governor could almost certainly be prevailed upon to pardon him. No

The Cabildo on Jackson Square in New Orleans.

satirist ever portrayed a more insane world of law and order than New Orleans was in reality.

In this volume numerous references have been made to the constant stream of immigrants which flowed into the city from 1820 to 1860, as indeed they flowed into all America; and a snap judgment would indicate that at any given time the percentage of foreign-born was very high, that being in part an explanation of the city's political corruption. Pious politicians and apologists to the contrary notwithstanding, in American cities of the nineteenth century the balance of political power usually lay in these groups of semi-literate but voting foreign-born. These groups *held* the balance of power but it was the men who controlled their votes who *used* that balance. New Orleans, like the rest of the South, like the rest of the country, had voting regulations, but they were chiefly for the convenience of the political machines, as the Louisiana laws are even today. Before the Civil War formal citizenship, especially in the cities, was probably the least of the considerations involving the franchise. But the confusing thing is that, according to the available figures, New Orleans did *not* have a comparatively high percentage of foreign-born. It was high, yes, as it was everywhere in America, but in itself it was not enough to account for any great part of the political mess. And invariably the men most conspicuously involved in New Orleans' scandals bore the same kind of names later found most prominently on Confederate honor rolls. One does not even find a preponderance of Creole and French names among them. Names in themselves certainly mean little in this respect. Yet one is likely to find a certain difference in attitude toward government in a town where the Joneses, Browns, and Smiths predominate over the Wozniaks, Ah Sings, Svendborgs, and Schultzes.

And yet in this matter of New Orleans' foreign-born it is quite probable that the statistics are all wrong. The figures seem to belie themselves. We are told that ten thousand immigrants from the West Indian islands alone settled in New Orleans around 1810, that later Irish and Germans came in at the rate of thirty thousand per year, though of course these latter, especially the Germans, did not all remain in the city. Other hordes came in lesser profusion. Not a few of these moved on, but even more of them must have stayed, for otherwise how account for the fact that by the fifties New Orleans' population had moved up to more than one hundred and fifty thousand? And yet the records indicate that both New York and St. Louis had much greater proportions of foreign-born; other cities were neck and neck with New Orleans. From casual observation the visitor in modern New Orleans easily gets the impression that it is a "foreign" city, and yet current census figures show that the ratio of foreign-born is surprisingly small. It is all very confusing.

No less confusing is the record of the Negro population, both slave and free. In the forties and fifties the slave population of New Orleans decreased by over 5,000. Where did they go? Well, undoubtedly many of them were sold into the outlands at high prices, but that is a surmise and there is no exact data. Those who believe in the efficacy of the non-importation law will say that the death rate took care of the decrease, but that theory won't hold water, for the higher birth rate canceled out the death rate. If that were not true there would be practically no Negroes in the United States now. By the same token the number of free Negroes in New Orleans decreased by half in the decade before the Civil War. Where did they go? There is no exact answer to that either, except that nobody knows.

The newspapers denied it, the public denied it, and the politicians denied it, but still New Orleans remained the most unhealthful city in America. The death rate per thousand, exclusive of deaths from contagious diseases, was two to three times the national average. Between the Louisiana Purchase and 1900 the city had no less than thirty-seven epidemics of yellow fever alone, to say nothing of the recurrent outbreaks of cholera, bubonic, and smallpox.

The city had suffered in the past, but the yellow-fever scourge of 1853 is still known as the Great Epidemic. It even extended into the summers of 1854 and 1855, carrying off some five thousand persons in these latter years, though it lay dormant during the winters.

Most records agree that the fever came in on shipboard during May of 1853, but by just which ship is not precisely known. In early May the *Northampton*, from Liverpool with several hundred Irish immigrants, arrived at New Orleans; she had had sickness aboard, and some deaths. Arrived also the bark *Siri*, having lost her captain and several crew members of yellow fever at Rio de Janeiro. Shortly afterward there arrived the *Camboden Castle*, and she had lost seven of her crew of the fever at Kingston, Jamaica. A shore crew sent to unload and clean the *Northampton* reported her very foul and with traces of black vomit, the yellow-fever sign, present in her hospital. This crew quit, another was hired, and several members of the second gang fell ill. On this same day, May 17, the *Augusta*, inbound from Bremen with two hundred immigrants, came into port in the same tow with the *Camboden Castle*. The *Augusta* moored alongside the already questionable *Northampton*. From all these ships the immigrants promptly went ashore, eager to be away from what was almost always crowded misery. The *Camboden Castle* was in turn moored alongside the *Saxon*, which had originally come in in the same tow with the diseased *Siri*.

Thus there were in port five vessels, to all five of which yellow fever could be traced to some extent. The immigrant passengers scattered all over the city, among relatives and friends, or found burrows of their own. The ships' crews went ashore and sought their favorite brothels, saloons, and boardinghouses. The city could hardly have been given a more thorough infection had it been planned.

Yet the disease did not manifest itself immediately. Two

victims of yellow fever died within a week or ten days, but they were not reported as such, even by the attending physicians. On May 27 one of the passengers off the *Northampton* was brought to Charity Hospital and next day died of the fever. The board of health was notified of the cause of death but again no public mention of it was made. A few cases developed through June, but nothing spectacular. For the week ending July 2, twenty-five deaths were recorded. The newspapers still ignored the situation and so did everyone else.

The city rocked along, trying to cure the disease by ignoring it. But in the end it refused to be ignored longer. For the week ending July 16 there were two hundred deaths from the fever, hundreds more had been taken ill, and indifference gradually became near-panic. Only twenty years had elapsed since the last great scourge and every adult of thirty or over had vivid and uncomfortable, even nightmarish memories of the last time.

During the week following July 16, Charity Hospital alone received up to one hundred patients per day and could not possibly care for them adequately. The Ursulines toiled unremittingly day and night, and still the sick spread over the floors and into the corridors.

The usual frantic exodus from the city began, and every means of transportation was taxed to the utmost. At the same time, of course, the very means of transportation decreased. Horse-drawn vehicles which left the city did not return, and steam packets one by one stopped running to the city at all. There was some railway mileage north and west of the city, but not enough to be of much real aid in evacuation.

To make matters worse it began to rain, the heavy, tropical, summer rains of New Orleans, and this time they were far worse than usual. It is said that it rained every day for two straight months, and even if that is an exaggeration the fall was still far more than normal. And in between the drenching rains the drying sun did not prevail as it usually did, the sky remaining overcast, the air chill and heavy with moisture. The many miles of still-unpaved streets again became morasses, and even funeral vehicles moved with the greatest difficulty. The old scenes of twenty-four-hour burial again took place in the cemeteries, and it became impossible to hire gravediggers at any price. Bodies, as usual, were dumped into the canals and the river. Public vehicles stopped in front of houses, especially in the thickly populated areas, while the drivers yelled a query as to whether there were bodies to be removed.

Men and women and children were struck down wherever they happened to be, some of them in the streets. Those caring for the ill collapsed and frequently died ahead of their patients. Whole family groups were wiped out and folk living alone, or in hotels and boardinghouses, died and their decaying corpses remained unnoticed for days or even weeks.

And still it rained incessantly. The streets were running streams and weeds grew shoulder high through the crevices of the banquettes and cobbled streets.

Everywhere the atmosphere of a charnel house gone mad prevailed. There was an air of near-insanity and mental depression that cannot be measured or described. The city authorities, no more misguided than other folk of the day, burned barrels of pitch and tar on the street corners, on the theory that the pall of black, stinking smoke had some effect on the disease. For the same reason cannon were fired day and night at regular intervals. From a distance the city appeared as though burning under an artillery bombardment, and everywhere the stench was almost overpowering.

Police and the volunteer firemen were of course stricken along with everyone else and were unable to go about their ordinary duties. People on the whole became more careless because they could not help themselves. Fire alarms went unanswered and probably only a miracle and the incessant rain prevented the city from being destroyed by fire. Wild,

[213]

blind drunkenness, incredible debauchery, and crime ran their course unchecked. Human ghouls of every sort made their appearance, and the homes of the dead were robbed before they could be buried. The plague scenes of medieval Europe paled in comparison.

And beside all this horror there was as usual the triumph of the human spirit over adversity. Doctors, nuns, priests, ministers, the meek little man from next door, and some of the toughest divekeepers rose magnificently to the emergency. They toiled against superhuman odds, asking only that they be given enough strength to carry on, and for the most part their heroism and devotion went unrecorded and uncelebrated. And of all contagious diseases yellow fever is one of the most hideous in its outward manifestations. Beside it smallpox and Spanish influenza are as nothing.

Through July and through August the pestilence roared on. The death rate mounted daily. There were fifteen hundred deaths per week. On August 22 there were officially two hundred and eighty-three deaths, one every five minutes, and there were unquestionably many which went unrecorded. But the next day there were twenty-five fewer deaths, and on the day following a still further decrease. By September 10 the number of daily deaths dropped below one hundred, and after that the decrease was steady until December, when it appeared that the disease had at last run its course.

Between June 1 and October 1 there were about eleven thousand official burials, though this is not by any means an exact record of the dead. During this year of 1853 there were about thirty thousand known cases of yellow fever in New Orleans, and deaths from *all* causes were about sixteen thousand. It is well known, of course, that in epidemics of this scope deaths from causes other than the contagion also increase greatly. In the summers of 1854 and 1855 the fever, still not completely stamped out, killed about five thousand persons, and to these must be added seventeen hundred and fifty deaths by cholera. The death rate per thousand from 1853 through 1855 was, respectively, 111, 72, and 73. Total deaths from all causes during the three years were about thirty-seven thousand, or four times New Orleans' normally high rate.

Of course the losses, both human and material, were enormous. The human suffering and misery were incalculable. And what did the city do about it? Well, not very much. Out of sight was out of mind with most Orleanians, and there were lost profits to be regained. They determined to study the situation as far as possible and decided upon compulsory quarantine in the future—should the need be really urgent, of course; that was about all.

The fact still remained that it was another forty years before the city got around to taking the sewage out of the streets and putting it where it belonged. And fifty years after that it could not truthfully say that its sanitary regulations were even as good as the average city of its size in the rest of the United States.

CHAPTER XIV

Before the Storm

HARDLY REALIZING IT, New Orleans had grown to be the metropolis of that part of the country which thought of itself as the South. No other Southern city compared with her in wealth and population—a statement as true today as it was before the Civil War. Yet one hesitates to say that she was the most influential city in the field of strictly Southern thought, as even now one would hesitate to say that about New York City and the rest of the United States. Richest and most populous as she was, New Orleans was also the South's most un-Southern city.

It is true that she had grown great on a slave economy, and the agrarian lands which sent her two million bales of cotton per year were the very body of the slave economy. Her publicists and newspapers were as stoutly and vocally in favor of the slave system as any group in the South. In fact, they went out of their way to repeat that theme at every possible opportunity. Orleanians, by their very temperaments, seemed of all people in the South those most likely to cling to the belief in Negro slavery as an institution.

But in New Orleans there was another side to the question, and it was a very large side indeed. It sheltered more people of alien race than any other city in the South, and the

majority of these people neither owned slaves nor believed
in the slave system. They had no personal liking for the
Negro, rather the contrary; it was the institution they were
opposed to, and they opposed it for the most part on economic grounds. In the preceding chapter it was stated that
New Orleans' slave population decreased by five thousand
in the decade before the Civil War, and economically these
slaves were replaced by immigrants. The Irish, for example,
liked the American concept of personal freedom but for
various reasons seemed best fitted for the manual labor
hitherto performed almost exclusively by the Negro.

There was the question of the free people of color. To
the world at large New Orleans maintained that they were
no problem at all—or if they were the problem would solve
itself in time. Yet in private many Orleanians were fully
aware of the acuteness of the problem, aware of its real
status and the way it adversely affected the moral fiber of
the whites. Orleanians had been more than casually interested in the various unsuccessful (for the most part) attempts
to resettle free Negroes somewhere in Africa. They had not
done much to solve the problem, it is true, but they were
certainly aware that something would have to be done about
it eventually.

Then there was the matter of commerce. Of all the cities
in the South New Orleans had had the longest profitable
relations with the East, and some of these ties were strong.
There were businessmen in the East who abhorred Negro
slavery and yet had nothing but the warmest feeling for their
New Orleans colleagues, and there were plenty of Orleanians
who felt the same way. Cotton and sugar had become the
darlings of New Orleans commerce, and in the North the
spreading railroads had bitten deep into her former spheres,
yet the volume of business which still came down the great
valley was enormous and not to be lightly thrown away.

This was the other side of the medal.

These were factors which influenced all the South to a

greater or lesser degree, but in New Orleans they were thrown into sharper focus than anywhere else in the South of the 1850s. In the end none of these factors mattered, what sober counsels there were found no listeners, and New Orleans and Louisiana were swept along with the rest of the South for better or worse. It was almost a foregone conclusion.

Civil wars are fascinating things in the sense that they provide the best possible theater for the display of every known variety of human activity, emotion, stupidity, and brilliance. Wars between national states are equally stupid but they seldom produce the brilliant interplay of emotion and cross-purposes created by even a minor civil war. A great many contemporary Americans see our own Civil War as merely something which happened and is best forgotten. They regard it as a great musty mass of names, dates, battles, and forgotten generals—a shadowy something from which the names of Lee, Grant, and Lincoln emerge chiefly as suitable objects for patriotic regard. That is a pity, for in many ways the American Civil War is one of the human masterpieces of all time.

The true motives of men who make civil wars are almost always obscure and are seldom the ones they profess for the benefit of the public at large. The motives of the leaders of the ante-bellum South were no exception. Their stupidities and self-deceptions are myriad, and yet it is hard to believe that at least some of them did not very clearly see the fundamental weaknesses of their position. Why they deliberately chose to ignore their known weaknesses is one of the obscurities. Perhaps their knowledge of them was overshadowed by a sincere belief that the North could not or would not fight, though that, too, was a fundamental error—one of many.

Of course it is easy to point out these flaws in judgment eighty years later, but it is also difficult to perceive why some of them were not deadly obvious in 1860. Not a few Confederate leaders were unable to comprehend cold reality. Some of them mistook wishful thinking for fact, and many of them were simply enchanted by their own rhetoric, but there were many who must have seen the truth clearly. It is these who are hardest to understand.

Both Northern and Southern historians have worked themselves into a lather trying to demonstrate that the American Civil War was not fought over the slavery issue and dilate at length over the business of states' rights. Yet what state rights were at issue except those involving slavery? And did not the Confederate Vice-President Alexander Stephens state the case exactly when he said: "Its [our government's] foundations are laid, its cornerstone rests upon, the great truth that the Negro is not equal to the white man; that slavery, subordination to the superior race, is his natural and normal condition. This, our new Government, is the first in the history of the world, based upon this great physical, philosophical, and moral truth." What could be clearer than that? Or was Mr. Stephens fighting one war and his colleagues another?

The South reiterated that she wanted nothing but honorable separation, that she wanted nothing which belonged to the despised and hated Federal government—and then proceeded to confiscate all Federal property she could lay hands on, even seizing and operating the U.S. Mint in New Orleans until the gold stock ran out.

One of the cardinal principles of the Confederation was the right of any of its members to secede, even as they all had done. Yet when some of her own states threatened exactly that, it was not secession but plain treason.

The South's leaders told their people that, "honor" and personal feeling aside, the South was economically indispensable not only to the North but to the rest of the world, whereas she herself was virtually self-sufficient and self-contained. The briefest examination of any comparative figures should have shown what an utter fallacy *that* was. And that was one of New Orleans' special weaknesses. The city believed that the great valley could not live without free access to its natural outlet at the foot of the Mississippi, whereas the truth was that the upper valley had been getting along more and more for years without New Orleans. The Crescent City had just never taken the trouble to learn that for herself.

These are generalizations about the South as a whole, but they are not superfluous here for every one of them applied to New Orleans in some degree. New Orleans was the one city in the South where a real divergence of opinion, concerning both secession and its aftermath, could be found. Had Louisiana—and New Orleans dominated the state—refused to secede, it is possible that her refusal would have made other states think twice. But there is a tide in these matters which, once started, must run its course. Louisiana had gone too far to back down, and when the time came she carried out the formalities as though glad to get through with them.

The first step toward secession was taken by Louisiana when her delegation, by an 8 to 2 vote, walked out of the Democratic Convention which later nominated Stephen A. Douglas for the Presidency.

The second step was the election which followed in the fall of 1860. This election was unique in American history in that Lincoln, the successful candidate, was not represented on the ballots of ten Southern states, one of which was Louisiana. The Louisiana vote was as follows: Douglas, 7,625; Breckinridge, 22,681; and Bell, 20,204. Thus it is quite correct to say that Lincoln did not get a single vote in Louisiana. What might have happened had his name been on the ballot is a matter for conjecture only. On this score alone could be based an argument that the vote did not reflect Louisiana's true sentiment, but there is more to it than that. The total vote cast was 50,510, whereas the population figure on which Louisiana claimed Congressional representation was 709,290. But, in order to give the Louisiana democracy every possible advantage, suppose the figure is broken down. Then it stands: free population, 376,280; slave, 333,010. Thus less than one seventh of the free population, less than one fourteenth of the total population, expressed its views on the Presidency. Louisiana's apologists explain that the total vote is unimportant, that the proportions are sufficient to indicate the state's true intentions. (One of the favorite deprecatory phrases is "mere numerical majorities," though that principle seemed to be quite all right when applied to the deliberations of the Confederacy.) Perhaps it is best to let the reader take his choice from among the figures.

But there is more. The Presidential vote, of course, did not in itself take Louisiana out of the Union, but the passing of the Ordinance of Secession did. The vote of the special secession convention, in January of 1861, was: for secession, 103; against, 17. But even that didn't settle the matter—quite. At least one New Orleans newspaper charged that some of the Union delegates to the special convention had repudiated their election pledges—as they did elsewhere in the South— and demanded that the convention examine the original vote for delegates and then submit its own 103 to 17 decision for popular approval. By dint of some hard work the convention finally concluded that the popular vote had been: for Union delegates, 17,296; for secession delegates, 20,448—which was a majority but still a long way from the 103 to 17 vote of the convention. By a vote of about two to one—after first refusing to consider the question at all—the convention also refused to submit the ordinance for popular approval.

(Throughout these figures those of the state rather than New Orleans are used, because they are more generally accessible; but it must be remembered that New Orleans contained about a third of the state's eligible voting population and so always held the balance if not the majority of power.)

Reduced to their simplest terms, the figures indicate that one eighteenth of the *voting* population took New Orleans and Louisiana out of the Union and into the four years of the Civil War. How can one resist the temptation to observe that New Orleans deserved whatever she received?

CHAPTER XV

The Mighty Is Fallen

IN THE BEGINNING the actuality of the war made little
impact on New Orleans.

State troops occupied Forts Jackson and St. Philip a few
miles above Head of Passes. Other troops seized the U.S.
Mint and the still-unfinished U.S. Custom House on Canal
Street, and the Federal-owned but unused barracks. Still other
troops, mostly the young bloods and those Orleanians who
were always ready to join any crusade, hurried North and
East to join the Confederate colors.

Otherwise the city went about her business much as she
had in the past. The Mississippi was open as far as Cairo,
much farther than that to all practical purposes, during the
first months of the conflict, and though there was talk of a
Federal coastal blockade, that was a long way off and few
Orleanians feared it anyway. The South still labored under
the delusion that England and France needed her cotton so
badly that they would send their merchantmen after it with
naval escorts which would brook no insolence from the
Yankees.

Indeed it is only through cotton that the first year of the
Confederate war effort is connected with New Orleans, and
that not very closely. From the beginning of the conflict the

Confederacy had neither money nor a financial policy worth the name. The only specie it ever held was that confiscated from Federal mints and customhouses at the start of the war. Later it floated certain domestic bond issues and these were paid for, as the Davis government wanted them to be, with cotton. In other words, the planter or patriot turned his cotton over to an agent of the Confederacy and accepted bonds in payment. In turn the Confederate government warehoused this cotton against the time when Europe would be willing to pay almost any price to get it. Thus the Davis government planned to partially finance the war from the proceeds of a gigantic cotton speculation. As far as the eventual increase in price was concerned, the government guessed correctly. The trouble was that by the time the government was willing to sell cotton, the blockade had become effective enough to prevent its delivery—and Europe showed a singular reluctance to come after it in force.

In the first year of the war, during which the Federal blockade was largely ineffective, the European market bought heavily though at no more than a normal increase in price. New Orleans carried forward this business as it always had. Thus the sharp demand and resultant price advance did not come nearly as soon as the Confederate government expected. That was a bad error, but so was its apparent conception of the amount of cotton necessary to control the market to any great extent. By 1860 New Orleans alone was handling two million bales annually, whereas the Confederate government never held title to more than 400,000 bales. It is true that after the start of the war production fell off sharply, but even so 400,000 bales was hardly a corner on the world cotton market.

The Confederacy tried several ingenious methods of turning its cotton stock into usable money, but never succeeded to the extent of more than a few million dollars, which were spent in British shipyards to no good purpose. Otherwise, when the Confederacy needed money it simply printed a new batch of greenbacks—yellowbacks, to be exact—each of which was more worthless than the last, since the earlier ones at least had confidence and hope behind them. Alexander Stephens had told the South that it was worth no less than twenty-two billion dollars. This was nothing but the wildest imaginings, though had the South actually been worth as much as one fourth of that sum there was still no way to use it in conducting a war. The time-honored theory that the South impoverished itself to support the war is simply not true. The truth was that when the war began the South as a whole was badly in debt, and while it did become impoverished it was not through financial support of the government. The people *were* the South, and they could not have aided the government greatly in a financial way had they wanted to. There were many individual exceptions, of course. Many a stanch Southerner can prove that his grandfather equipped this or that company from his own pocket, donated his horseflesh, or turned the ancestral home into a hospital, but in comparison with the total war needs of an entire people these things were as nothing.

In the aggregate New Orleans probably suffered less from the prosecution of the war than any other Southern city of consequence. Richmond, Atlanta, Savannah, Charleston, Vicksburg, and Chattanooga saw property worth millions destroyed as direct results of the hostilities. New Orleans did not. What physical loss she suffered—and it was very little—was inflicted by her own citizens.

Through the last eight months of 1861, during which the war was being fought with increasing bitterness elsewhere, New Orleans moved her cotton as usual and at a better-than-average price. The city itself had as yet felt little of the war's real impact, though the time was not far off when she would.

But while the Federal government had its hands full in Virginia, Kentucky, and Tennessee, it had not forgotten the city of New Orleans by any means. It was merely a question of time, as it had been with the British in 1814. The Federal government was and had been perfectly aware of New Orleans' strategic value, though it appears that the Confederates were not. Or if they were they did little to demonstrate their concern. Certain steps had been taken, it is true. Forts Jackson and St. Philip—for years hardly more than token fortifications under the Federal regime—had been rebuilt, regunned, and fully manned by the Confederates. The city itself was garrisoned, though not heavily, and there were military forces at the outlying posts on the Mississippi and Lakes Borgne and Pontchartrain. A chain-and-cable barrier mounted on schooner hulks had been thrown across the Mississippi in the vicinity of the two lower forts and was commanded by their guns. (The city and the military had the greatest confidence in that fence, though there has seldom been an instance in military history where such a barrier has been worth the effort of erecting.) In addition there were in the Lower Mississippi and the Gulf a miscellaneous fleet, made up mostly of converted packets and ocean steam vessels. The number of Confederate troops in the Department of New Orleans was, as of January 1, 1862, 10,318. These troops were of course distributed as above. Such was the extent of New Orleans' preparedness for invasion.

But these were thought to be enough and New Orleans, confident as always, had no active fear of invasion. The city was not easily approachable by any route except the river. Neither highways nor railroads, such as they were, offered good attack routes, and the Mississippi was securely Confederate as far up as Memphis until sometime after New Orleans itself had fallen. The use of the invasion route through Lakes Borgne and Pontchartrain was discounted because the defenders felt the Federals would remember the lesson of the British fiasco there. In this instance that failure was heeded by the Union commanders, though it might not have been. Strategic military precedent on both sides in the Civil War was shattered and remade many times for the rest of the military world to ponder in the future, though that is beside the point here.

Even today there is a tradition in New Orleans—the South still reveres these Civil War traditions whereas the North has almost forgotten they ever existed—that the city fell to the Union forces only because she had willingly stripped herself of man power for service in the North and East. Of course that is only moth-eaten conjecture, but even if it had been true it only proved that the Confederacy committed a grave error in allowing such a strategically important position to remain inadequately defended.

The expeditionary force which was to undertake the capture of New Orleans was under way by the latter part of February 1862, its objective supposed to be a matter of great secrecy. The naval force was commanded by David Farragut, a gentleman of some fifty years' service in the U.S. Navy. The land force was headed by Benjamin F. Butler of Massachusetts, lawyer, Democratic politician who had voted forty times for Jefferson Davis as Presidential nominee at the Charleston convention, politically appointed general, scoundrel of parts, and one of the most contradictory personalities in the entire panorama of the Civil War.

Farragut's fleet contained about fifty vessels of all sizes, from small two-masted bomb ketches and schooners to the heaviest ships of the line such as the *Pensacola, Richmond, Brooklyn, Hartford,* and *Mississippi.* Butler's original land force consisted of about 15,000 men originally, and en route he was to pick up sufficient other units to bring the total to around 18,000. (That cautious soul, George B. McClellan, had estimated that the capture of New Orleans would require at least 50,000 men, though he apparently had no idea what a navy was for.) Strange how this force, except for some superiority on the military side, corresponded almost exactly with that of Cockburn and Pakenham in 1814 against New Orleans—and stranger still to compare the results of the two expeditions!

The Mighty Is Fallen

The Union force was equipped with every possible means of achieving its objective, including a set of orders from General McClellan, who from his swivel chair had as usual planned everything except the way to win the objective. In the long run Butler and Farragut—though mostly Farragut—simply ignored McClellan's long-distance strategy and went ahead as the circumstances dictated.

The Yankee naval fleet was off the mouth of Southwest Pass late in March, sizing up the situation and preparing to overcome the first obstacle—the ever-present and damnable bar!

In the meantime New Orleans had been learning what war was. Slowly but inexorably the Federal blockade made itself felt—at New Orleans especially. The mouths of the river were sealed by the Union navy; trade from upriver was more and more curtailed as the active fighting front moved southward from Cairo. Little by little traffic in the harbor thinned almost to the vanishing point. The majestic packets were doing transport service upriver or gone to more prosperous fields; a long line of them was moored on the west bank of the river opposite the city, out of business for the duration. A few towboats—they were slim but sturdy vessels, like their modern counterparts built with maximum power plants and minimum everything else—had been mounted with guns and licensed as privateers, though that was not an especially profitable game. Here and there was a fisherman's boat, the ferries, and a few craft engaged in Confederate military service; otherwise one of the busiest harbors in the world appeared to be dying, its wharves silent and deserted.

Little by little the general cargo warehouses emptied, not to be refilled. Their doors were shut and the locks began to gather rust and cobwebs. Some rice, sugar, and cotton moved in, mostly that which was due the merchants on account of crop loans. The city itself could use the sugar and rice; the cotton was little good for anything. Already it jammed the warehouses and presses of New Orleans and all the South, while Confederate soldiers in the field went without everything which manufactured cotton could have given them in the way of aid and comfort.

Specie as a circulating medium vanished entirely. In its place there was first Confederate currency, then state, city, and private bank currency, until in the end the city was using streetcar tickets in lieu of small change. In fact, things were so tough that petty crooks went to the trouble of splitting these streetcar tickets, making them worth a dime instead of a nickel. Even saloons issued their private currency. The joke about using cigar coupons for money might have been true had there been such a thing as cigar coupons. As it was George Cable, then a boy of fourteen, has written that the labels from a popular brand of olive oil filled all the requirements of a currency—they were greasy, colored, dirty, smelled bad, and bore a signature. As usual prices began to skyrocket, the poor suffered most, and provision dealers balked at accepting the near-worthless currency until the city council forced them to take it—that was simpler and cheaper than maintaining bread lines.

Actually, there was probably more specie in New Orleans than in any other Southern city, if only for the reason that it had had more to start with, but it went one of two places: to a foreign haven—in not a few cases New York or Boston— or into local hiding places. Certainly little or none of it found its way into the empty coffers of the Davis government.

Crime went on as usual, though somewhat more viciously because the pickings were slimmer. A crook had to work hard to get a living, much less make any real profit.

Physically, the city was going to pieces and everything had been neglected since the beginning of the war. This had been an especially wet spring and the river was running almost levee full. With levee engineering at the stage of development it was then, these bulwarks had to be watched and reenforced continually, but now they were not. Nobody cared. Decay in that climate had always to be guarded against, yet now many of the uncared-for wharves were already so rotten that what incoming vessels there were had to look twice to be sure of their moorings.

Of course the city was fully aware, as soon as Farragut's fleet came in sight off the river mouths, that an attempt was to be made against it; but still it didn't worry. It had supreme confidence that no fleet on earth could pass the forts and the barrier on the river; these failing—though that was impossible!—no army could get through the surrounding swamps. Moreover, the city was repeatedly told these things by authorities who might be supposed to know—in fact, the city was told some very strange things indeed.

In order to allay any fear that *might* be abroad, the New Orleans *Picayune* of April 5, 1862, stated, in part:

Forts Jackson and St. Philip are armed with one hundred seventy heavy guns (sixty-three pounders, rifled by Barkley Britton, and received from England). The navigation of the river is stopped by a dam of about a quarter of a mile [*sic*] from the above forts. No flotilla on earth could force that dam in less than two hours, during which it would be within short and cross range of one hundred and seventy guns of the heaviest caliber, many of which would be served with red-hot shot. . . .

. . . Between New Orleans and the forts there is a constant succession of earthworks. At the Plain of Chalmette, near Janin's property, there are redoubts, armed with rifled cannon, which have been found to be effective at five miles' range. . . .

In Forts St. Philip and Jackson, there are three thousand men, of whom a goodly portion are experienced artillerymen, and gunners who have served in the navy.

At New Orleans itself we have *thirty-two thousand* infantry, and *as many more* [italics all author's] quartered in the immediate neighborhood. In discipline and drill they are far superior to the Yankees. We have two very able and active generals, who possess our entire confidence, General Mansfield Lovell, and Brigadier-General Ruggles. . . .

Actually the two forts had considerably fewer than one hundred and seventy guns, and only a small portion of them were modern. There were batteries at Chalmette, but at no other point between the forts and New Orleans, and Farragut's ships silenced the Chalmette battery in about twenty minutes, without, in fact, stopping in their passage up the river. As stated before, the official record shows 10,318 Confederate troops in the Department of New Orleans (not all of these were present for duty) as of January 1, 1862. As of January 1, 1863, the Department of the Gulf, a much larger area, had a complement of 10,489 men—which seems to tally fairly well, since very few men from the military forces were lost at New Orleans and about the same units remained stationed in the general area after the occupation of the city, though of course they were farther away.

(A substantial case can be made for the theory that the only lesson history teaches is that it teaches nothing; but it isn't because the lessons aren't there. And now as this is written. in 1942 the thought of Singapore, "impregnable Singapore" which fell in ten days, comes irresistibly to mind.)

Farragut's heavier ships had a rough time at the Mississippi bar, consuming a month's time and an extra thousand tons of coal before getting into the river with the entire fleet. The regular pilots from near-by Pilot Town were pressed into service, but after they hung a couple of big vessels securely on the bar, whether intentionally or not, the fleet's navigating officers took matters into their own hands and got the ships through.

The most careful consideration was given the disposal of the mortar vessels which were expected to silence the forts. A party under command of F. H. Gerdes, of the Coast Survey vessel *Sachem*, surveyed the lower river exactly. Mortar ranges were calculated to the yard and the position each mortar vessel was to occupy was marked by a flag on the riverbank. The flags even carried the names of the corresponding vessels, and they had absolute orders not to move a foot once they were fixed in position. These mortar boats were ranged in two single lines on either bank of the river and anchored as close inshore as possible, each line having its fire fixed on the fort on the corresponding bank of the river. Farragut's mobile units were drawn up at a point further down, out of effective range of the forts, and a section of Butler's transports waited still further below the naval vessels. With everything thus in readiness, the bombardment by the mortar boats began on the morning of April 18.

As a pyrotechnic display nothing else like it had ever been seen on the Continent, but the accounts of the resultant damage vary considerably. The mortar shells were thirteen inches in diameter and weighed about two hundred and fifteen pounds. By a direct hit they were capable of doing fearful damage; on the other hand, they floated through the air like black balloons and an agile man, supposing he had room to move in, could almost always get out of their way. Admiral David Porter of the U.S. Navy calculated that 16,800 of these shells were thrown at the Confederate works. A Confederate officer in one of the forts reported 25,000, but still another source says the total was nearer 5,000. Whatever the total was, only a small portion of it registered as direct hits on the forts. Some damage was done, of course, but on the whole it was ridiculously small considering the weight of metal thrown and the length of time the bombardment was maintained—five full days and nights. Unprotected wooden structures within the forts were demolished and set on fire; some guns were put out of action entirely and others temporarily; a considerable number of men were killed and wounded. But the forts were not put out of action by the mortar fire, either during the general bombardment or later. Federal officers who later accepted the surrender of the forts testified that the major defense works and guns were comparatively undamaged and could have held out indefinitely.

On the other hand, the Federal fleet was little damaged by the almost equally heavy fire from the forts. One mortar

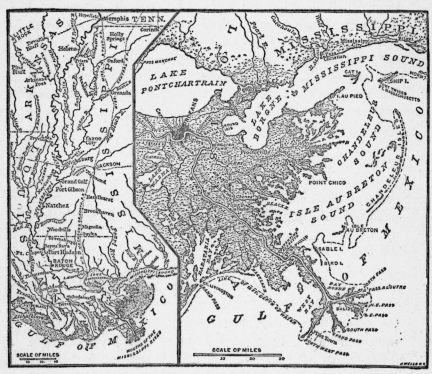

Maps of the Lower Mississippi region, showing railroads, towns, etc., as they were in 1862.

schooner suffered a direct hit and sank within twenty minutes, though without loss of life. Damage to other vessels was slight, as were the casualties.

During the night of April 20 a force under command of Captain Bell successfully managed to cut the cable barring the river. This cable was laid on floats made of dismasted schooners. The schooner hulls in turn were filled with logs and anchored both upstream and down. With the cable in mind the attacking force had brought along a newfangled explosive device, with its inventor to do the actual exploding. But this was a failure, and in the end sledge hammers and cold chisels did the job. The gunboat *Itasca*, Captain Caldwell, was lashed alongside the center hulk, and the cables severed by his crew in a half-hour. The raiding party was discovered and the guns of Fort Jackson opened on them, but the damage to the raiders was nil. With the main cable cut and the hulk's anchor cables slipped, the two vessels were whirled away by the current and went aground before the *Itasca* could regain control. But luckily the hulk was on the inside, and when the lashings were cast off the *Pinola* came up and, after several tries, managed to free the *Itasca*. In the meantime the center stay of the barrier was gone, and under the pressure of the current the hulks at either side of the center pulled their anchors and swung around against those hulks still holding, leaving a great hole in the center of the "impassable" barricade. The Confederates made no effort to repair the breach, though of course any repair job would have been a far more costly matter than the cutting operation.

Opinions varied as to just how much the forts had been damaged, but on the twenty-third it was decided that the flotilla must run the gantlet of the fort guns now or eventually be forced to give up the idea. After five days and nights the mortar ammunition was running low and the mortar boats themselves were in a fair way to kick their timbers apart. Accordingly, it was decided that the active flotilla, as yet hardly touched by the action, should attempt to run the forts early on the morning of the twenty-fourth.

The Federal fleet was in motion about 2:30 A.M. on April 24 and was divided into three sections with the three heaviest vessels, under Farragut himself, in the center. Those mortar vessels, which were propelled by steam, five of them, pulled up to a point just below Fort Jackson, anchored, and laid a blanket of canister and shrapnel over the fort's water batteries. This fire also acted as a screen between the fort and the moving Union fleet near the center of the river.

Followed then one of the most savage ship-and-shore encounters of the entire war. The terribly outnumbered Confederate fleet—with the exception of the heavily armed but clumsy floating battery *Louisiana*, which remained under the lee of Fort St. Philip until the shooting was over—attacked furiously and with no regard for the odds, and seldom have naval men given a better account of themselves. Captain Beverley Kennon, of the Confederate ship *Governor Moore*, depressed his heavy bow gun, in order to reach the attacking Federal *Varuna*, to a point where he was shooting through his own fore deck. The *Governor Moore* was under almost continuous fire for three hours, lost fifty-seven men killed and seventeen wounded, of whom four later died in hospital. In the darkness and heavy smoke Confederate vessels took broadside after broadside at distances as short as twenty yards. When dawn came and the smoke lifted it was seen that the riverbank was lined with Confederate craft, practically all of them too small to have expected to cope successfully with the Union fleet.

The consensus of opinion among Union naval officers was that had the Confederates had a unified plan of defense, under a unified command, the fleet could never have run the river and the entire expedition would have failed—for no one supposed for a moment that Butler was general enough to have succeeded by land alone. The trouble was that each of the forts was under a separate command, and the vessels of the

The Mighty Is Fallen

Confederate fleet operated both independently of the forts and each other. Fifty years earlier New Orleans was saved through the blunders of the attackers; now it was lost by failure on the part of its defenders.

The bulk of Farragut's fleet passed on up the river, smashed the batteries at Chalmette on the morning of the twenty-fifth, and between one and two in the afternoon of the same day anchored in the harbor at New Orleans itself.

Some of Butler's land forces had in the meantime approached the forts from the Gulf side, that is from the rear, arriving in time to receive their surrender. The forts were still in first-class fighting shape and it is extremely doubtful that Butler's forces could have stormed them successfully. But the heart had gone out of the defenders. When Farragut's ships successfully ran the river the usefulness of the forts was at an end. They were cut off in every direction and lengthy resistance would have served no purpose.

The capture of New Orleans was first and last a naval operation and Butler's military force had the city handed to them on a platter. Of course the *Picayune's* thirty-two thousand infantry in the city was sheer myth, and to all intents and purposes General Mansfield Lovell's actual eight or nine thousand men might as well have been somewhere else. As a military leader General Lovell was a fine horseman, but he never fired a shot in defense of New Orleans. The troops he had at New Orleans could have made the difference between victory and defeat for Johnston and Beauregard at Shiloh on the sixth and seventh of April, whereas in New Orleans they weren't worth their ration allowances.

What happened thereafter was not without its humor, but the city was in no mood to enjoy it and in fact never has.

CHAPTER XVI

New Orleans *vs.* General Butler

NEWS that the Union fleet had passed the forts reached New Orleans about the time the event occurred on the twenty-fourth, probably before Farragut's men destroyed the telegraph line which ran down the east bank of the river to Quarantine, just above Bolivar Point. The city alarm bells were rung and numbers of the home guards hurried to their posts—though exactly what happened to them after that is a mystery. Hysteria was the order of the day, and the streets were thronged with crowds who knew neither where they were going nor what they intended to do. By afternoon men, mules, and drays were hauling cotton from presses and warehouses, piling it on the open wharves and setting fire to it. This process went on until far into the night, and the flames could be seen thirty miles away, on the farther shore of Lake Pontchartrain. The fires burned all night and far into the next day. As in the days of pestilence there was a frantic exodus from the city by those who had the means to get away. General Lovell withdrew every last Confederate soldier from the city, not even leaving a company or two to help the police preserve order. The police were, as usual, either powerless or conspicuous by their absence. The only active police force was a group known as the Foreign Legion, made up of foreigners and members of the consular staffs—that is, those men who did business and owned property in New Orleans but publicly and honestly retained their various citizenships. Their prime objective, of course, was the protection of their property and the property of the firms they represented, but undoubtedly their presence and regular patrols prevented worse public disorders than there were.

On the morning of the twenty-fifth there was a good deal of looting at the steamboat wharves, especially in foodstuffs and liquors. On this morning also a number of empty vessels were set afire and cast adrift on the river. A few of these were sunk by the Federal fleet below the city. The point of all this destruction of property—mostly other people's property, incidentally—was to keep it from falling into Yankee hands, though in reality it was nothing more than blind hysteria. There was no good reason to suppose that the Yankees wanted the particular property that was destroyed, and even if they had, that portion which was destroyed, large as it was, was but a fraction of the city's total resources—a very minute fraction.

When the Federal fleet moved up to Canal Street the long levee was empty of shipping but lined with thousands of Orleanians, apparently come to witness their downfall in person. It poured rain that day as the fleet moved in, and in a few places the river trickled over the top of the levee. In the rigging and along the ships' rails bluejackets grinned at the townsfolk who yelled occasional imprecations at them—not a few of these sailormen knew New Orleans of old.

The squadron received no official greeting from the city authorities—New Orleans was determined to be different. Presumably Farragut thought it necessary to make some official gesture of taking over the city, and General Butler was still somewhere down the river. But Farragut did—or permitted—an odd thing. To accept, or demand, the city's surrender, he sent ashore only two men. The senior officer was Captain Theodorus Bailey, who had led the first fleet unit past the forts, and the other Lieutenant G. H. Perkins, and their escort accompanied them only as far as the furious mob on the levee. (Maybe Bailey looked upon New Orleans as the Texas Ranger looked upon the riot the authorities had asked help in putting down. When he arrived alone and the helpless authorities expressed surprise, the Ranger said mildly, "Well, there's only one riot, ain't there?") Followed by the howling mob, which sometimes walked at their heels and sometimes surrounded them entirely, many of the mob with weapons in their hands, the two officers calmly made their way to the City Hall. It was perfectly true that the fleet's broadsides were trained on the city, but even so——

After a little trouble the two officers managed to find Mayor Monroe and politely told him why they were there. Whereupon Monroe informed them that the city was in the hands of General Lovell, and that he, Monroe, had no authority to surrender it. Captain Bailey was agreeable and suggested that Monroe produce General Lovell, and oddly enough the mayor did—oddly, because these negotiations were *not* conducted under a formal truce. The Confederate troops had been withdrawn but Lovell must have been lingering around the corner from City Hall, for he made his appearance in short order. When Bailey asked that Lovell surrender the city, since Monroe would not and the general had evacuated it to all intents and purposes, Lovell replied that he, too, refused to surrender the city, and that while he was momentarily stymied by the presence of the fleet, he intended to fight to the last man on shore. He said he had withdrawn the troops only in order to avoid endangering the lives of the folk in the city. As for himself, he was returning to his troops and—— Exactly what else he didn't say. Thus Lovell, having put himself in a position to deny that he had ever surrendered the city of New Orleans, passed the ball back to Mayor Monroe. The mayor then told Bailey that he would have to discuss the matter with the City Council, and that he would have to let Farragut know what they decided. Having done what they could, Bailey and Perkins returned to the fleet and reported.

Farragut's chief feeling was amusement tinged with irritation. The only Orleanians with authority were apparently trying to turn the situation into a bad joke. But Farragut knew exactly where New Orleans stood strategically and his own job was done. Butler was the man who would have to deal personally with the Orleanians—and with Lovell if that gentleman really intended to make trouble. Farragut knew very well that Lovell could make no trouble for *him*.

Very early on the following morning Mayor Monroe sent word to Farragut that the council would meet at ten o'clock, and that he would let Farragut know what they decided. But Captain Farragut was losing patience fast. He informed Monroe that all non-Union flags would have to be removed by noon, that he demanded the unconditional surrender of the city and the raising of the Union flag over the Mint, the Custom House, and the City Hall.

The council met and heard Mayor Monroe, argued and discussed, and eventually passed some resolutions. Farragut, meanwhile, had gone up the river to Carrollton to see about the shore fortifications there and did not receive the mayor's answer until the following morning, Sunday.

Monroe and the council said, in effect, that the war was a matter between the Union and Confederate governments, and that even the council had no authority to deal with Farragut. *But,* on the other hand, they had no objection to Farragut's taking over the city on whatever terms he chose to name, since the city had no way of resisting him. It was a sort of Chinese victory in which everybody won and nobody lost. It is hard to know whether to admire the mayor and his council or to laugh at the absurdity of the whole thing.

Farragut ordered Captain Morris of the *Pensacola*, which was anchored off Esplanade Avenue, to send a party ashore and hoist the Union flag over the U.S. Mint, located at the foot of Esplanade Avenue. This was done, and the officer in charge of the party warned the curious onlookers ashore that the *Pensacola's* guns were trained on the Mint and would be used if necessary. This was at eight in the morning. About eleven, while the devout of the fleet were about the usual Sunday-morning services, a party of four men, headed by one W. B. Mumford, appeared, hauled down the flag, dragged it through the streets to the delight of the onlookers, and eventually destroyed it. One of the *Pensacola's* maintop howitzers did open fire, but the shooting was bad and no one was hurt.

Farragut was inclined to let the whole matter rest there. But on Monday the *Picayune* not only published a eulogistic account of the affair but gave the names of the men involved in it. Quite possibly the Federals could have discovered the names if they had wanted to, but the news account saved them the trouble. Farragut was really somewhat embarrassed, since he was only holding his finger on the knot of New Orleans until Butler should arrive to tie it.

When Butler arrived in New Orleans and learned what had happened he threatened to hang Mumford, and did. It was a stupid business all around and no credit attaches to anyone involved in it. Still, this was civil war in earnest, and the results of certain acts could have been predicted easily enough had men bothered to reason. Mumford was a civilian and had a wife and three children. When the incident occurred the Union forces had not formally declared their jurisdiction over New Orleans, and even if they had it is doubtful whether Butler could have drummed up any faintly legal justification for such a drastic sentence. On the other hand, Mumford, like the revolutionists so summarily dealt with by O'Reilly a hundred years earlier, knew what the consequences of his act might be. It is hard to sympathize with senseless exhibitionism at this distance.

The Union troops landed in New Orleans on May 1. General Butler (in his travels up and down the river he had been using the transport *Saxon* and one wonders if it was the same *Saxon* that had figured in bringing yellow jack to the city in

1853) took up quarters at the St. Charles Hotel, the city's best, and New Orleans was to learn more of what war could be!

Of New Orleans and its doings a great many books have been written, and there are as many kinds of them as there are writers; but a singular characteristic of many of these volumes is the way they have studiously avoided any account of the four years of the Civil War. Many have pointedly ignored it altogether, others have made a few names and dates suffice. There are several reasons, but one is that, complicated as the city's history has been generally, the Civil War years present an especially intricate mass of contradictions. To write an errorless account of those four years is next to impossible; to compress any fair account into a comparatively few thousand words is extremely difficult. Yet some accounting of those four years belongs in any attempt to portray New Orleans as it was. By the very nature of things much of the city's war story has been shown against the background of General Butler, because the doings of scoundrels usually make the best reading. But as a matter of fact Butler's reign in the city lasted only from May 1 to December 15, 1862, a period of seven and one half months out of a total of four years. This is an attempt to tell a little of all of it.

Butler's Union troops were landed without any untoward incidents, and shortly afterward Farragut and most of the fleet left for the campaign against Baton Rouge.

Whatever else may be said of General Butler, his worst enemies must have admitted that he was probably the most industrious man in New Orleans. The very quantity of his affairs was enormous. Of course all his letters, except the most personal, and orders were written by clerks—that is, he was spared the manual labor of composition—but he was inclined to be wordy, to explain everything down to the last detail, and the amount of time he spent in dictation alone would have floored most men. His capacity as an executive was considerable. Anyone who has spent any time over the records of the Civil War political generals, and knows something of their previous backgrounds, recognizes the fact that Benjamin Butler's intellectual range was far above the average. In addition he was a good lawyer from a state which habitually produced good ones. This is not to say that the general had a complete understanding of every situation in which he was involved; far from it. But he never hesitated to tackle problems which would have left many a military man in despair, problems which the layman, even with the explanations of both sides before him, finds hard to follow. New Orleans itself was a problem different from every other in the South, and a man in Butler's position had to deal with matters of military administration; state, national, and international law; banking and business transactions of all kinds; public health and sanitation; consular relations; the rights of nationals; international trade regulations; his relations with the Washington government; and all the distortions of these things necessarily caused by a state of civil war. Some of Butler's rulings were more unfortunate than unjust, more loyal to the letter of force than to the spirit of compromise. If his *public* attitude is to be believed at all, and there is no reason why it shouldn't be, Butler considered the Civil War a rebellion in fact and that the best way to get it over was to treat it as such. That was also General Sherman's attitude precisely. Once having adopted this point of view—its validity will be debated a hundred years from now—then all else followed.

One of Butler's first acts—on May 4—was to issue an order to the effect that shipments of sugar, cotton, and provisions could be consigned to New Orleans as before. Vessels, that is steamboats, carrying such cargoes would be given passage through the Union lines, providing they carried only their normal crews and the owners or agents of the owners of the cargo, and their safe return guaranteed. On the surface this was a laudable effort to restore a vanished commerce. Butler's detractors claimed that, through his brother "Colonel" Andrew Jackson Butler, he merely wanted to do some cotton and sugar business on his own account. Probably both were true, but one thing is certain—Orleanians themselves couldn't do business unless produce came in, and the only way it could get in was through the medium of such an order. There seems little doubt that General Butler did some business in these commodities, or rather "Colonel" Butler did it for his brother's account. But so did Orleanians, and, aside from the moral issues involved, the Butlers were merely competitors who occupied a preferred position.

There was more to it. Under the terms of the government rental contract, the privately owned troop transports were to be returned to their owners in ballast, it being supposed that there was no cargo of any kind available. But there was no ballast to be had in New Orleans either. General Butler claimed that if he adhered to the contract the ballast would have to be hauled several hundred miles at great expense. This was only partially true, but it was a basis for argument. Furthermore, the rental of the transports was a huge swindle in the first place. For some of these vessels the government was paying a rental as high as fifteen hundred dollars *per day*. For the use of some of these vessels in the New Orleans expedition the government paid in rental three and four times their total value, but the Union record is full of that kind of thing and it was no doing of Butler's.

Thus, Butler reasoned, since the ships had to be returned in ballast, why not ballast them with something useful? Sugar was three cents a pound in New Orleans but New York and Boston were crying for it at six. But even if the government only broke even on the sugar and cotton it would be saved the cost of procuring the ballast from a distance, plus the even more costly delay in returning the ships. There again the idea was perfectly logical—except that somewhere along the line the government's brokerage accounts became badly tangled with the Butler accounts, and the good in the idea was lost in the private wrangle over the profit motive. All this, of course, was a matter between General Butler and the government, and had nothing to do with the welfare of New Orleans. To add a crowning touch to the whole business the shipowners demanded that freight on the cargo be paid for at the regular rates, in spite of the fact that they were already collecting up to fifteen hundred dollars per day for use of the vessels! There was no lack of patriots on either side.

Followed then the notorious Woman Order, which was brought about by the fact that, so the general said, the ladies of New Orleans went out of their way to insult the Federal soldiery at every possible opportunity. The evidence indicates that they did exactly that, though it seems that the boys from Wisconsin and Maine and Connecticut might have borne up under it. But whether Order Number 28 was the way to correct the abuse (?) is something else. At least six million words have been spilled in proving how mistaken it was. The order read:

Head-quarters, Department of the Gulf,
New Orleans, May 15, 1862.

General Order No. 28:

As the officers and soldiers of the United States have been subject to repeated insults from the women (calling themselves ladies) of New Orleans, in return for the most scrupulous non-interference and courtesy on our part, it is ordered that hereafter when any female shall, by word, gesture, or movement, insult or show contempt for any officer or soldier of the United States, she shall be regarded and held liable to be treated as a woman of the town plying her vocation.

Major-General Butler.

By command of
Geo. C. Strong, A.A.G., Chief of Staff.

Order Number 28 gave Butler an international reputation and the reverberations echoed far and wide, even in the holier-than-thou British House of Commons. That the order was wide open to abuse is unquestionable; there is no evidence to show that it was abused in fact. One of the curious things about it was that the women in New Orleans who might have been expected to be most liable, that is the professional prostitutes who were accustomed to being haled into court now and then, were the most insulted by the order. Leaving all the hullabaloo aside, it appears that the order achieved its original purpose; but it also led to complications of a really more serious kind.

According to Butler's original statement of intentions, the city was to go on functioning as before, subject to certain exceptions inherent in a state of war. Admittedly there were plenty of these exceptions but probably that was unavoidable. However, the city government hadn't been notably effective in any department, and it wasn't to have much of a chance now. It was the Woman Order which caused the break—or at least was used as an excuse.

As spokesman for the city Mayor Monroe was in a position where he had to protest the Woman Order or forever lose face in New Orleans. One point of difference led to another, and the upshot of the whole argument was that General Butler summarily ordered the imprisonment at Fort Jackson of Mayor Monroe, the chief of police, and two other members of the city government. Thus the city was deprived of its executive heads and a proclamation of Butler's, signed by the military commandant General G. F. Shepley, did the rest. The kernel of the order was in the paragraphs which read:

The functions of the chief of police will be exercised by Captain Jonas H. French, provost-marshal, to whom all police officers will report immediately. He is entrusted with the duty of organizing the police force of the city, and will continue in office those found to be trustworthy, honest and loyal.

The several recorders [in New Orleans they acted somewhat in the capacity of police judges] are hereby suspended from the discharge of the functions of their offices, and Major Joseph M. Bell, provost judge, will hear and determine all complaints for the violation of the peace and good order of the city, of its ordinances or of the laws of the United States.

[245]

The Port of New Orleans

The laws and general ordinances of the city of New Orleans, excepting such as may be inconsistent with the constitution and laws of the United States, or with any general order issued by the commanding general of this department, or with this order, are hereby continued in force. . . .

Since the mayor and chief of police were out of office, Shepley decided that everyone in their respective departments was likewise out—as they probably would have been had the administration lost at the election which was shortly due but wasn't held. At any rate, the vacant offices, including the entire police force, were promptly filled with Union adherents—or those who claimed to be—and professed Union sympathies were admittedly the chief qualification. It followed that these men were naturally feared, hated, and despised by the great majority of Orleanians. The result was what might have been expected. Without casting doubt on the personal integrity of Bell, French, or Shepley, who after all were acting under orders, it is possible that the abuses of the system were endless. These officers in the very nature of things were forced to act on the word of their subordinates, and New Orleans got its introduction to carpetbagging government in advance of the rest of the South.

In June the drumhead court-martial got around to finding Mumford guilty. He was hung before the Mint where he had pulled down the flag, and that didn't make New Orleans feel any better either.

(The Mumford affair had a strange aftermath. That Jefferson Davis, because of it, proclaimed Butler an outlaw and "common enemy of mankind," and ordered that in the event of his capture he was to be hanged immediately, is well known. There were other things in the order but in the matter of General Butler reference was made primarily to the Mumford case. The keeper of Southern chivalry and honor wasn't even going to give Butler a trial! But there was more. All commissioned officers serving under Butler, if and when captured, were to be treated the same way! The exact words were, *reserved for execution*—which was plain enough. Few orders issued by the head of a supposedly civilized government have been more drastic or all-inclusive. But the curious thing was that the order was not issued until late in December, a week after Butler was actually relieved of the New Orleans command, long after Davis himself knew that Butler was to be relieved—he is alleged to have known of it before Butler did—and seven months after the Mumford execution. Davis represented that the delay occurred because he had tried to get the Federal government to act against its servant Butler—but had been unable to get satisfaction. Be that as it may, the whole affair, from the probably unwarranted hanging of Mumford to the certainly unwarranted blanket death sentence, had an extremely bad odor.)

In war it is usually the poor who suffer first from high prices, stoppage of trade, and kindred ills, and the poor of New Orleans were no exception. And because the city was the largest in the Confederacy its destitute were numbered accordingly. Not all of New Orleans was dependent on the cotton trade for a living, but it was a very large factor, and in the season of 1860–61 the city exported 1,915,000 bales. In 1861–62 that figure dropped to 28,000 bales. Traffic in other commodities showed a corresponding decline, and as usual it was the poor who felt the pinch first.

Since he had taken over the city government, General Butler had likewise acquired the problem of the hungry poor. Because it was a municipal problem, the municipality would ordinarily have been called upon to shoulder the burden. This would have meant taxation of some sort, and of course at least part of the tax would have fallen on the poor as well as the wealthy. But the general had other ideas. When the city was in danger of Federal attack, a defense fund, in the form of a bond issue, had been subscribed. This fund amounted to $1,250,000. So Butler decided that if these firms and persons could afford to support a defense fund they could also support a relief fund. Since taking over the city he had acquired the original subscription list, and now each name on the list was assessed one fourth of the amount originally subscribed to the defense fund. From this group $312,716.25 was taken. They winced—but paid up.

Sometime before the Federal occupation, ninety-five firms and individuals in the New Orleans cotton trade had joined in an effort to prevent the consignment of cotton to the city. They even induced the state government to forcibly prevent shipment by rail and river. This was plainly cutting off their own noses, but the theory was that at the moment selling cotton out of New Orleans was more of an aid to the North than the South. Butler held that these persons and firms, through their efforts in curtailing normal trade, were largely responsible for the destitution in the city. Therefore they, too, should subscribe to the relief fund. They were assessed arbitrary amounts, but none nearly so large as the first group. This "B" list brought in $29,200.

With plenty of money on hand for the purpose, the Federals hired all comers and set them to work cleaning the always-filthy streets. There were two reasons—one simply to provide needed work with pay that would help feed a family, the other a step toward combating the summer danger of yellow fever. Like everybody else, Butler had some very erroneous ideas about the fever, but as a beginning he couldn't go far wrong in cleaning the streets and open sewers. How many friends the general made by this work project is impossible to judge, but certainly they must have been many. Among the illiterate poor, and for that matter the illiterate rich though for slightly varied reasons, political feelings are likely to be pretty close to the stomach.

Of course the sum expended in this way served only as meager temporary relief, but the Union officers made it last until the following December, when a duplicate assessment was made. Orleanians paid grudgingly enough, and yet the resentment over this was less than in some other matters— perhaps because they supposed that if the poor were hungry

View of New Orleans in 1852 from St. Patrick's Church.

long enough they might have taken more forcible means to satisfy their needs.

It was this levy for the poor, among other things, which started the general in his continuous war with the foreign consuls of New Orleans, though the first difference of opinion was with the acting British consul over the British unit of the Foreign Legion. General Butler had publicly acknowledged the useful services of the Foreign Legion, but of course after the Federal occupation there was no further excuse for such an armed force. The various units of it disbanded of their own free will. But when the British unit of some fifty or sixty men voted to dissolve they also voted to send their arms and equipment to General P. G. T. Beauregard in the field forces of the C.S.A. They made no secret of it, and presently the news came to Butler. He sent for Captain Barrows, former commander of the company, and Barrows readily admitted the disposition of the equipment. Thereupon Butler gave Barrows and the company twenty-four hours in which to leave the city. Apparently Barrows didn't argue the point. It was a clear enough case of neutrals giving material aid to the enemies of the United States while under the latter's protection, though it was also a merely friendly gesture on the part of the Britishers, many of whom knew and admired Beauregard, an Orleanian, personally. Barrows evidently realized that their position was legally untenable and merely asked that those members of the company not present and not voting at the meeting be exempted, and to this Butler agreed. The result was that all the company except Barrows and one other left town, and these last two Butler arrested and imprisoned at Fort Jackson.

Coppell, the British consul, then entered the case and defended the company on the ground that they "had meant no harm." Butler was righteously angry. What, he demanded, did Coppell and the others think constituted "harm" if the delivery of military supplies did not? For the fact was that the equipment had actually been shipped. Perhaps the general would have been more lenient with the mere announcement of intention. Coppell then took the matter up with Lord Lyons, British minister at Washington, with the result that the State Department requested—requested, not ordered— Butler to review the case of the two imprisoned men. Of course Butler took the hint, and the men were released from Fort Jackson.

Legally Butler had been quite right, but from the standpoint of Union foreign policy he was quite wrong. It was intricacies of this sort which made New Orleans far harder to deal with than any inland city occupied by Union troops, where the problems were purely domestic. Most of Butler's later troubles with other consuls came about through his inability, or refusal, to recognize when it was wise to overlook certain things which were technically illegal. As has been mentioned before, civil war has few established precedents.

It is true that in New Orleans there were a great many legitimate foreign nationals, but it was the bogus ones who caused most of the trouble. Butler once said that if everyone claiming foreign citizenship in New Orleans were legitimate there would have been no Americans left. An exaggeration, of course, but it made the point. It is said that at this time no less than thirty thousand persons in the city claimed French citizenship, to say nothing of other nationalities. Most of the consuls were Southern in sympathies, and it wasn't too difficult to wangle a certificate of citizenship which could later be conveniently forgotten. And under international law such a certificate naturally allowed exemptions from the harsher aspects of martial law but did not much restrict the holder's actions otherwise.

The rigid enforcement of quarantine regulations also caused friction with the consuls. Butler was determined that there would be no yellow fever this year if he could prevent it. Yellow jack could do more damage to his troops than a Confederate army corps. So quarantine of incoming vessels

was rigidly enforced. Lack of such enforcement, as in the
Great Epidemic of 1853, had played a major role in admitting
contagion to the city. Butler enforced quarantine with a
vengeance, and as a result suspicious vessels were sometimes
held at the station above Fort Jackson for three or four weeks.
Naturally such delays played hob with the delivery of passengers and cargo, but of course it couldn't be helped and
no civilized port in the world questions the need for such
regulations today. But certain of the consuls didn't agree.
They held that Butler was being arbitrary and discriminating
for reasons which had nothing to do with possible contagion
and threatened to hold American bottoms in their own ports
for a retaliatory period—the phrase they used was "quarantine
reciprocity"—regardless of the ships' state of health. The argument was carried so far that a Spanish vessel out of Havana,
the *Cardenas*, ran past the quarantine station without stopping,
landed at a spot some three miles below the regular New Orleans landing, and put ashore her passengers without benefit
of customs or passport inspection. Naturally, Butler was
furious, and matters weren't helped any when the Spanish
consul blandly stated that there couldn't be much wrong
with the disembarking because the Federals hadn't objected
to it! They had not objected, of course, because the unloading
was done at dusk, three miles below the regular landing, and
nobody had known the *Cardenas* was there in the first place.
(Butler contended that the vessel had disembarked certain
notorious Confederate agents who were on their way home
from purchasing expeditions in Havana, but there was no
proof of that.) As a matter of fact, the forts would have fired
on the *Cardenas* except that she was mistaken for the army
supply ship *Connecticut*, which had been expected. When the
Connecticut did appear a few hours later and went on without
stopping, the fort guns promptly opened fire on her. It was
this sort of thing which kept the general under a continuous
fire of censure, and when he was in the wrong his enemies
took every advantage of their opportunities.

The fact remains that there were but few known cases
of yellow fever in the city during that summer season of 1862.

The general had a fertile imagination and was always willing
to put it to practical use. For the sake of the gaiety of nations
it is a pity that he didn't have the opportunity of carrying
out his investigations in the field of international slavery
laws. Since he had the problem of a great number of slave-
holding foreign nationals, or at least those claiming foreign
citizenship, on his hands, it occurred to him to investigate
the French and British anti-slavery laws. The discoveries
were interesting indeed. Englishmen were, under English
law, subject to heavy penalties for each slave owned; and
French ownership of slaves had been illegal since 1848,
though a period of grace after that date, under certain circumstances, was allowed under French law. Even this period,
however, had long since expired. Thus the possibilities for
causing international red faces were boundless, but unfortunately Butler was recalled before he had a chance to go
into that.

In May, after the Federal occupation but before the sup-
pression of the city government by Butler, the Municipal
Council had done something which from that time raised
this issue of international law and international courtesies.
At the time of the land and water battles for the lower forts
a French naval vessel had been present in the Mississippi. In
fact, its officers had taken it on themselves to advise Farragut
against attempting to run the forts at all. After Farragut's
success in that operation the Frenchman moved on to New
Orleans, and since there actually were a large number of
French nationals in the city the Frenchman had every right
to be there. But after the occupation of the city the council
was informed (though incorrectly) that a French *fleet* would
shortly visit the city. Thereupon the council passed a resolution welcoming this fleet and giving it the freedom of the
city—a city which, rightly or wrongly, they continued to
govern only in part and that part by sufferance. In other

words, the council, which never professed to be anything but Confederate in thought and feeling, invited a foreign fleet to make itself at home in a port which was actually held by a third power. The legitimate presence of a French war vessel was one thing, but the *invitation* of a fleet was something else entirely. It so happened that the fleet didn't materialize, but that didn't alter the fact of the invitation and Butler's opinion of the council's action can be imagined. There were other clashes, all more or less unimportant, between the general and certain British and Spanish men of war. Of course Britain and Spain were both neutral in fact, but their officers were almost to a man Southern in sympathies, and their too-ready expression of their private feelings didn't help the tranquillity of the general situation.

The New Orleans business dealings of the general and his brother have been rehashed again and again, mostly without any evidence to back up the charges and innuendoes. There is no doubt whatever that A. J. Butler made a great deal of money in New Orleans in a very short time, some say as much as two million dollars. General Butler admitted that his brother had made *some* money. It also appears that he made a great deal of money for the general, some say as much as three million dollars. One account has it that A. J. Butler was in silent partnership with the New Orleans gambling houses, that without his permission they couldn't operate. It could be—but there isn't a shred of evidence to that effect. There is also a great deal to the effect that he sold contraband to the Confederates and that it was passed through the lines only by the consent of the general himself. That could be also and probably was, though again there is no proof of wrongdoing. For this business of buying and selling from and to the Confederacy was a very long way from being a crime *per se*. Everyone who knows anything about the Civil War knows that. Under certain circumstances "trade with the enemy" was not only permitted but encouraged, and the encouragement came straight out of the White House. For reasons of public policy that was not made common knowledge in either the North or the South, but every army commander on both sides was well aware of it. For other reasons of policy neither government insisted that its field commanders allow this trade to go on without restriction. Some of the army men themselves were dead against it—Grant was, for instance—and acted accordingly. Yet it was no secret in some circles that the very occupation of certain Southern ports, New Orleans for one, was done in order to expedite this trade. That wasn't what the folks back home were told, but it was nonetheless true. So regardless of how much business A. J. Butler did with the enemy, none of it was necessarily illegal.

All this is by no means an attempt to whitewash the record of General Butler, but rather is offered in the spirit of inquiry —an attempt to discover just why Butler's enemies so hated him. That the general and his brother both made considerable fortunes in New Orleans is granted. That this was a distinct breach of a certain kind of trust is freely admitted, and Butler warrants all due criticism on that score. Yet all this doesn't account for the fact that he was "Beast" Butler to New Orleans and probably the most hated man in the city's history. His military rule of the city was sometimes harsh to an extreme, but so was Andrew Jackson's. On the other hand, Butler was never indicted for any alleged crime. He was admittedly neither a libertine nor a drunkard and no one ever suggested that he took personal pecuniary advantage of a single individual Orleanian. Admittedly he left the city in better physical shape than he found it. On his own admission Sherman in Georgia did a hundred million dollars' worth of damage and his name was anathema in Georgia for two generations if not longer, and yet Sherman was never hated with the same kind of hate awarded Butler.

It is worth hazarding a guess that the whole business was rooted in the unfortunate Woman Order. It touched some elemental, sensitive spot in men that was only vaguely recognized. Men were angered for a reason they themselves couldn't understand, and Butler, whom most of them wouldn't have recognized in church, was made the visible object of their anger. (Confederate officers often admitted that the only thing they ever knew about Butler was the Woman Order.) He was, if it is any comfort to Orleanians, almost as much hated in the North as in the South. General Nathan Forrest, who in the North was considered responsible for the "massacre" of white and Negro Union troops at Fort Pillow, was never accorded a fraction of the animosity the North gave General Benjamin Franklin Butler of Lowell, Massachusetts.

Steps toward Butler's recall probably were first taken early in the autumn of 1862, though when the general inquired about rumors to that effect General Halleck wrote, on September 14, that there was nothing in the rumors. Stanton in general had approved of what Butler had done, and at the moment there was no friction between Butler and the War Department. The order relieving Butler was dated at Washington on November 9 and was eventually delivered to Butler by his successor, General Nathan P. Banks.

War Department,
Adjutant-General's Office,
Washington, November 9, 1862.
General Order No. 184.

By direction of the president of the United States, Major-General Banks is assigned to the command of the Department of the Gulf, including the state of Texas.

By order of the Secretary of War.
E. D. Thomas, Assistant Adjutant-General.
H. W. Halleck, General-in-Chief.

There it was, and it could hardly have been more to the point.

Of course according to the order it originated with President Lincoln, but then reference to him in the body of the order could have been more or less a matter of form. But it is also obvious that no reason was given for Butler's recall. Butler turned his command over to Banks about the middle of December and left for the East the latter part of the same month. It is a curious thing that Butler never was told the exact reasons for his recall—or if he was the reasons were never made public. When he asked Lincoln, the President told him that the step had been recommended by both Seward and Stanton. When he asked Stanton, he was put off without a definite answer. The secretary was cordial personally but simply wasn't talking. Butler seems to have taken the situation in good humor. He hadn't explained some of the things he did in New Orleans either.

It appeared later that he was recalled because of pressure brought by the French government, which rightly or wrongly seemed to have a tender regard for New Orleans. Otherwise Seward apparently would not have had a hand in it. That Washington did not lack confidence in Butler is sufficiently demonstrated by the fact that he was later assigned to another command of importance. It is perfectly true that he was not a conspicuous success in his later assignment, anything but that, in fact, and was removed at Grant's express demand, but that had nothing to do with New Orleans.

Every American historian of note, and some not so noteworthy, has called Butler some sort of scoundrel, and in view of that, and the fact that he seems to be regarded as so much greater a scoundrel than any of his colleagues on both sides of the Civil War, it is surprising how much evidence there is on his side of the argument.

CHAPTER XVII

The War and After

THE CITY had little fault to find with Butler's successors, no fault, that is, except their very presence. While Butler's memory is still despised in New Orleans his successors, Generals Banks, Baird, E. R. S. Canby, Hurlbut, and even the redoubtable Phil Sheridan himself, as commander of the Department of the Gulf, are scarcely remembered by anyone save the history professors.

For New Orleans the Civil War neither began at Fort Sumter nor ended definitely at Appomattox. The city saw no actual hostilities after April 1862, but it was not finally rid of Federal troops until long after the last Confederate units had surrendered and come home. In the meantime much of its old life went on, subject to certain limitations, of course, very much as before. Its political life, naturally, functioned on a very different plane.

After Butler took over the municipal government in 1862 there were no general elections in the city until after the war, although there were elections. Under Butler two members of Congress were elected in 1862, and that they were solid Union men goes without saying. It has been claimed that no restrictions were placed on voters, *except* that they take the oath of allegiance to the United States (Negroes were *not* allowed to vote in Louisiana or anywhere else in even the carpetbag South until some time after the Emancipation Proclamation), but for a great many people that restriction was quite enough. No other regulations mattered. At times much has been made of the fact that the vote for these Union Congressmen was, even in 1862, greater than the original New Orleans vote in favor of Secession, but no reasonable person supposes that the figures had any important meaning. For years elections in New Orleans had been farces more or less, and for ten years after the Civil War they continued to be, though for entirely different reasons.

In other cities and states in the South elections before the Civil War were conducted on as high a plane as any which prevailed in the United States, then or now, and so the effect of the carpetbag corruption after the war can be pretty accurately measured. After the war Louisiana and New Orleans also took a terrible beating at the hands of carpetbaggers, all-around scoundrels, and illiterate Negroes, but here, because the city had such a record for previous corruption, the real effect is harder to judge. The city's outcries against the Northern corruptionists would have been received a bit more sympathetically if her hands had been cleaner to start with. Because of that, too, it is harder to say just who, after the war, the corruptionists in New Orleans were. If that seems unfair it must be pointed out that in New Orleans after the war almost the only variation in the old forms of politics was the addition of the Negro as a factor.

During the war the respectable social life was of course greatly curtailed in both quantity and quality, for New Orleans did furnish a very large number of men to the Confederate field forces, as well as government officials and general officers of the caliber of Judah P. Benjamin and General P. G. T. Beauregard, the former probably the shrewdest advisor Jefferson Davis had. It is a curious fact, however, that of all the Southern states, except those known definitely as "border" states, Louisiana is credited officially with furnishing more troops (exclusive of Negroes) to the Union cause than any other—which illustrates the danger of being too dogmatic about sentiment in this region.

As for the unrespectable social life of the underworld and half-world, it flourished as never before. The brothels, saloons, and gambling houses liked the troops' money just as well as they did that of the steamboaters and deep-water sailors. Which is not to say that the Union troops were an army of libertines and drunkards. But they were barred from the ordinary social life of the city and it was only natural that they should spend their money and time where they were most welcome, even if the welcome was purely commercial. In 1864, however, General Stephen A. Hurlbut, who succeeded Banks, made a gesture toward closing the gambling houses, chiefly on the grounds that they were crooked and didn't give the soldiery an even break for their money.

As for the "trade with the enemy" (it was that from the point of view of both sides), that went on just the same after the departure of General Butler and his shadowy brother. As a matter of fact, George Denison, who acted as agent and collector for the U.S. Treasury in New Orleans during the Butler regime and afterward, believed that contraband trade in that area was better regulated under Butler than his successor Banks—and Denison was no special friend of Butler's. Maybe Butler managed the trade better than Banks because so much of it passed through his own hands, whereas under Banks it was every man for himself. (Banks had been in New Orleans hardly more than a month when Lincoln stated that everyone would be better off if Butler were sent back to take over the city—providing that Butler would have been in command of the city alone and not the entire Department of the Gulf.)

Personalities aside, it must be admitted that the trade in cotton, sugar, and other commodities, whether contraband or not, and regardless of exactly who made the big war profits, redounded to the benefit of New Orleans at large. The speculators, even supposing they were all Northern interlopers, which they were not, might loll at their ease over cool drinks on the long veranda of the St. Charles Hotel, but the benefits worked down through the various economic strata as always. The speculators reaped the huge profits, but the little men—draymen, clerks, checkers, samplers, warehousemen, the folk who owned warehouses and dock facilities—were back where they had been in the normal course of peacetime trade. They were not better off but they made a living—and a living was all the little men had ever made. Admittedly the speculators made a great deal of money, but it was a false profit, that is a profit which the South itself would not and could not have made in normal times. And the "spurious" profit was made by Southerners as well as Northern interlopers. In fact, Orleanians had a considerable edge on the trade to begin with.

In the East toward the end of 1864 cotton went to the astronomical price of $1.90 per pound, Federal currency. But at the same time cotton in the Confederacy was selling for sixty cents per pound on the basis of the same currency valuation (Federal as well as Confederate currency was badly depressed), or about twenty cents gold. The difference in Northern and Southern price, the speculators' profit, was obviously enormous. But certainly the planter had never before received such a price either. The point is usually made that these prices did the South no good because it had no cotton to sell, but that simply was not true as a whole except in a relative sense.

The South boasted frequently of how its slaves had loyally kept on producing at home during the four years of the war, even after the Emancipation Proclamation. A great deal of that talk can be ascribed to sheer sentimentality, but the figures back it up to a certain extent. During the years 1862–64 inclusive 541,000 bales of cotton were sent to Europe, while the amount consumed in the North was even larger. This is admittedly a far cry from the quantities shipped from New Orleans alone before the war, but, taking into consideration the enormous price advance, the South was by no means deprived of its cotton income to the extent generally supposed. All this has been pointed out at some length because of one thing: Wilmington, North Carolina, and New Orleans were the two Southern ports which profited from that portion of the cotton and sugar trade carried on by sea.

It is true that the South—and New Orleans—did not profit *lastingly* from this trade as it would have under normal conditions, but that is a truism which applied to the North as well, indeed to almost any country ever the victim of inflationary prices. Too, the South converted not a little of its profits to war purposes of one kind and another, because this was almost all the outside income it had.

The poor devils who went home to Richmond, Atlanta, Vicksburg, and Charleston after the close of the war in 1865 found their cities in ruins, their very homes in thousands of instances no longer existing. But the war-weary thousands who returned to New Orleans found the Crescent City doing business at the same old stand, not a bullet mark to be seen except those which were the result of old election and personal feuds, physically unaltered otherwise—except that it had actually grown a little!

Politically it was changed. Ah yes! The city still housed Federal troops and would for some time to come—and yet it appears that the returned Confederate veterans did not greatly resent the Union troops. Certainly they did not relish the presence of the blue uniforms, but, on the other hand, they must have understood that the country youths from Maine and Iowa, most of them, were just as anxious to go home as New Orleans was to be rid of them. No, the wrath of the returning veterans was not directed against the men in uniform, who otherwise were very much like themselves and in time would also go home, but against the carpetbaggers, usurpers, and illiterate blacks, aided and abetted by the Federal government, who were apparently dug in for life.

The Port of New Orleans

Four full years of civil war and bloodshed had been required to get the city into such a mess; it would require at least that long and some bloodshed, though hardly as much, to clean it up.

The worst affair of blood did not occur until 1866. The fight between Congress and President Andrew Johnson was in full swing, with the postwar South and its future the chief bone of contention. Feeling ran high everywhere in the South, and nowhere higher than in New Orleans.

By July 1866 both state and city government had—subject of course to the rules of occupation—come nearly under the control of the natives. The word is not the best, but its meaning is plain enough. But there was still a very strong carpet-bag-Negro party, more or less determined to control the state regardless of legality—and this group was certain that it had the backing of a large lump of Congressional sentiment, which it probably did. Through this party the Constitutional Convention of 1864 was to be reconvened with the specific intention of admitting the Negroes to full suffrage. Some days before the convention met a mass meeting, attended largely by Negroes but addressed by white speakers, was held in Lafayette Square. Threats of violence were there made openly and the city was naturally on edge, the presence of Federal troops probably tending to preserve a semblance of tranquillity.

On the day the convention met at Mechanics' Hall a procession of Negroes formed for the purpose of marching to the hall. There was some shooting during the procession, but the marchers managed to reach the hall intact. In the meantime both police and Federal troops were called out. The police arrived in a hurry but the troops did not—through a misunderstanding (?) they did not arrive until after the shooting was over. The police opened fire through the windows of the hall and in a short time the occupants hung out a white flag. Then the police entered the building with drawn weapons, and exactly what happened then is somewhat obscure. (This account is necessarily brief. The record of the Congressional investigation which followed fills a volume of almost six hundred pages.) At any rate, the shooting began, and when it was over the casualties were: on the white-Negro side, forty killed and one hundred and thirty-six wounded; on the side of the police, one killed and ten wounded. That it was a massacre seems obvious, even without the emphatic testimony to that effect by General Phil Sheridan, who at the time commanded the Department of the Gulf with headquarters at New Orleans.

Regardless of the provocation, such an occurrence, horrible enough at any time, was especially unfortunate at the moment and probably postponed the stabilization of the state and city governments for at least six years, possibly longer. The best thing that can be said of it is that nothing of the sort was to occur again.

In May 1865 all trade restrictions caused by the Civil War were removed, and to all intents and purposes New Orleans was a going concern. But it was a going concern with a difference, and she was never again to be the supreme outlet for the great valley.

Let none suppose that the Civil War as such was the sole cause of this future decline. The conflict speeded up the process but it had been under way long before 1861. New Orleans had simply refused to take notice. At the end of 1865 there were only two railroads running into New Orleans, and only one of these, the New Orleans, Jackson & Great Northern, connected with the upper valley. But in the great factory and granary of the Middle West railroad building had actually increased during the war years. The transcontinental lines were advancing across Iowa, Nebraska, Minnesota, and Kansas. Furthermore, shippers in the vast area west of the Alleghenies had gotten into the habit of using the railroads and the Great Lakes when the South was cut off. The habit had been growing before the war and the conflict simply added impetus to it. True, the rail rates to seaboard were far higher than the old water rates to New Orleans, but speed had become a factor as never before. And ocean freight rates to Europe were cheaper from the East than they ever had been from New Orleans, thus making up in part for the higher rates from farm and factory to seaboard. Then, too, the character of freight shipments, the great majority of tonnage that is, had changed. The railroads were better fitted physically to haul shipments of coal and lumber and grain. The splendid packets had been ideal for clean baled cotton, barreled sugar, and package freight in small lots, but how could the old *Sultana, Southern Belle,* or *Duke of Orleans* handle three thousand tons of coal or five thousand tons of shelled corn?

Somewhat less to the point, but a factor nonetheless, was the depressing truth that there was no longer a fraction of the steam packets that would have been required to carry the vast produce of the great valley. Most of the packets constructed during the Civil War were built in the North primarily for war purposes, gunboats and such, whereas the packet losses for the same period were great—just how great no one knows. Some were shelled and sunk; many were burned; many simply wore out from hard driving and lack of necessary repairs and upkeep—this last was especially true in the South, where all sorts of mechanical equipment simply could not be had at any price.

Physically, the steam packet was a curious mechanism—perhaps it is not too far-fetched to compare it with a boy's paper-and-stick kite. Given care and skill in handling, there is no reason why either should not perform its function indefinitely; abused and in unskilled hands, they will go to pieces with amazing rapidity. Many a packet, for example, made only a few trips before it was burned, smashed, blown up, or otherwise rendered useless. On the other hand, there is the case of the old *Gouldsboro.* She saw service originally as a Civil War gunboat, and in 1940—after a good many transformations, of course—she was actively in service as a car ferry for the Texas & Pacific Railway at Terpsichore Street on the New Orleans river front! Surely there are few ocean vessels and pieces of land transport which can better that record. This is an extreme example, of course, but many packets had enviable records. Almost any packet which survived until the 1920s and 1930s—and there were more of them than is popularly supposed—was certain to be venerable with age if not actually ancient.

There are still packets on the rivers, but if they are the genuine article they are necessarily survivors of another generation. There are many boats on the rivers of the Mississippi Valley that to the uninitiated resemble the steamboat of a Currier & Ives print—in fact, these boats, with New Orleans as their home port, are still an important part of Louisiana's intrastate transportation system. But these craft, powered by gas and Diesel motors and in many cases using screw propellers, and the powerful modern river towboats of the barge lines, only superficially resemble the once-resplendent steam monarchs. The kind of skill and craftsmanship which went into the river packet vanished along with the skill which built the horse-drawn vehicles that bore such exotic but now unrecognizable names as jagger, Eureka jump seat, loop calash, and gazelle.

Thus the reasons for New Orleans' commercial decline become evident. Yet it was decline, not total eclipse by any means. For one thing, there was always cotton. Both New Orleans and the South realized that cotton was no longer king, if indeed it ever really had been, but it was still a very lively citizen for all that.

In time the towboats and huge river barges would help bring back some of New Orleans' lost river trade, but the time was not yet. For decades after the war the one- or two-man flatboat would be a feature of the Mississippi, but these were stubborn survivors of another age and had no real bearing on the newer movements of freight. Of course the steam

packet did not, by any means, die with the war. If it had
New Orleans would almost certainly have died with it; it
was merely that its eventually fatal disease was contracted
during the war. As railroad mileage increased—and it increased
steadily even in Louisiana—the packet trade fell off. One by
one the old packets simply disappeared. New packets were
built, of course, up to the 1890s, and the tendency was to
build them even larger and more powerful than before, yet
the number of new ones put in service did not begin to keep
pace with those abandoned. The shift was so gradual as to be
almost imperceptible, but it was there.

Towboats and barges were in general use on the Ohio long
before they were at all common in the New Orleans trade.
In 1875 there were but four towboats and thirty barges in
service between St. Louis and New Orleans, and in 1887
there were sixteen towboats and one hundred and twenty
barges. This was a respectable increase, of course, but still
one hundred and twenty barges could not handle more than
a tiny fraction of the great commodity movement in the
West, and it was the prosperity of New Orleans which suffered most—for of course the freight was moved in spite of
New Orleans.

There is a theory, which unfortunately this writer is not
competent to discuss in detail, that for geographical and commercial reasons the great railroad systems of North America
should never have been built as they were from east to west;
that by all rules of logic the great trunk lines of the Mississippi
Valley, and including that portion of Canada which is contiguous, should run from north to south. It seems logical.
And if that had been planned, or if it had happened acciden-
tally, New Orleans would undoubtedly be a world metropolis,
perhaps even *the* world metropolis. But of course human
foresight of that caliber would have prevented all the major
human catastrophes up to and including World Wars I and
II, and this is too much to expect by far. Nevertheless, if
this transportation theory is valid, and it seems that it ought

to be, then the Civil War may be responsible for this failure also. For New Orleans *was* the metropolis of the South (still is, for that matter) and as such was a natural magnet, and if events had been allowed to take their course without interference it is possible, just possible, that the country would have followed this logic by accident.

Incidentally, if it seems that an undue amount of space has been given here to the Civil War, it is only because that conflict had such a far-reaching effect on all the South. It was Mark Twain who told the story which makes the point as well as any. A young New Yorker was visiting in New Orleans and remarked that the moonlight down there was marvelous. An old Negro woman sighed and said, "Ah, bless yo' heart, honey, you ought to seen dat moon befo' de waw!"

So much, in brief, for the city's relations with the interior. Beyond that, with almost any other natural port in America, there would have been only the ordinary business of the sea. Not so with New Orleans; she had problems in both directions.

It was the ever-present but now more than ever acute problem of the mud-and-gravel bar across the multiple mouths of the Mississippi which added to the postwar confusion.

Until the second decade of the nineteenth century Pass à la Outre was the entrance to the Mississippi most regularly used by ocean vessels. At its Gulf exit was a tiny settlement on stilts, which had been there since Bienville's time. It was known as Balise or Balize, and since the time of the French and Spanish had been both fortification and pilot station, and the name Balize was synonymous with the whole New Orleans area. Because the settlement was the first human thing seen in the Delta by inbound seafarers, vessels for New Orleans were commonly known as "bound for Balize." But in time Pass à la Outre shoaled, and at the same time Southwest Pass deepened. Balize was eventually abandoned and the present village of Pilot Town took its place, and until the late 1870s Southwest Pass was the river's main outlet.

The Port of New Orleans

But, outside, there was always the huge and unpredictable bar. Always bad, it became worse even as ships became larger, and of course during the war no one thought of doing anything about it. During the 1850s certain surveys had been made with a view toward solving the problem, but the war ended that too. During these same 1850s the side-wheel steam tug had been the only power that could cope with the bar, and of course it was by no means a solution. Sometimes the tugs were able to haul a vessel with a sixteen-foot draft over a spot on the bar where there was only fourteen feet of natural clearance, but they also frequently failed. More than a few times vessels were badly or entirely wrecked on the bar, and on one memorable occasion a vessel stayed aground there for three months. Often two or three ebb tides were needed to move a tight ship across, and frequently an extra towboat or two had to be called in to finish the job.

In the earlier days of the steam towboat service competition was keen and it was the usual custom for a tow captain to contract to haul a vessel over the bar for a flat fee, in which case it was up to him to do the job one way or another. But after the war the towboatmen became aware that they'd had a good thing all the time but hadn't realized it. Accordingly, the Towboat Association was formed, and thereafter the passage of the bar became not only a navigation but a human problem. Towage rates went up to one hundred dollars per hour—and if one tug couldn't do the job the price was still one hundred dollars per hour for each tug required. Now of course there was no law which prevented a master from trying the bar on his own, but the association had an answer to that also. If the rash skipper tried and failed, only luck and Providence could get him off. No association tug would take the job—and there were, one may be sure, no non-association tugs. When an untowed vessel went aground and was refused towage, the grounded vessel frequently blocked the channel for everybody else. There were occasions when as many as thirty vessels of all sizes were held up for weeks.

Of course from any reasonable point of view the situation was intolerable. The bar itself kept the newest, fastest, and most economical ships from the New Orleans trade, and those which could and would work the trade were subjected to systematic brigandage. One wonders why New Orleans commercial interests did not rise in their wrath—they weren't doing too well anyway—and *do* something. They didn't. As usual a few angry and vocal men tried to do something about the situation, but they had little success. Most Orleanians merely shrugged and muttered something about "politics." In New Orleans politics, meaning some mysterious, sinister, and uncontrollable force, is always a convenient scapegoat for anything seriously wrong with public affairs.

For these various reasons freight rates were outrageously high and the city's commerce suffered accordingly.

Yet in spite of New Orleans' general lethargy help was on the way, both from Congress and Captain James Eads of St. Louis. Under orders from Congress the army engineers had taken a hand in the situation and knew, so they thought, what the solution was. Of course these engineers were familiar with the jetty systems in use at the mouths of certain European rivers, and they were absolutely convinced, for reasons too complicated to go into here—though as it happens they were all wrong—that jetties were impossible in the Delta. Instead they proposed to dig a canal from a point on the river near Fort St. Philip to Breton Sound, which a glance at the map will show as a part of the Gulf. The distance to salt water here was about four miles. At the river end of this canal they proposed to build a gigantic granite lock, five hundred feet long and large enough to accommodate the largest expected ships, to compensate for the natural rise and fall of the Mississippi as against the fixed level of the Gulf waters. The cost of this entire project was estimated at $8,000,000 and it was highly favored by most Orleanians, few of whom had any real conception of the engineering problems involved.

The argument over the control of the river mouths was of course widespread, for a great many people other than Orleanians were legitimately interested in the sea gate of the Mississippi.

To the eternal good fortune of the valley it was at this stage that Eads took a hand. Captain James Buchanan Eads was one of those Yankee accidents of genius which only happen now and then. He was without formal education in any branch of engineering, even mathematics, but as a very young man in St. Louis had become interested in the river. That led to a steamboat salvage business which, because of his natural genius, was so successful that he was able to retire in his thirties, independently wealthy. At the beginning of the Civil War he came out of retirement and performed a near-miracle in the construction of river gunboats for the Federal government—an achievement especially noteworthy in comparison with the fumbling and corruption in naval construction and management in general. The war over, he tackled the problem of a bridge over the river at St. Louis. When Congress authorized the bridge there they didn't know whether they really wanted it or not, and so made the conditions so tough that every engineer in the country, and some noted experts from abroad, insisted that its construction was impossible. Every engineer, that is, except rule-of-thumb Eads. He not only could but did build the "impossible" bridge, and it's still as good as ever for he even saw to it that repairs and replacement of parts were fully accounted for. Furthermore, Eads, in his salvage work, had perfected a diving bell which he used personally on steamboat wrecks, and there was a good deal of truth in the statement that he had personally walked over every yard of the Mississippi bed from Vicksburg to St. Louis. To Eads the river was not only a means of livelihood but a fascinating hobby, and it is simple

Philip Gendreau, New York

The Laffite blacksmith shop. Said to have been the headquarters of the famous pirates Jean Laffite and his brother Pierre. Now a café in the *vieux carré* of New Orleans.

truth to say that he knew more about the Mississippi than any other man alive, for he proved it time and again.

So Eads entered the argument by coming out in favor of jetties in the Passes and flatly against the canal and lock. He tried to show that, even if the granite lock could be successfully built on the Delta alluvium, a sudden rampage of the river might easily obliterate both canal and lock. His faith in the jetties was based on a solid understanding of the enormous power inherent in the river itself—and it was a power, Eads knew, which could create as well as destroy.

There is not space here for any lengthy description of the Mississippi jetty system, but to all practical purposes the dictionary definition is close enough. Jetty: a projection into a river for narrowing it and raising the water, or for causing it to carry out gathering sediment and thus to deepen its channel. To that it is only necessary to add that in the case of the Mississippi the process was extended to include the bar which was the main cause of the sediment gathering in the channel.

To the lay landsman it may appear that much ado has been made over the problem of the bar. But the Mississippi bar was no submerged streak of mud in the creek back of the barn. Consider these things: The sediment discharged annually by the Mississippi, mostly through the Passes, is (about) 406,500,000 *tons*. This is roughly equivalent to 46,000 tons per hour—23,000 two-ton truckloads of earth, sand, and gravel being dumped into the river below New Orleans every hour, night and day, year after year. No small part of that load, especially the layer nearest the river bed, clung to and became part of the bar. Is it any wonder that it was a thing too big for many men to comprehend? It is worth adding that the average discharge of the Mississippi system is about 175,000 cubic feet of water *per second;* the total annual cubic feet of discharge is a figure a great number of people can't even decipher. Thus the problem was to cause this giant flow of water to act usefully against the equally giant deposit of sediment.

The opposition to Eads's ideas was widespread and bitter. Ordinary citizens opposed him because of ignorance—and to call the opposition of the college engineers anything else is mere courtesy. Eads had achieved the "impossible" before, but that was apparently written off as sheer luck. Some of the opposition to Eads's jetty plans would have been comical had they not been so in earnest. One group in New Orleans (could they have been inspired by the Towboat Association?) pleaded with Congress not to heed the mad Eads, on the ground that the jetties would cause the Mississippi to back up and literally annihilate the helpless city! The old-timers on the lower river knew that Eads was wrong. Why? Well, they just *knew!* This writer has the greatest respect for the real and peculiar knowledge of the Mississippi that veteran rivermen have; and yet in the Delta I have been solemnly assured that the Mississippi, as any well-behaved river should, becomes wider as it nears the Passes—wider in the sense that its width gradually increases from source to mouth. It is a peculiarity of the Mississippi that this is untrue, and these rivermen should see her at Cairo!

But Eads went his critics a great deal better. He offered to build the jetty system and create a twenty-eight-foot channel through Southwest Pass into the Gulf *at his own risk.* The price for the impossible would be ten million dollars. He asked that one million be paid him when twenty feet was an accomplished fact, then one million for each two feet up to twenty-eight. The remaining five million was to be paid at the rate of a half million per year, during which period he would continue to guarantee the full channel depth. Probably the United States never received a fairer proposition. The government engineers' own estimate of the mere cost of building the jetties, which they insisted would not work anyway, was $16,000,000.

And yet what followed was a classic example of how the American Congress can do things which are masterpieces of the illogical. A House committee reported Eads's original proposition favorably, but the collective body of farmers rejected that and instead appropriated $8,000,000 for the St. Philip Canal. Then the Senate would have none of that but instead appointed a committee to investigate—not content, of course, with the acres of reports already at hand. When the final report came in it stated that the canal would cost $11,500,000, jetties at Southwest Pass $16,000,000, and at South Pass $8,000,000. Of these it recommended that the South Pass jetties be built because they were cheaper!

Regardless of the money involved—for he was literally not interested in making any profit from the job—Eads insisted that the South Pass theory was all wrong, on the ground that it was shallower and narrower and carried a much smaller volume of water than Southwest Pass, that the bar at South Pass was just as tremendous as at Southwest Pass whereas the volume of flow directed against it would necessarily be much smaller. Eads even offered to reduce the price of the Southwest Pass jetties to $8,000,000 if in addition he be allowed $150,000 per year maintenance after they were proved successful. This time the House was thoroughly convinced but the Senate wasn't—it had been the Senate's committee. Instead the Senate offered Eads $5,250,000 for building the South Pass system and $100,000 per year maintenance for twenty years—in other words, a total of three quarters of a million dollars less than its own committee had estimated the original cost of construction. In addition the government would withhold one million dollars of the original cost (to bear 5 per cent interest, however) as a guarantee of performance, half to be paid at the end of ten years, and the balance at the end of twenty—providing everything was satisfactory. And this was the Congress which only a few years before had lavished money and land grants on the railroads in a spending spree not equaled before or since except by the New Deal!

Captain Eads was by no means certain that he could break even on the job; no man could have been sure. There were too many unknown factors, not the least of which was yellow fever—it defeated the French in their Panama effort and for a time in 1878 brought the work in South Pass to a standstill. But Eads had come this far. He had superb confidence in himself—and he accepted the Senate's terms for better or worse.

The enabling act was passed March 3, 1875, and on July 8, 1879 (though vessels were actually using Eads's unfinished channel in 1876), Captain Brown, the government inspector in charge, certified that there was a clear channel of thirty feet, regardless of width, from Head of Passes to the Gulf of Mexico. The task had been herculean, but it had been accomplished exactly as Eads had said it would be. Within twenty years Congress had authorized the same operation for Southwest Pass, as Eads had wanted to do it in the first place. And this time the work was handled by the now-convinced army engineer corps. Today both South and Southwest Passes are continuously maintained, but even as Eads predicted it is Southwest Pass which carries the heavy traffic.

In New Orleans Eads's monument, in name at least, is the paved area, usually full of parked automobiles, where Canal Street joins the Mississippi. It is the most conspicuous spot on the New Orleans river front, and officially it is Eads Square, but to most people it is simply the foot of Canal Street, the city terminal of the Algiers ferry.

In passing one wonders what the effect on New Orleans' future would have been if the jetties had been constructed forty years earlier, when the bar first became a major New Orleans problem. From an engineering standpoint they could have been built then—had there been an Eads to do it. Of course the cost was finally borne, and no doubt rightfully, by the Federal government—and this within ten years of the close of the Civil War, when Congress was supposed to be treating all the South like an illegitimate orphan. And yet New Orleans could have paid every cent of the cost and scarcely missed it, while her gain otherwise would almost certainly have been enormous.

CHAPTER XVIII

Slack-Water Times

THE SUCCESSFUL COMPLETION of the jetty system was a boon to New Orleans commerce, but it could not restore the city's one-time supremacy. Somehow, somewhere, the city had grown tired and lost its old ambition. It may have been the war, in part, though it seems unreasonable to blame the war for everything.

The city continued to grow, but the growth had become steady and was no longer the headlong rush of the forties and fifties. New Orleans found time to take stock of itself, to contemplate its way of life, and on the whole to find it good. It was not the way fancied by Pittsburgh and Detroit and Boston, but what did that matter? It suited New Orleans. The city had sampled the rich but wasteful profits of the prewar days, and now most of the money was long since spent. It had yielded to the temptation of ambition in the bright days of 1860 and learned that a revolution lost is far worse than none at all. It had dreamed of being one of the world's greatest cities, and yet watched Chicago, nine hundred miles to the north, grow from an upstart village to a city five times the size of New Orleans. At times it was all very confusing, so to a great extent New Orleans gave up worrying about it.

The Port of New Orleans

There were men in New Orleans who of course were still relentlessly ambitious, and while the city didn't hold that against them it refused to be a party to any more ambitious schemes.

It was still a city of strange contrasts and ways misunderstood by the stranger. It had to its credit the invention of such alcoholic delights as the crusta, the Ramos gin fizz, and the Sazerac cocktail, and its bars had served the first regular free lunch in the United States. It lavished money and care on its churches and seemed utterly oblivious of its reputation (justly deserved) as the brothel of the Mississippi Valley. It had the dirtiest and most unkempt thoroughfares in America, and yet every householder cared meticulously for his own small plot of earth, worried more over his hibiscus and orange trees and lilies than the state of municipal morals. The huge ground-level cisterns were still an adjunct of nearly every household, and drinking water was hauled from the Mississippi above the city, to be filtered at home for drinking. Foreign tongues were used everywhere, and in the Old City especially French was spoken as commonly as English, and shop signs and such were more likely to be French than English. Yet practically everyone knew English, or at least what passed for English, and one was as likely to find French spoken in Carrollton or West End as on Chartres Street.

In New Orleans the whole matter of language and dialect is a thing apart from the rest of the United States. The species of Louisiana French known as "gumbo" or "gombo" has been discussed and diagnosed at length by experts; its origins are pretty well known and its peculiarities catalogued. It is not a language at all common nowadays, though there is one rural region in Louisiana where the Negroes still use it almost exclusively. The younger generation of Orleanians, except in rare cases, knows only an occasional word of gombo, and these the words which might be called part of New Orleans "tourist" tradition, the idea of being "different." But with Orleanians whose memories go back to the eighties and nineties it is quite different. Addressed in a sentence of gombo they will frequently answer without hesitation, sometimes replying in the same language almost automatically. And in the next instant, if in public, they are apt to be sheepish or self-conscious about the whole thing. Most of them, as a matter of fact, could not go on with a commonplace conversation in the same language, but to words, phrases, or even sentences some subterranean memory reacts easily. Pressed for an explanation, the modern Orleanian will probably insist he does not know where or when he learned what little of the language he does know. He will insist further that when he *tries* to remember it it eludes him more completely. He will tell you further that, even when *he* reacts to it accurately, he cannot give *you* a free translation. And all this is true. For it was not a written but a spoken speech, and where it is preserved in print at all it is mainly as a curiosity. Until a few years ago there was always at least one French-language newspaper or periodical published in New Orleans, but of course their scholarly editors scorned the use of gumbo French except in the sense that the English press prints Negro jokes in alleged Negro dialect. So likewise the English-language publications stuck to what they believed was English —it often was not, but that is another story.

All the peculiarities of New Orleans French have been dissected by experts, and for the reader who is interested and can understand the technicalities, the essays on the subject by Lafcadio Hearn are among the best. For that matter Hearn was unquestionably the best proseman who ever concerned himself with the kaleidoscope of New Orleans life. The pieces he wrote for the New Orleans newspapers of the latter seventies are today as fresh and crisp as they were then, without a trace of the simpering Victorianisms which cluttered most of the contemporary writing in English. It seemed that Hearn could not write badly if he tried, and because he was an original himself he hadn't the slightest regard for the literary fashions of the period. In the latter portion of the nineteenth century George W. Cable was probably the best-known literary man of New Orleans. There were more than a few Orleanians who considered Cable an incompetent hack, though they themselves couldn't do as well. Cable was uninspired and a little pedestrian, but he was industrious and made himself heard, and Hearn at least professed to have a great respect for his abilities. But Hearn was too modest. He could take a sentence or an idea from Cable and polish it, re-form it, examine it from a dozen new angles, until it scintillated in a way that Cable could never achieve. Proof of his skill lies in the fact that Hearn died with an international reputation which has grown after his death, while Cable, when he is remembered at all, is recalled as a mildly talented American regionalist.

But the matter of New Orleans English speech is a curious thing and one to which students have given no great amount of attention. New Orleans speech is Southern, yes, but it is not the same as any *other* Southern speech. Few Orleanians can tell from a man's speech alone whether he is from Savannah or Houston or Nashville, but they almost certainly can tell whether or not he is a fellow Orleanian. Now a certain amount of this is very obvious: one does not expect a Bostonian to talk the same as a man from Kansas City. But the New Orleans speech distinction is sharper than that. One *does* expect the man from Kansas City to resemble a St. Louisan in his talk, but the Orleanian knows he does not use the same speech as the man from Baton Rouge, and Baton Rouge is only eighty miles up the Mississippi and is as Southern as New Orleans if not more so. Orleanians are apt to say, "Well, New Orleans is a great seaport—that accounts for it." But it doesn't account for it—quite. Comparisons in such matters are hardly ever exactly to the point, and yet the nearest one can come to describing New Orleans speech is to say that it sounds like Brooklynese spoken with what is commonly thought of as a Southern accent. Colloquialisms and inflections are different but as a generality likely to be generally understood the comparison is valid. *Why* it is that way is another matter and one not easily explained. It may have something to do with its relation to gumbo French, but the mere fact that New Orleans is a seaport explains nothing at all.

In another field New Orleans has for decades been the living refutation of a once-popular American theory that the arts in America suffered because of American preoccupation with materialism, lack of leisure, and lack of an indigenous culture that was understood and appreciated. Now New Orleans could be said to have these qualities in reverse. After the war the rush of trade was conspicuously absent in the city. Orleanians had no objection to making a profit, far from it in fact, but the old roaring atmosphere of commercialism was gone. There just wasn't that kind of business to be had and the city as yet had few industrial enterprises. Thus the leisure was the by-product of that state, plus the climate, but it was no less leisure for all that. And as for the culture, that was as old as any in America, and certainly as definitely formed. Yet New Orleans was no great shakes as a mother of the arts; in that respect she was as much on the short side as any American city of comparable size, and this in spite of her worldliness and sophistication.

The best of her native writers, artists, and musicians, with but few exceptions, have been third rate by any international standard. Of course she produced many men and women of fine talents, but invariably they were talents on a miniature scale. Even the writers who wrote best of New Orleans were not what the city thinks of as "native." And New Orleans has always attracted artists and writers in droves—time was when the French Quarter was as well regarded a bohemia as New York's Greenwich Village. Even now any sunny autumn morning will find the cool entrances to Royal Street patios cluttered with easels and paint kits, and the tools will be used by every species of artist from the finest dry-point men in the business to angular, retired maiden schoolteachers with a vague talent for water color and the urge for self-expression. For a hundred years the city has attracted writers of national, international, and no reputation at all.

A writer's personal life was incomplete unless he could speak familiarly about the city by the Gulf, and almost all of them had their say about the city, some of them extremely well indeed. Even now during the winter months New Orleans can muster almost as many alleged writers to the square block as Hollywood, New York, or Santa Fe. And that was always the trouble: the city attracted them but did not produce them. As observers many of these writers were extremely acute, but somewhere, somehow, the essence of New Orleans escaped them, and most of them were wise enough to know it. It is a curious but true thing that no really good and honest and intelligent major novel has ever been written about the city, and when and if it ever is it should be a very fine thing indeed. Until now most writers have been content to deal with the superficial trappings of the city's "atmosphere"—and that is about as penetrating as delineating the true character of a department-store Santa Claus by describing his artificial beard and red flannel suit.

But if New Orleans lacked distinction in some of the so-called higher arts that is not to say that she was without means of aesthetic expression. The great mass outpouring of New Orleans' collective spirit was of course Mardi Gras. Dormant during the Civil War years, it came back to life in even greater splendor and elegance during the seventies—and with more honest sentiment behind it. Mark Twain, who liked New Orleans very much, was inclined to ridicule what he called the "girly-girly romance" of the Mardi Gras, but while Mark was wittily eloquent more often than not, he was also badly mistaken on numerous occasions. Other people, good Orleanians, too, have belabored Mardi Gras as senseless rigmarole and, lately, commercialism, but these charges were not always valid. The carnival was always as legitimate a celebration as Fourth-of-July bombardments, fireworks on Christmas, or alcoholic New Year's festivities, and tradition has endeared it to the hearts of Orleanians.

There was hardly ever a time when New Orleans didn't love a parade—the Mardi Gras was and is half parade—and it never missed an opportunity to stage one. For that matter it doesn't now. Canal Street echoes with the music of brass bands and marching feet, and Orleanians never fail to stop and watch with appreciation, though chances are three quarters of them will have no idea what the occasion may be. Before and after the Civil War one of the especially elegant parades was the annual Fourth-of-March turnout of the Volunteer Fire Department, or, as it preferred to be called, the Firemen's Charitable Association. On these occasions, as the newspapers invariably put it, the "beauty and chivalry of the city" were always present in force. The department was not volunteer in the sense that it worked for nothing, but it was not city-controlled until the nineties and it behooved the folk to show their respect and admiration.

(A neat example of the boys' eye for business is the case of the ship *Tornado*. She caught fire at her wharf in February 1878, and efforts to whip the fire ended by opening her sea cocks and sinking her. Two days later the *Tornado's* master entered some sort of agreement with Chief Engineer O'Connor of the F.C.A. to pump out the ship and raise her. When the F.C.A. put in a claim for salvage due the *Tornado's* master refused to pay it, on the ground that he could not be charged for services of the municipal fire department. Thereupon Chief O'Connor attached the vessel and enumerated the claims against her. The *Tornado* was charged with fifteen days' service of twelve steam pumpers, two hook-and-ladder companies, and a whacking bill for hose and other materials supposedly expended in the operation. And what is more the *Tornado* had to pay it, for the fire fighters and equipment as such were *not* under contract to the city. The city contract was let to the F.C.A., and the latter organization in turn hired the firemen. Thus the de-

[281]

partment was bound to fight all fires, but there was nothing to keep them from engaging in other activities if they did not interfere.)

As fire fighters the boys were frequently no great success but at parades and funerals they were champions. The following condensation from the *History of the New Orleans Fire Department*, by former Chief O'Connor, conveys some of the elegance of the Fourth-of-March parades, which celebrated the anniversary of the department's founding:

. . . The most careful attention was given to the decoration and beautifying of the engines. Every shining part was polished like a mirror, and silver plating was renewed if there was the slightest excuse for it. The engines were newly-painted, and particular attention was given to the wheels, in the painting of which large sums of money were expended. . . . Then they took down their trophies of various kinds from the walls of the engine house, and mounted them on the engine—awards won in many contests, trumpets, horns, ribbons, sets of silver plate—and as time went on and these trophies accumulated, they could make only a selection of the most recent or the most distinguishing. . . . Wreaths of flowers to be used as garlands, rosettes for the horses, bouquets both big and little, for men and machines, streamers of bunting and banners of silk, some of them intricate pieces of exquisite needle-work, were among the contributions of the ladies to the general appearance of festivity.

There were pyramids of variegated flowers to rise from the smoke stacks; or urns surmounted with massive bouquets or plumes in which silver and gold were freely intermingled; silk cushions for the driver's seat; saddles of colored satin for the fire horses. . . . Above all it was common to see perched the company emblem, whether the Eagle, the Dove, the figure of Hope or Columbia, or the portrait of some martyr of whom only the name remained as an inspiration to those who followed his example and in his path.

It was through a tumultuous and vociferous multitude of spectators that the procession made its way over the route designated. Crowds came from other cities to witness the event, and many came accompanying the visiting fire companies from other cities, of which there were nearly always representatives in the annual parades. The parade ended, the line was dismissed, and the engines were taken back separately to their houses. . . . There was an interval during which opportunity was afforded for a few words of felicitation from the ladies, before it was necessary to adjourn to the festivities with which the firemen brought the day to a close. . . . Now they separated into companies, each company spreading its sumptuous supper table where it would. The public rooms were taxed to accommodate the revelers, and in many quarters of the city there was the sound of revelry until far into the night.

In other words, a really elegant clambake!

Another annual New Orleans procession had its roots in a more honest sentiment. One of the city's numerous eccentrics had been John McDonogh, a pious Scot who made a fortune in the slave trade and lived by a set of dry maxims in which Andrew Carnegie would have rejoiced. McDonogh was refused (so tradition has it) by the Michaela Almonaster who became the Baroness Pontalba, died a bachelor, and left his considerable fortune to the New Orleans public-school system—which certainly needed it! Even now the school children of the city make an annual pilgrimage to the statue erected in memory of John McDonogh.

All Saints' Day found the cemeteries of New Orleans bedecked as lavishly as any in the world, and because of their natural peculiarities they present an unusually striking appearance on that day. And on St. Joseph's Day strangers were made welcome in the homes of New Orleans Catholics who could possibly afford a St. Joseph's altar.

The city was what is known as a good sporting town and there a man could get a bet down on practically anything, from a steamboat race to the weather. A race track had been considered an absolute necessity—though sewers were not—and the newspapers featured prize-fight news along with national politics, and there was more of it. Under most circumstances prize fighting was illegal, but the police usually

[283]

managed to refrain from any arrests until a decision was reached in the ring, and fights were held the year round. Cockfighting was good box office in the eighties and nineties and is still practiced surreptitiously.

After the Civil War gambling in general was more widespread than ever, and in New Orleans there were probably more gambling houses than grocery stores. As a matter of fact, gambling in practically all forms was legalized by the carpetbag legislature of 1869, and the sporting fraternity rejoiced exceedingly. But not for long, for the influx of professionals from outside was so large that the local boys suffered terribly from the ruinous competition. The vice was in a fair way to destroy itself when the New Orleans professionals asked the legislature to repeal the license law! It was an almost unheard-of thing, but the legislature complied willingly. They seldom got paid for doing something morally approved. With the license law repealed, the police ran the outsiders out of town and in a short time the local boys were back in business again, paying toll to the police rather than to the state. The police weren't any cheaper but they were easier to co-operate with.

The same legislature in 1868 granted a charter for twenty-five years to the Louisiana State Lottery Company, and the charter remained in force long after the other gambling laws went out of existence. Because of competition in other Southern states the New Orleans company did not do so well for a number of years, but by 1880 it was going great guns and its annual income was enormous. At one time it offered a semi-annual prize of $600,000 on a forty-dollar winning ticket, with daily, weekly, and monthly prizes running into the thousands. To enhance its prestige and reputation for honesty the Louisiana Lottery paid ex-Confederate heroes Beauregard and Early annual salaries of thirty thousand dollars each to supervise the monthly drawings. And the financial reputation of the lottery was so good that winning tickets could be as readily cashed anywhere in the country as certified checks or express money orders, and it would probably be running yet had it not been for the Federal government. In 1907 (the name had been changed to Honduras Lottery Company) its tickets and printed matter containing its advertisements were successfully barred from the mails, and interstate movement of tickets was forbidden by the Interstate Commerce Commission.

In a city where such affairs were carried on so openly and semi-legally it was only natural that other vices so dear to the so-called "sporting classes" should flourish. Prostitution was widespread in every decade of New Orleans' history until the period of World War I, and it staged a mild comeback after that conflict was over and Federal pressure removed. Off and on for sixty years the city had passed ordinances saying where brothels could and could not be operated, and in a way such zoning amounted to legalizing, though the city did reserve the right to punish harlotry as such. But once, in 1857, the city went so far as licensing both brothels and their inmates—it was the only city in the country ever to attempt such a scheme—though in time the courts held the licensing illegal and ordered the fees returned. During Reconstruction Basin Street achieved an international reputation that was deserved, and it remained a gaudy brothel district for many years, probably reaching its height of notoriety in the eighties and nineties. It is a mildly amusing fact that, through the agency of a still-popular blues tune and incidentally one which is a near-classic ("Basin Street Blues"), the street still retains that reputation, though as a matter of fact Basin Street has long since ceased to exist as such. (It is even more amusing that several generations of otherwise fairly chaste American adolescents learned to strum "Basin Street" on the piano, danced to its beat in high-school gymnasiums, and sang its more or less meaningless words without having the least notion of Basin Street's real character.) Above Canal Street it is now known as Elk Place, and below Canal it can hardly be called a street, since

The Port of New Orleans

at the Canal Street junction the Southern Railway Station was plunked down in the middle of Basin, filling it from sidewalk to sidewalk, and behind the depot a double track uses up most of the street.

To say that prostitution has never died out in New Orleans is to be almost naïve. It will never disappear in New Orleans any more than it will vanish from any other city. That is not only a matter of morals and geography but of human nature. It is true, however, that prostitution's outward characteristics have changed greatly and, in New Orleans at least, it no longer is so tightly organized. In New Orleans prostitution probably (though not certainly) dwindled with Prohibition and revived to a certain extent with Repeal, though that is a personal opinion and there are no statistics to prove that opinion either right or wrong. When conscription went into effect in 1940 New Orleans became once more the center of a network of training camps, and the army itself, in line with its current morale policy, not only permitted all soldiers to visit New Orleans freely, but encouraged it by providing transportation in army vehicles and setting up a so-called rest camp on the shore of near-by Lake Pontchartrain. That there would again be a rise in the city's prostitute population was inevitable—but it is still true that the business operates pretty much on a free-lance basis. With a state of war an actual fact it may be that the army will become more strict, but that is a matter not likely to be much publicized. The city's attitude, in any case, is likely to be carefully neutral. That is it will neither quarrel with the army nor do anything about its own morals.

New Orleans was always a city in which life went on in a series of orbits within orbits. First there was the cleavage between the French and Spanish, then between the French, Spanish, *and* Americans. Later other racial factions, such as the Italians and Irish, formed their own social pools. And then there were the water-front and Delta folk, who were parts of these other factions and yet a group apart in another way. Of course these factions always overlapped in many ways, though municipal affairs and the Catholic Church were probably the two most binding influences.

And there were always certain small groups who were in New Orleans but not necessarily of it. The Filipinos were one such group, for example, and the Latin Americans of temporary residence were another. These last were for the most part exiles, at least temporarily, and that was the one thing they had in common. Hondurans, Cubans, Mexicans, Venezuelans, San Domingans—they did not share their political troubles except in a general way, but their very presence in the city for a common reason tended to draw them together.

New Orleans was the one American city familiar to all Central and South Americans, the one city in America where they could feel at home with the least effort, and the American city which was geographically closest to their homelands. These criminal and political exiles came and went through New Orleans for a hundred years, and for that matter still do, though nowadays, since political restrictions of all kinds are probably tighter than they ever were, the coming and going are much more clandestine. The city, of course, was for long a mecca for adventuring filibusters— frequently they were idolized public figures—but aside from any American participation New Orleans was always the natural base of operations for revolutionary exiles. Probably more political turmoil has been planned there than in any other American city, not even excepting New York.

A century ago the meeting place was Maspero's Exchange, at the corner of St. Louis and Chartres streets in the French Quarter, later the site of the more famous St. Louis Hotel. From there it moved to Banks' Arcade on Magazine Street, like Maspero's near the river front. And later still the most popular rendezvous were the Café des Émigrés and the Café des Exiles, the latter at the corner of Royal and St. Ann streets, barely a half block from St. Louis Cathedral. These two latter were operated by refugees for refugees, and the character, or at least the general intention, of their customers was commonly known in New Orleans. When revolution in Latin America became a less popular interest and the United States government began to take a sterner and more official attitude toward affairs south of the border, these places also lost their popularity. Lost it, that is, in the sense that they became too public for their main purpose. Activities were transferred to dingier cafés in more obscure back streets, but they went on just the same. Time was when it was well known in certain circles that any revolutionary Latin American in the United States could be found, or at least a message passed on to him, through certain cafés in San Antonio, New York, and New Orleans. The San Antonio address was mostly favored by Mexicans, with the rest of the trade going largely to the place in New Orleans.

Nor was the city looked upon with less favor by Latin Americans intent solely on doing a peaceful and profitable business. To most of them New Orleans was *the* city of the United States. It was a fortunate coincidence that New Orleans was at once the city they knew best and the one best fitted temperamentally to get along with them. But there the good fortune more or less ended. With its interests properly organized—and by this is meant more than the mere business of buying and selling—the city should have had a monopoly on Latin-American affairs. Yet it does not. Somewhere in the process it failed. It was not complete failure, of course, but the result past and present has fallen far short of what it could so easily have been. And that is not so much to blame New Orleans as to be a little sorry for her sake.

Books about New Orleans almost invariably fall into one of two categories. In one the writer dwells almost lovingly on the city's manifold and obvious iniquities—probably for the same reason newspapers feature gory murders in front-page headlines and bury accounts of minor good works next to the classified ads. In the other class fall the books which dwell with equal rapture upon the New Orleans of filmy, moon-struck, pseudo-romantic trappings that has no connection with reality. But oddly enough something of a case can be made for each approach.

If the city drank to excess it also invented concoctions aimed to make the process as pleasant as possible; if it sinned greatly it repented in the same way. Its vice was vice with a capital V, yet it carried it off with a careless air of grace, a sort of "I know I'm stealing your wallet but we might as well be friends in other things" attitude. It was a Latin attitude that the rest of the country found difficult to understand, and it probably stemmed from the fact that at times so much of New Orleans' entire population was involved in affairs which would have been at least frowned upon in most parts of the United States that had passed the frontier stage. And a part of it came from the city's almost amazing quality of tolerance—or, more specifically, the willingness to judge its citizens by *all* the parts of their character. It saw no reason why men should not be saloonkeepers and gamblers and still make excellent aldermen, husbands and fathers, and church members. It is an attitude by far more typical of New Orleans than any other part of the South, and certainly is *not* an attitude very common in the North, especially in the smaller towns. New Orleans simply refused to worry about that particular kind of social distinction, and that after all is a pretty fair example of one kind of democracy.

Probably in no other way does New Orleans' singular character show to better advantage than in the way she has named her streets. As far as I know no one has tried to illustrate the sameness of the production-line Industrial Age by calling attention to the way American cities are so devoid of imagination that they must resort to numbering or lettering their streets rather than naming them, but it might be a point. Identical rows of unimaginative dwellings and apartment houses in New York, Chicago, Cleveland, and Washington face streets exquisitely named Second, Ninth, or Ninety-second, and even villages do the same thing. At least one city in Illinois has staggered the creative imagination by calling all the thoroughfares running east and west numbered streets and those running north and south numbered avenues. Even Washington, where Congressmen frequently let their imaginations run riot, had to fall back on the alphabet.

But not New Orleans!

The choice of names in the original French city was more or less obvious. Rue Royale was the principal street, or king's way, and Chartres, Burgundy, Toulouse, Orleans, and Conti were French ruling families, as was Dumaine (Du Maine). Iberville (once Custom House), Ursulines, and Levee are self-explanatory, as are also Barracks, St. Louis, and Esplanade. Canal Street actually was at one time a canal, or at least a moat, and Rampart is on the site of the original city line, later a fortified wall of earth. Gallatin, Madison, Decatur, Wilkinson, Clinton, Clay, also in the French Quarter, are the result of the War of 1812 period and after.

When the American city began to grow above Canal Street and the Suburb Marigny to thrive below the French Quarter, the ex-governors and mayors came in for their just dues, so came into being Carondelet, Girod, Peters, Kerlerec, Macarty, and Galvez. Tchoupitoulas and Perdido are of course of Indian origin. In due time came those which were standard American or particularly New Orleans—Jefferson, Jackson, Franklin, Washington, Villere, Calhoun, La Freniere, St. Denis, Marigny, Lizardi, Forstall, Poydras, Freret, Howard, Tulane, Gallier, Perrier, Louisiana, Napoleon, Derbigny, a host of other such. The Church of course came in for its full share by way of Saints Claude, Peter, Philip, Roch, Charles, Thomas, Ann, Andrew, Maurice, James, and Thomas. So much is more or less commonplace but still a cut above numbers and letters.

But then New Orleans let its imagination go—and put the muses to use with Clio, Erato, Thalia, Melpomene, Terpsichore, Euterpe, and Polymnia. They named one street for

Mayor Joseph Shakespeare, but to make up for it to the memory of the bard they went above Carrollton Avenue and arranged Shakespeare, Milton, Pope, Addison, Moore, Goldsmith, Walter Scott, Byron, and Dryden. Where else could you find Peoples Avenue followed by Rabbits Street, and that by Beer? And then within a few blocks come Painters, Arts, Music, and Room. Not far away are Patriot, Benefit, Abundance, Pleasure, Humanity, Treasure, Agriculture, Industry, and Law. Piety is followed by Desire, or vice versa, and not far away is Love Street!

Both nations and cities are remembered with Mexico, Spain, America, Poland, France, Roman, Dublin, Edinburgh, Constantinople, Madrid, and Vienna. The Greeks and other ancients come in for Athis, Mithras, Dryades, Copernicus, Ptolemy, Newton, Americus, Magellan, Balboa, and Socrates. The Church was remembered again in Nuns, Felicity, and Annunciation streets, and for variety there are Lowerline, Upperline, Lurline, Sisters, Calliope, and Coliseum, Elysian Fields, and Austerlitz. Then not to be too unusual the city numbered a group of streets from First through Ninth, inserting Washington Avenue in place of Fifth Street, but even these are a flight of fancy, for neither First nor Ninth has any meaning in the sense that they begin, end, or bound any particular area. And then to add a typical New Orleans touch, they liked some of the names so well that they used variants of them all over town, so that the stranger must be very sure whether he wants Philip or St. Philip Street; Peters or St. Peter; Clay Street or Henry Clay Avenue; Washington Avenue, Square or Street; Orleans Boulevard, Street or Alley.

Let no one suppose that a city which can perform with such virtuosity is without a soul—no matter how shopworn.

CHAPTER XIX

A Seaport Grown Up

ONCE THEIR IMPORTANCE in the general scheme of things was established, life for most American seaports became stable in the sense that their prosperity rose or fell with the prosperity of the nation as a whole, but not New Orleans. For various reasons she had gone her own peculiar way regardless of what the rest of the country might be doing. During the period of the embargo and War of 1812, for example, the wharves of Eastern seaports were either empty or lined with shipping which had no place to go, whereas New Orleans was hardly aware that there was an embargo or a war. During the first year and a half of the Civil War New Orleans' wharves became emptier while those in Eastern ports hummed with activity. With the growth of "trade with the enemy" and the rebirth of some of the otherwise lawful trade, the latter years of the war saw some improvement, though it was only a token. But with the war finally over, the city awakened to the painful fact that the prewar trade wasn't coming back, at least not to its previous extent.

Some of the reasons for that—decline of the steamboat traffic and growth of the Northern railroad systems, the trouble at the mouth of the Mississippi—have been discussed in previous chapters. The increase of rail traffic into New Orleans, the successful completion of the jetty system, and the use of towboats and barges in the river service were factors which helped offset the city's misfortunes. But these were only a temporary relief, not a cure. The fact remained that the city had lost her one-time supremacy and seemed unlikely to get it back.

Now if this had been merely a matter of the comparative prosperity of a city of two hundred thousand, after all only a drop in the great bucket of America, it would have been important only to New Orleans. Actually, it was a change of great import and one which to a large extent affected the whole of the Mississippi Valley. It must be remembered that New Orleans had not been a seaport of merely provincial importance, but one of the great commercial gateways of the world. By 1840 the tonnage and tonnage valuation of New Orleans were exceeded in the United States only by New York, and in the rest of the entire world only by London and Liverpool. Thus what happened to New Orleans as a seaport was of consequence in a great many places beyond the boundaries of Orleans Parish, Louisiana.

Prior to the Civil War commercial figures everywhere were far less accurate than they have become since, when, in the United States in particular, every county is acutely aware of how many pigs or cabbages or wagon wheels it annually produces and ships. In New Orleans during 1860, the last great year of trade before the Civil War, it was generally considered that the business of the port exceeded $300,000,-000. The population of the United States was at that time about 31,000,000.

During the several decades after the war the city's commerce dwindled until New Orleans was no longer even mentioned in connection with the world's important seaports. In fact, fifty years went by before the city's port trade again approached the figure of 1860. The year was 1912 and the value of combined imports and exports was

$299,450,727, but that figure included also the trade of Baton Rouge. And even though the figure does equal that of 1860 the comparison is still hardly accurate as regards New Orleans' importance as a port. First, the figure included Baton Rouge; further, the comparison is made on a value basis, and in general far more goods could be shipped for less money in 1860, and the population of the United States —and therefore the population of the New Orleans trade area—had at least trebled. So New Orleans' relationship to the country as a whole was still far away from its old place. The reaching of the old high-water mark, on paper at least, was something to crow about, but there were plenty of people who knew that New Orleans still had a long way to go. Not even the loudest booster could claim that this achievement put the city back anywhere near the top of the heap.

The foregoing comparison is made on a value basis, and for the point at issue it is as good as any, but the fact was that some years previously the city had exceeded her old tonnage record. That is to say that the tonnage handled by New Orleans in 1889, which was 4,000,000 plus chiefly as the result of grain movement south from St. Louis, was greater than any previous annual tonnage, though the value was not nearly so large. All figures concerning the tonnage of water-borne shipping are tricky and in the hands of an expert can be made to prove a variety of things. (As, for instance, the figures which, on tonnage alone, show Pittsburgh as being the busiest port in the United States.) There is no direct relationship between tonnage and valuation—consider the difference between an Alaskan port shipping gold and one shipping gravel or coal. Or compare the per-ton prices of three such common commodities as coal, wheat, and cotton. The ratio of money value is per ton usually in this order—5: 35: 120; this will vary under different conditions, of course, but is near enough. At first glance it might appear that a tonnage turnover of high valuation would be desirable, but this is not necessarily so, in fact seldom is. A *balanced* tonnage is as important to the healthy economic life of a seaport as to a nation at large.

Probably this is as good a place as any to say a word about "tonnage" as applied to sea trade and to ships in particular. The fact is that the word "ton" as applied to ships came originally from the word "tun" and had nothing whatever to do with the weight unit of 2,000 pounds. Few landsmen— and for that matter few enough seamen—can form any accurate idea of a ship's size from the sort of tonnage figures ordinarily used in newspaper accounts of shipping.

As this is written in 1942, the Navy Department has recently ruled that, in order to avoid giving useful information to the enemy, the tonnage of ships sunk by submarines will no longer be published; instead the ships so lost will be described as small, medium, or large. And as a matter of fact that is just about the most accurate way, for most purposes, any vessel can be described, whether for the American newspaper reader or the German navy. To the German Ministry of Information it will be far more useful to know that a "large" vessel has been sunk, than to be quoted tonnage figures which in themselves mean very little. This is even more true of ship sinkings caused by planes. When a bomber pilot reports that he sank a vessel of 5,000 tons, his estimate of the vessel's size is probably worth exactly nothing. In the first place, an air pilot is likely to be a rotten judge of ship size at any distance, let alone from several thousand feet in the air, and in the second place the tonnage figure is so utterly misleading.

To quote a few examples of the confusion apt to engulf the landsman—one of the largest steam packets ever used in the West was the *City of Louisville*, and she was rated as having a net tonnage of 1,142. An ocean cargo vessel of about the same size as the *City of Louisville* would be considered as having a net tonnage of about 2,000. Yet the ocean vessel would carry about three tons of cargo for each ton of rating, whereas the best the packet could do was one to one and a half for each ton of rating, a great part of the variation of course being in the vast difference in draft. Likewise the ocean vessel would use about two thirds of one horsepower per net ton, but the steam packet would require one and one half horsepower per net ton. Following the same lines of reasoning, most large seagoing tugs would actually have a rating of *minus* tons, as would the powerful towboats now in use on the Mississippi system. The tonnage ratings of sailing craft are still more complicated, some of them having a cargo capacity of about ton for ton with rating, but others, notably some of the very fast American clippers of the 1850s, carried less cargo than their tonnage ratings. All this is obviously quite confusing and is not meant to be an explanation of what tonnage means under any circumstances but an example of how impossible it is to make ordinary comparisons.

The cargo *moving* capacity of the river towboat as compared with the ocean vessel is interesting, though it proves nothing much except that they are two distinct means of transportation. The old steam towboat *Sprague*, with a rated horsepower of 1,800, which compares well with that of an ordinary tramp steamer hauling 7,000 cargo tons of coal, has on numerous occasions come into New Orleans with a barge tow carrying 60,000 tons of coal—a downstream haul, of course. Nevertheless, it would require twelve average 100-car trains, for example, to carry the coal that the *Sprague* has moved in one tow. On other occasions the *Sprague* has towed *upstream* an oil cargo of 224,000 barrels, or the equivalent of around 45,000 tons! That these figures and the river tows have a definite bearing on the business of New Orleans will be shown a little further on, so they have a certain relevance here.

With business no brisker than it was in the period following the Civil War, there was little incentive for New Orleans to improve the harbor. She had never taken any pains with it when the business there was enormous—it was natural that she should take even fewer pains with it now, for it was difficult for the city to do anything when she had all the incentive in the world.

The harbor had certain natural advantages—no tug service was needed, for docking at least, and it was tideless. It was also located at the city itself, which is not always the case in combined river- and seaports.

On the other side of the ledger there was a good deal to be said about it. As time went on the wooden wharves became more decrepit—a little neglect could go a long way in the New Orleans climate. Dock services were of course nowhere comparable with what they are now, and in New Orleans they could be depended upon to be as bad as the worst. Until the late nineties the fire-protection service was weak to say the least—fireboats were in use in Eastern ports long before New Orleans could boast one—and a skipper could never be quite sure of what he was getting in the way of fresh-water supply. The rats, both rodent and human, seemed bent on setting a population record, and the port officials in general had a moral standard not much above the rest of the city government. Having loaded a cargo, a skipper had to watch it if he expected to sail with everything his manifest called for. A smart vessel waiting to load cotton for Liverpool might have a broken-down Mexican cattle boat, reeking with the smell of manure, for neighbor on one side and a fleet of luggers reeking with the stench of oyster-shell on the other. So a certain portion of any vessel's crew might look forward to the red-light glitter of Basin Street, but an earnest-minded master bent on his ship's best business interests was not likely to look forward happily to a spell in New Orleans—and in the summer season everything was likely to be worse.

It was not to be expected that New Orleans would worry any more about her harbor welfare than about any of her other problems.

The body which changed all that was the Board of Com-

missioners of the Port of New Orleans, created and given
authority by the state in 1896, though the commission did
not assume full control of all facilities until 1901. Before this
the water front had been nominally owned by the city but
leased to private companies and individuals, whose rental
rates were computed on the basis of how much they agreed
to spend in the way of improving their leaseholds. Probably
it would have been hard to find a poorer way of managing
the facilities of a port with pretensions to world importance.

The Dock Board (the usual term for the commission) was
authorized to do the following:

To regulate the commerce and traffic of the port and harbor
in such manner as may, in their judgment, be best for its maintenance and development.

To enjoy all the rights, powers, and immunities incident to cor-
porations.

To take charge of and administer the public wharves and landings.

To construct new wharves where necessary, and to erect sheds
on the wharves and landings.

To place and keep the wharves and landings in good condition.

To maintain sufficient depth of water.

To provide for lighting and policing.

To collect a fee from vessels using the harbor and shipping
facilities.

To purchase and expropriate property, wharves, or landings
necessary for the benefit of the commerce of the port and harbor.

The Dock Board is an instrument of the state of Louisiana
and it is certainly the most public kind of knowledge that
Louisiana's public institutions have in the past given some
extremely—well, eccentric performances. Time was when
the country's newspapers carried a daily running account of
what was new in Louisiana politics, and it would be too
much to say that the Dock Board has always been altogether

free of what is usually called "politics." On the other hand, it is the simplest kind of justice to say that it has performed its primary function with every possible credit to itself.

Without going too deeply into the philosophy of governmental commissions it may be pertinent to remark that the Dock Board has been influenced by the fact that it has had to deal with the world at large, and not primarily with the citizenry of New Orleans and Louisiana. It is an extremely important part of modern New Orleans and yet the great body of citizenry not directly concerned with shipping has little knowledge of how it works and not much interest in finding out.

The power given the board to purchase and expropriate water-front property for its use was and is important and is one of the reasons the board has functioned so well. The board has jurisdiction over a far greater area of water front and water-front facilities than it owns, but it owns enough key property to make its other jurisdiction peculiarly effective. The property purchased was financed by bond issues, to be retired out of income and not by tax levies—the board has no taxing power whatever—and in general this has been a good thing for the state, the investors, and the board. The standing of its bonds is not the final proof of an institution's good administration, but it is one indication of a good administration, and on this score the board rates high.

Confining the board's activities to the scope permitted by its normal income has probably been a very good thing. Since its income is directly concerned with the state of trade in general, the board has of necessity geared itself to the expected flow of trade, the same as any other successful business must but as governmental bodies in the United States seldom have. Furthermore, its income has been determined to a certain extent by competition—that is the charges for port service are to a great extent determined by those in effect elsewhere. New Orleans' rates may be higher or lower than those in effect in other comparable ports, but it is obvious that there are strict limitations, both up and down, beyond which these charges may not reasonably go.

At times the board has fretted under the restraint imposed by its income limits, and undoubtedly it has been occasionally denied beneficial things because of that restraint. On the other hand, the New Orleans Dock Board has never been any more infallible than any other body of men, and probably the income limitations have prevented it from making at least a *few* mistakes.

That the board has been successful has been attested by the rising flow of port commerce since it took over, and by the esteem in which it is generally held by shipping interests. Since 1912, a year previously used as a comparison, the commerce of the port has never fallen below the three-hundred-million mark—though that is a rather poor way of stating the case. Actually, the port trade since 1912 has in only eight years fallen below the *five*-hundred-million mark and in general has ranged far above that, and once, in 1920, passed the billion line—that, of course, in an era of high prices, though the tonnage that year was also very high. What it will do during the current war years and after is any man's guess, though like the rest of American shipping that will depend a good deal on what bottoms are available. Curiously enough, or perhaps naturally, the tonnage of New Orleans has six times since exceeded the 1920 mark which produced the billion-dollar valuation, and has at least six times approached it very closely. Yet the highest recorded tonnage—thirteen million-odd in 1937—had a valuation of considerably less than three quarters of a billion. Let the students of economic mysteries draw what moral they will from these figures—they are intended here only as an extension of previously mentioned tonnage vagaries.

No steamship company or shipper, with a few exceptions, owns dock facilities in New Orleans proper, and as near as can be determined they are all happy about it. A priorities system, the first-call-on-berth privilege, is in use, and most lines running regularly into New Orleans pay a fee for that privilege at designated docks; all New Orleans home lines do. The privilege by no means includes exclusive use of a given wharf, and when the particular wharf is not in actual use vessels from other lines may be assigned to it. But because the dock facilities are so extensive and have never been used at anywhere near capacity, friction over the question of privilege is so rare as to be almost non-existent.

A very few dock facilities within the city are leased outright on an exclusive basis. Those at Press Street, for example, are used by inland waterway craft which arrive and depart numerous times weekly, and so are in a class slightly different from those used for ocean and coastwise traffic. Likewise the Stuyvesant Docks are owned by the Illinois Central Railroad and part of them used exclusively for cargo carried to New Orleans by the road or consigned to the city in particular care of the road. Even part of the Stuyvesant Docks, however, are available for public use.

By this system shippers and shipping companies are for a nominal fee provided with every facility within the power of the Dock Board and its purse. Everybody gets an even break, the huge concerns have no advantage over the little man, and shipping interests are relieved of all worries connected with the extremely important matter of dock facilities. What wouldn't the American railroads give for that kind of relief!

Not the least of the Dock Board's achievements is the Inner Harbor Navigation Canal, which provides a deep-water connection between the Mississippi and Lake Pontchartrain. According to the board the canal was "created primarily to provide deep-water frontage for unlimited industrial development, and to provide the port with an inner harbor in which the commercial wharf system could be extended with the advantage of a constant water level." All of which is true enough, but the canal is also an all-important link in the Intracoastal Canal System, by which the entire Gulf coast is provided with what amounts to a water highway free from the uncertainties of deep water. The route eastward from New Orleans runs by way of the Inner Harbor Canal, Lake Pontchartrain, Lake Borgne, and Mississippi Sound to Mobile; and the water distance from Mobile to the Mississippi at New Orleans is thereby shortened by perhaps three hundred miles, plus the advantage of being more or less weather free.

Canals have always been a familiar part of the New Orleans landscape, but at normal high water in the river there is a twenty-foot variation between the level of the river and that of Lake Pontchartrain. Thus the old canals extended into the city from Lake Pontchartrain but never dared make the connection with the river. Until modern engineering made the inner harbor and its lock system possible, a canal connection with the Mississippi might well have been a means of annihilating New Orleans during some of the worst flood periods. The Inner Harbor of course provides deep water only within its own length and does not extend into Lake Pontchartrain, for the latter is simply not that kind of a lake.

During World War I New Orleans was a most important embarkation point, and accordingly an army supply base, what was probably the largest dock unit in the city, was built by the Federal government. It was planned as though the war might last indefinitely, was not completed until the war was over, and thereafter fell into the disuse which is usually the common fate of American military establishments in peacetime. The base was not only the largest dock facility in the city, but probably the largest structural group of any kind—at least at the time—and contained some fifteen million square feet of floor space exclusive of the wharf and runway areas.

Eventually a portion of it was leased by the Dock Board. They, in turn, leased part of it to a couple of manufacturers and in another part set up what was called a Permanent Trade Exposition. The army still used a corner of the estab-

lishment and the rest of it became a storehouse for the para-
phernalia of the WPA.

Lend-Lease changed all that, however, and in a few months
tanks, trucks, and airplanes were spilling out of the buildings
and onto the docks, old tenants were vacating hurriedly, and
army engineers were furiously at work filling in along the
riverbank and creating new wharf space.

With the growth of American military interest in the
Caribbean area it was inevitable that this base and New Orleans' shipping facilities as a whole should acquire a fresh
importance.

In the long period prior to 1900 the great bulk of New
Orleans' sea commerce was export, but since then the trade
has leveled off and now one year will see an export balance
and the next an excess of imports. New Orleans' importance
was always that of a transshipment center, for until the last
two decades the city processed very little raw material herself.

Before the Civil War the steam packet and the flatboat in
all its bewildering variety carried cargo to and from New
Orleans, but after the war the railroad gradually replaced
almost all other means of transportation. Almost is the word,
for water-borne commerce never dies out entirely where
there is water to be used. But the United States, possessing
in the Mississippi the world's most magnificent river system,
came closer than any other country to destroying its river
commerce. To repeat, the traffic on the Mississippi system
never died completely—but in comparison with the total
amount of goods in transit it sank almost to the vanishing
point. From being the first and frequently only means of
transportation it became not even a means of last resort.
Thought of the rivers vanished from the minds of men who
did not live within sight of them, and even the latter forgot
to think of them as highways open to anyone who would
use them.

The Port of New Orleans

It is true that year by year, as the great timber areas of the Mississippi Valley were logged off and more thousands of acres came under the plow, the Mississippi system became more precarious to navigation. Did the Mississippi shoal terribly at Plum Point and Stack Island? Of course. Did navigation on the Wabash and a host of other little rivers become impossible for even the smallest of steamboats? Again of course. But the answer was that nobody cared. Somehow it was taken for granted that the railroad could serve America better. It could go anywhere and railroad management, not government, had to maintain it. That both government and the people had been and were paying for the railroads either could not or would not be understood. It was not the first nor last time the country deliberately ignored or abused its great natural resources.

A few people, chiefly those directly in the path of their flood rampages, remembered the rivers and insisted something be done about them. Something was done, but it was only a token of what was necessary to regulate the rivers as they should have been. Everything that happened to the rivers after the Civil War could have been prevented by an expenditure far less than that spent on uneconomic rail lines. The Mississippi River Commission, charged with both flood control and improvement of navigation, came into being in 1879, but it had very limited resources simply because the great majority of the public no longer were interested in the state of the rivers. In the first twenty-seven years of its existence the Mississippi River Commission spent, on the Mississippi between Cairo, Illinois, and Head of Passes, $52,-500,000—or less than was stolen from any one of half-a-dozen railroads by stock manipulation or rate frauds during the same period.

It is a waste of time to blame Congress for the neglect, for while that body has made plenty of mistakes on its own account it has always yielded to the people when the people really made up their minds that they wanted something. So

A Seaport Grown Up

Congress did little about the river systems because the people at large wanted nothing done about them. For that matter the people at large still don't care whether anything is done. Railroad bonds which will probably never be retired and stocks which skip dividends year after year are still far more important than the rivers which belong to all the people.

It was this decline in the use and usefulness of the rivers which above all caused New Orleans' fall from commercial supremacy in the great valley—and New Orleans herself, more's the pity, never did much about it.

In Europe, both past and present, rivers are regarded as gifts of Providence, and the river front of any European city is likely to be, in part at least, the city's show place. In American cities, both past and present, the river front is likely to compare well with the city's dirtiest alley, although New Orleans, because her river front is also her harbor and is under the jurisdiction of the Dock Board, has escaped that state more than most. New Orleans is fortunate in that she has a body of men responsible for her river front, though that happens to a certain extent to be an accident. In most American cities *nobody* is responsible for what happens to the river front.

Now this is no plea for beautifying the water fronts of American cities, though that is no bad idea in itself, but an attempt to point out that the erection of commercial and dock facilities on these river fronts would be at once an aid to river commerce, a species of flood control and protection, and incidentally an improvement in appearance. A row of docks, even the most utilitarian kind, is bound to be an improvement over an ash heap or a junk yard full of discarded automobiles and tin cans.

Waterside terminal facilities are something which river traffic must have. Barges can't unload structural steel, or flour, or citrus fruits on a mudbank, but satisfactory docks can be built on them. Docks which, if built, would pay for themselves over and over again in freight-rate savings! It is in the very nature of river traffic that the barge lines, those devoted to public use, can't possibly provide terminal facilities themselves, although, on the other hand, they cannot operate without them. Even the Federal Barge Lines, the strongest single influence in the renewed life of river commerce, can't do much about the matter of terminal facilities. They do not have the money to build terminals even if the law under which they are incorporated would permit it, which it does not. There is no question of the savings possible in water transportation. The waterways' claim of 20 per cent savings in rates has been proven over and over again and the possibilities of the traffic have hardly been touched as yet.

In the through traffic to New Orleans during the eighties and nineties towboats and barges came into much wider use, but there were limitations beyond which they could not go. Shippers were reluctant to use them, in spite of their cheaper rates, because of a lack of wharf facilities, and there were not wharf facilities because shippers declined to use them and thereby provide the money for them. It was a perfect vicious circle. In this period Mississippi barge traffic had as its backbone the movement of grain from St. Louis to New Orleans, and this it hauled much more cheaply than the railroads could in spite of its somewhat less efficient unloading facilities at New Orleans. At that time neither the suction unloader nor its predecessor, the bucket-type conveyor, was in common use anywhere.

The lack of proper channels in the rivers was also a hindrance to the fullest development of heavy river traffic, but that was not the fault of the barge lines, and even that drawback was being eliminated, though slowly, to be sure, by the Mississippi River Commission. And always the need was for more wharf facilities, but the cry was never great, because even the bargemen seemed to have no vast amount of faith in their cause.

This indeterminate state of affairs lasted until the entry of the United States into World War I, when it became apparent that the railroads simply were not equal to the demands made on them. A motley collection of river craft was pressed into service by the United States Railroad Administration, did a noble job, and in 1920 was handed over to the War Department—then as now in charge of rivers and harbors—to be operated as the Inland & Coastwise Waterways Service. Barges had proved themselves, if any proof was necessary, in spite of the railroads' objection to competition. They continued to prove themselves, and in 1924 the Inland & Coastwise became the Inland Waterways Corporation with a capital of five million dollars, later increased to fifteen million. Since then the Federal Barge Lines—the collective name of the several lines operated by the Inland Waterways Corporation—have enjoyed the best of health. Their officials are likely to call the success of the Federal Lines "spectacular," though that is hardly the word for it. It has had a steady growth under what is essentially a conservative management, but it has been hampered by lack of capital. In some ways the successful operation of the Federal Lines, over distances of several thousand miles and considering the great tonnage moved, with the capital available, has been a great job. With capital and terminal facilities commensurate with its possibilities, its growth could indeed be spectacular.

But the anti-waterways pressure is always there, making itself felt in any effort to increase the scope of the barge lines. There is pressure in favor of the waterways, too, but so far it has made only minor headway against the railroads and the capital interests behind them. Railroad spokesmen may deny any antagonism toward the waterways, though it is inherent, and point to the fact that many railroads in the Mississippi Valley have co-operated with the barge lines in establishing joint rail-water rates, so that the inland shipper may consign his cargo to the nearest barge terminal and still enjoy whatever savings in freight rates the barge lines may afford. That the shipper may do this is undeniable, but the fact remains that most shippers don't know it, and the railroad is the place where they are least likely to be given the information unless they manage to blast it out for themselves. It is only natural that this be so, for in the original battle for position between the waterways and railroads the railroads won, and now they can't be expected to deliberately talk themselves out of business they need so badly.

It is a pity that this should be so, for in a reasonably arranged transportation system there would be no great rivalry between railroads and waterways, but each would have its logical place in the overall scheme. To the dyed-in-the-wool riverman there is something ironically tragic in the sight of a long train-load of coal and other bulk goods lumbering along beside a broad river empty of useful traffic from bank to bank for miles.

From all this it must not be inferred by any means that the Federal Lines operate the only regular barge service into New Orleans—far from it, in fact. But Federal, Union, and American Barge Lines operate almost the only *through* lines available for public use, and the Federal Lines are the only ones who have done much to make the modern public waterway conscious. The economic value of barge service in general is attested by the great number of such craft in use by private concerns, especially on the Ohio and between Pittsburgh and New Orleans. Jones & Laughlin Steel, for instance, operate nearly a hundred barges. Carnegie Steel, Standard Oil of Louisiana, and a host of lesser-known concerns operate their own waterway delivery service. But these people use the waterways for their own private benefit, and rightly so, because the rivers are there for the use of everyone. Given the co-operation of shippers, ten times the public capacity could be utilized.

In time barge tows should be hauling cotton and citrus fruit from the Gulf coast to St. Louis, Minneapolis, Chicago, and Pittsburgh by way of the Intracoastal Canal, New Orleans, and the Mississippi system, and the benefits of savings in freight passed on to the consumer.

A Seaport Grown Up

As this is written the East coast of the United States faces oil and gasoline rationing because of tanker sinkings and a lack of tank cars the railroads claimed to have but didn't when the push came. But from New Orleans, Baton Rouge, Lake Charles, and Shreveport—all important oil ports—the barges still plow the rivers to Pittsburgh. *They* can haul oil—given barges and power! A fleet of oil barges can be built for the price of *one* tanker, and far more quickly. By the time this reaches print something may be done about that, for the rivers have been there all the time, waiting to be used, and it required a war originally to bring the Inland Waterways Corporation into existence.

(Since the above paragraph was written, and as these pages are about to go to press, the oil-delivery controversy has waxed much hotter and coastwise tanker sinkings have reached an appalling total. On the Atlantic seaboard oil rationing is a fact and may go into effect elsewhere shortly, so it may be pertinent to add to these original remarks concerning oil shipments via the inland waterways.

It is unfortunate, from the point of view of the public, at least, that most of the discussion about oil transportation by barge has been carried on by newspaper columnists who mean well, who sensed that the barge lines were not being adequately used, but who did not properly understand all the factors involved. It was, I believe, the late General Hugh Johnson who first suggested increased oil transportation by barge—but he thought of it as a means of releasing coastwise tankers for foreign service. The domestic problem was not then so acute. Since then other publicists have taken up the cudgels, though from the point of view of the problem as it now stands. It is something of a pity that, because of their lack of knowledge, they managed to give the public an erroneous idea of what is in reality a useful theory.

When the question of oil delivery was first agitated and a shortage predicted, spokesmen for the railroads insisted hotly that there were more than enough tank cars to deliver all the oil we could possibly use. They spoke of tank cars available by the thousands, and the public was led to believe that these figures meant *surplus* cars, whereas it later developed that the figures were intended to mean total cars. It appears now that the railroads were merely seizing an opportunity to boast of a prowess they didn't have—as stated above it was just such a previous failure which necessitated the creation of the Federal barge lines originally. But that aside, and with no reference to the fact that rail rates are forcing oil companies to sell crude oil on the seaboard at less than delivered cost, the railroads have fallen down on the job completely. That was, for physical reasons, unavoidable. Where they were at fault was in assuring both public and government that they could do something which was manifestly impossible.

Since rationing, because of this failure, is a necessity, the government has sought to soften the blow by creating the impression that the rationing is a good thing because it conserves passenger-car rubber. That may be so, but passenger-car gasoline consumption is only one small phase of the problem—and who believes that rationing would have been put into effect for the sole purpose of conserving rubber? Passenger-car rationing, in the East or anywhere else, leaves out of account the thousand-and-one other, and more necessary, uses of petroleum products everywhere in the United States. These uses must go on even if every passenger car stops running altogether. You can't ration the use of vital machine lubricants or fuel for shipping.

Now obviously the inland waterways cannot carry oil directly to landbound areas, and certainly not directly to the seaboard. So much is elementary. The problem is one of co-ordination, of using every last foot of transportation capacity to the fullest advantage, with a minimum of lost motion and duplication. Thus those towns and cities located on navigable inland waterways should not be allowed to receive one gallon of oil from a tank car which could be sent on over the Alleghenies to the seaboard. Tank cars should not be allowed to go for a load to any point farther than the nearest feasible rail-waterway transshipment point. As the emergency stands now the nation is not concerned with the competitive rights of any form of transportation. Railroads, waterways, and truck lines have, or should have, complemented each other. None, under our present system, is all-sufficient; we need them all.

No city in the Mississippi Valley should be allowed to receive a gallon of oil by truck or tank car if it can possibly be delivered by water; and no city anywhere should receive oil by truck or rail from a point farther away than the nearest water distribution point. Therein lies the usefulness of the inland waterways, not only in the present emergency but always.

It is true that such a program would require far more transfer facilities at these distribution points than we have now, but that problem is not insurmountable. Storage tanks and dock facilities can be built, at least for temporary use, of materials other than vital steel—steel which apparently can't be released for the construction of extra pipelines.

Much of the newspaper discussion of the problem has treated the barge lines as an end in themselves, the solution to the whole problem, which they are not and cannot be. The problem remains one of co-ordination of *all* transportation facilities, with the barge lines playing only their proper, but currently neglected, role in the overall scheme.)

Any growth in the activity on the inland waterways is sure to be reflected in New Orleans, for it was her location at the vital exit of the entire Mississippi system which made the city originally. New Orleans knows this and looks forward to it again, though with not too much optimism. There are times when it appears that more of New Orleans is concerned with garnering the pin money of the visiting tourist than in promoting her welfare in the general economic scheme of things. Orleanians are apt to mutter "politics" and let it go at that.

Of the inland waterways and New Orleans one last impression. Some of the barge tows which come into New Orleans are almost a thousand feet long and between two and three hundred feet in width. (The overall length of the *Normandie*, the world's longest vessel, is 1,029 feet.) It is worth an all-night excursion to see these behemoths put into the Upper Yard at New Orleans, though not many Orleanians go in for such sight-seeing. Somehow these tows convey a feeling of immense power, a feeling of America at work, that is as tremendous as these barge trains themselves. (Which is not to imply that these tows are uniquely American; the English Thames and German Rhine have long carried tows equally large.)

On the roof of the towboat's pilothouse—the towboats are always *behind* the barges—searchlights with a half-mile range pierce the heavy darkness, or it may be fog, of the river as the pilot, a fifth of a mile behind the bow of the leading row of barges, *feels* for the landing. You experience an almost weird feeling as the bow corner of the tow edges for the bank, for this huge thing is gliding almost silently. It is true that the towboat, literally a floating powerhouse, is throbbing with a heavy, steady beat, but it is a thousand feet away from where you watch and appears to have no connection with this moving mass. Only the stabbing, probing fingers of the searchlights connect the power plant at the stern with this dark, moving mountain. Then suddenly she—vessels are traditionally feminine but it is hard to think of this mass of floating islands in that gender—is in with a deceptively gentle bump, waiting men are running the mooring lines to the wharf cleats, and forty thousand-odd tons of cargo are safely in port. For a moment you reflect upon the fact of that moving mass and the minus-thousand miles of river that lie between here and Cairo. But isn't that river from a half-mile to a mile wide up there, with the Corps of Engineers, U.S. Army, providing a marked and lighted channel all the way?

A barge train ought to *float* down that highway of its own accord. The relaxed pilot smokes a cigarette, swigs his coffee,

and nods in solemn agreement. He knows you are kidding—
that is you are if you know anything at all about this mighty
river. And if you don't know he feels there isn't much point
in trying to explain. He will not tell you, for such comparisons
are out of his line, that manipulating that thousand feet of live
weight through a bend with only yards of channel to spare at
either end of the curve is something like docking a battleship
by hand—except that in the Cairo–New Orleans run it's likely
to be an almost hourly experience. He won't explain the feeling when the fog settles down so thick you can almost scoop
it up in a bucket, when the marker lights on the shores vanish
and there are still forty thousand tons moving like an avalanche
there in the void ahead of you, and there's nothing to steer by
except an absolute knowledge of the river amounting almost
to instinct, and a prayer!

All this doesn't matter now. In a few days there will be the
upriver trip with exactly the same hazards present in reverse.
But meanwhile, over there behind the wall of levee is fabulous
New Orleans!

CHAPTER XX

And So, New Orleans . . .

WITH NEW ORLEANS for his subject any writer must of necessity concern himself with the French Quarter sooner or later. He may twist and turn and try to avoid the hackneyed obvious, but eventually he will have to return to it, for it has a fascination he would not be able to resist if he wanted to.

Every city of character has its hallmark, its badge of identification by which it is most specifically known to the rest of the world. In New York it is perhaps what is known as "Broadway"; in Moscow the Kremlin; in Chicago the Loop and the Michigan Avenue lake front; in Shanghai the Bund; in New Orleans the French Quarter.

The Quarter is of course not all of New Orleans, is perhaps not even typical of the modern city. It is not the center of the city geographically or in any other way nowadays—except perhaps for a certain portion of the tourist trade, though it was the original Nouvelle Orleans, that from which all the rest of the city sprang. Originally it occupied an area of six by eleven short blocks, though it is now a little larger because of the new ground created by the shifting of the Mississippi's bank—the rest of New Orleans occupies an area of just under two hundred square miles. For the record, this little plot of ground bore one of the first, if not *the* first, permanent white settlements in the Mississippi Valley. Until the Louisiana Purchase the area was not the French Quarter but all of New Orleans, and was not thought of as being especially French—in population it was almost as much Spanish—until after the Americans, for various reasons, chose the area above Canal Street for their own. Predominantly French and Spanish it remained until after the Civil War, and it was in every way self-sufficient.

There were ancient Creoles and their ladies who, a decade after the Civil War, could boast that they had never so much as visited the bustling American city above Canal Street. The Quarter contained all that remained of original New Orleans, though after the devastating fires of the late eighteenth century there was nothing left of the original except tradition and the memory of a city that was no doubt the better for the burning. Even those who loved it best agreed there was little of human creation there that was worth preserving.

The Quarter had its great days. Within its boundaries had stood the institutions which were the very essence of New Orleans, or which were at least the outward expression of that essence. There was the Place d'Armes and its flanking three blocks containing the Pontalba Buildings, St. Louis Cathedral, the Presbytère, and the Cabildo. There were the St. Louis Hotel which was later the state capitol; the French Opera House; the original Ursuline Convent; the famous (?) Quadroon Ballroom on Orleans Street; Exchange Alley, also known variously as the Passage de la Bourse and the Street of the Fencing Masters. Here were the homes, few of them outwardly very pretentious, of the rich and powerful folk of the city. Here had lived the sometimes proud and haughty French and Spanish governors. Here five flags had sometime been the symbol of sovereignty: the lilies of the French monarchy, the flag of Imperial Spain, the Republican tri-color of France, the American Stars and Stripes, and the Confederate States Stars and Bars. Here Burr had seen the heart of his dream empire; Father Antoine Sedella had allegedly plotted for the greater glory of Holy Church in the New World; Andrew Jackson had enjoyed the triumph of the Battle of New Orleans; here bloody duels were fought in St. Anthony's Close, a few yards from the Cathedral altar; fabulous sums of money changed hands across the green tables, and discreet sin lived more or less in harmony with the strictest French code of family morals. Within this area occurred almost every important event of New Orleans' first century and a half of existence; so these very streets are heavy with a weight of tradition unmatched in any of the city's two hundred other square miles.

The period of the Quarter's decline in prestige must in general be established as the Civil War, though of course the decline was a lengthy process, as are almost all social changes, and in the case of the French Quarter the change neither began nor ended with 1861. Gallatin Street of infamous memory was in its heyday for a long period before the war. Barracks Street, not far from Gallatin, was hardly a quiet residential street, and Decatur Street, formerly Levee, was a typical water-front thoroughfare, though probably never as tough as Tchoupitoulas Street. Under the terms of the 1857 ordinance governing prostitution a part of the Quarter, that portion of it nearest Canal Street, became officially a part of the vice district. Theoretically, the ordinance prohibited prostitution in this area under certain circumstances, but in practice it increased it. That is by licensing the business in the restricted areas it tacitly forbade it elsewhere.

But vice districts like to move around, and when Basin Street, which was outside the Quarter, was enjoying its greatest prosperity Gallatin's toughness had for the most part vanished and the size of the brothel area within the Quarter was greatly reduced.

It was after this that the real decline of the Quarter began. Old families with sufficient means gradually moved elsewhere, and the old city fell slowly into physical as well as social decay. The fine, closely built homes went without repairs except those absolutely required to hold them together, and rents declined accordingly. With rents thus becoming cheaper a part of the Quarter was occupied by Negroes, other parts by immigrant Italians, and still others by those who simply found the area both cheap and convenient to live in. There remained, of course, and still remains, a smattering of the older families who had no place to go.

So the French Quarter became in a sense a slum. But only in a sense, because the word "slum" carries a meaning, perhaps of degradation of spirit as well as physical well-being, that was never completely true of the Quarter. Usually a slum is a place where people live because they must, but always a great many people lived in the Quarter merely because they wanted to. A great deal of New Orleans is "poor" in the sense that incomes are small, and of course this is especially true of the Negro population. And yet, without making any sort of plea for poverty as a way of life, it is true that poverty in New Orleans seems to be less an abject state than is usual in cities of comparable size and importance in America. Cold statistics would probably show that this is an utterly false impression, and that the poor of New Orleans have a great many things to be abject about; no doubt they do—but at least they *seem* to be in less need of uplift.

But regardless of the French Quarter's social and commercial state it remained what George Cable called "the most classic spot in the Mississippi Valley, the most picturesque group of façades, roofs, and spires in New Orleans." It still is. Time, of course, was to a certain extent a destroyer of these things, and the New Orleans climate is no preservative in any case—the city has known nine-inch rainfalls in one twenty-four-hour day. But time mellows, too, and the results of that are here also.

It was only after World War I that New Orleans discovered what a tourist asset it had in the French Quarter, and nowadays it makes the most of that asset commercially. And yet even a highly organized tourist trade, complete with barkers, guides, rubberneck busses, praline-selling black mammies in costume, postcard racks in every shop, and Visitors' Welcome signs, has not managed to destroy the really honest charm of the old city. There is much more here than meets the casual tourist eye, and the ballyhooed tours cover only a fraction of the Quarter's total area. The passing visitor sees Royal Street and its antique shops; Jackson Square; the Bourbon Street night-club belt of five or six blocks—around which, incidentally, clusters the only considerable brothel area in the Quarter nowadays. That part of the Quarter not directly concerned with the tourist trade goes serenely and obliviously about the business of living, only a little irritated at times by the gape-mouthed visitors snapping masterpieces with their Brownies or cluttering the sidewalks while the spielers retell the old ghost stories over and over, not infrequently adding embellishments of their own.

In the streets of the Quarter Negresses still wear the brightly colored *tignon* which was once a symbol of caste. Negresses still carry bundles nonchalantly on their heads in the immemorial way; Negro children carry their books to school in the same way. Decrepit wagons and wagoneers hawk coal from house to house—it seems that every building in the Quarter has its fireplace in every room—and the grocery stores sell little bags of coal for a dime and bundles of kindling for a nickel. Housewives and shopkeepers retain the morning and evening rite of sluicing porches, balconies, and sidewalks for coolness, and the one-time slave quarters and detached kitchens behind many of the older houses are as much lived in as ever, though nowadays as much by whites as blacks.

The Chartres Street side of St. Louis Cathedral is always lined with tourist cars and busses during the season, whereas the loveliest view of the building, the only good one in fact, is from the rear, looking down Orleans Street into St. Anthony's Square, with its towering sycamores and flowering

hibiscus and the fragile-appearing openwork iron cross on the
rear of the building itself. On Orleans Street of a late afternoon
one can see the colored nuns of the Sisters of the Holy Family
—the building was once the scene of New Orleans' notorious
Quadroon Balls—watching from their balcony as their small-
fry black charges strut in the street below to the music of the
school's brass band.

Because practically all the houses in the Quarter are built
directly on the sidewalk line (though New Orleans still likes
to call its sidewalks banquettes) louvered wooden shutters are
very much a part of almost every dwelling. In their day, of
course, they were the ideal means of providing at once ventilation and privacy, and in New Orleans they still do—next to
the iron balconies the wooden shutters are probably the most
obvious feature of French-Quarter architecture. But in addition they manage to create a mood. In the night hours, when
folk are still awake but the streets are quiet and semi-deserted
—and some of the Quarter's streets are extraordinarily empty
at night—light from these shuttered windows and doors gives
the pedestrian a strange sense of being in the midst of a
thronging life which he feels rather than hears or sees, a feeling utterly different from that created by batteries of lighted
apartment-house windows.

The guidebooks bristle with the addresses of publicized
patios and courtyards, for the Quarter is largely built around
these patios and some of them are lovely. But there are a great
many which are, for good and sufficient reasons having to do
with a natural desire for privacy, not publicized at all—and
these are usually the loveliest of all. A large part of the Quarter's population lives not on the streets where they have their
addresses, but rather on the *inside* of the squares, and generally
the façade of a building is absolutely no indication of what
may lie behind it. It may be a pile of three-dollar-a-week
unfurnished rooms, or a private house rich with everything
money can buy and install—and the two extremes are quite

likely to be next door to each other. The Quarter exercises its fascination on the well to do along with the poor.

In a sudden drenching rain the tiled roofs and bewildering multitude of chimney pots are astonishingly like the many-angled roofs of Paris, though the pedestrians in the streets below are not the same by any means. In New Orleans a sudden downpour often doesn't even cause the pedestrian to move out of his sauntering gait. He knows from experience that the rain will probably stop shortly, and in any case he always has the protection of the overhanging balconies.

It is a curious thing but to most of the people who have read or heard of the Quarter but who have never seen it, and to many of those who have seen it, it is either a brothel district or a sort of art colony. To a greater or lesser degree it has in the past been a little of both, but only a very little in comparison with the whole. It happens to be the oldest and most picturesque part of New Orleans, with perhaps 95 per cent of its residents being neither prostitutes nor artists but living here because they like it and in many cases because they have never lived anywhere else.

Old residents of the Quarter, when they are at all aware of these incongruous outside impressions, are likely to be more tolerantly amused than angered. They could, if they cared to take the trouble, point out that the Quarter contains one of New Orleans' best hotels; St. Louis Cathedral flanked by two state museums; the New Orleans Criminal Courts Building and the Louisiana Department of Conservation; practically all of the city's really famous restaurants, and Solari's equally famous food emporium; *and* the American Legion Building. They could point out that the old U.S. Mint is now a Federal jail; that Decatur Street's business houses cater to the sober and utilitarian needs of that portion of the water front; and that the world-famous French Market and its coffeehouse does business at the same old stand, also on Decatur Street. They could tell you all these things and many more, but to someone with another sort of impression it probably wouldn't make much difference. So most of the French Quarter's permanent residents know what they know and keep on living there and enjoying the process exceedingly—at least insofar as their surroundings contribute to their enjoyment.

And what of New Orleans' other two hundred square miles?

Well, they have their full quota of taxis, streetcars, automobiles, radio stations, hamburger stands, department and chain stores, parks, railroad stations, WPA projects, churches, moving-picture houses—and a "progress"-minded chamber of commerce. In other words, it has all the standard model appurtenances of modern American civilization, plus a number of differences of its own. Few observant strangers, suddenly deposited in almost any section of the city, would make the mistake of supposing this to be Akron or Omaha or Seattle or Baltimore. They might not immediately recognize the surroundings as being New Orleans but they would not mistake it for any other American place.

In Canal Street it has one of the great thoroughfares of the world, with St. Charles Avenue not far behind in impressiveness—and it probably has more miles of unpaved, and most certainly more one-way, streets than any other American city of comparable size.

It has newspapers which are probably adequate for the public they serve, but they have little personality of their own and are distinguished for what must be some of the world's worst proofreading.

In New Orleans the Negro is everywhere and always present, for the most part regarded by the city with a sort of good-humored tolerance, with relations in a kind of suspended truce which both parties understand but almost never discuss, even among themselves. Most Southern cities have more than one so-called black belt, but New Orleans is notable for its extraordinary number of them. Small Negro communities crop up in the strangest juxtaposition to otherwise completely white neighborhoods, and to the stranger the transition is sometimes a little surprising. He takes for granted that the Negro population is large, but he hardly expects to find parts of it living around what seems every fifth or sixth corner. This is not an accident, and the fact that this is so is a commentary on the whole matter of racial relations in the Deep South. For physical reasons streets are usually the actual boundary lines between black and white areas, and it is probable that New Orleans has more miles of these border lines than Chicago or New York. The Orleanian will explain with disarming candor that this is merely proof that the South is more realistically tolerant in these matters than it usually gets credit for being— and that is true but only within strict limitations. There is a bit more to it than that.

New Orleans, at bottom, prefers to have its Negro population scattered, not because it likes the increased contact between whites and blacks, but because it fears, or at least pretends to fear, the results of concentration. There are as many theories about what the results of such concentration might be as there are people with theories, and whether or not this fear has any validity it certainly has a practical effect on the racial distribution. Not many Orleanians have any real understanding of the Negro social organization, nor want any, and of course this can be described also as one form of tolerance. Probably the Negro prefers it that way. It is by no means a solution of any of his basic problems, and always he is inferior socially, politically, and economically. But if it comes down to a choice between being driven and regimented or being ignored he much prefers the latter.

In comparison with other American cities New Orleans has always had a very low ratio of persons per dwelling, and that still holds good. The present result of that low ratio, or at least one result, is the city's very large area in comparison with its population. For both climatic and social reasons the Orleanian does not like apartment houses. He will live in a two- or four-apartment building if he must, but he vastly

And So, New Orleans . . .

delectable mountains of food at the French Market stalls . . . some of the world's truly fine restaurants . . . Negro jazz in small back-street cafés . . . the liquid pleasantness of true New Orleans speech . . . the greenery of weeping willows overhanging time-mellowed plaster walls . . . New Orleans coffee at its best . . . the docks with their ceaseless sights, sounds, and smells . . . Canal Street jam-packed with Orleanians watching any parade . . . the tiny perfumers' shops . . . the fact that a dime is practically an unknown coin—it is always two nickels . . . the super-de luxe antique shops of Royal Street . . . the sailors from the Algiers naval base looking over the tattoo selection at the shop on wheels near the Canal Street ferry landing. . . . Small things these, but they add up to a good deal in the way of pleasant but still not riotous New Orleans living.

Some years ago the city went to a great deal of trouble and expense to create on the shore of Lake Pontchartrain one of the South's really good airports. And when it was done New Orleans gave it the name of one of the late Huey Long's ablest henchmen. In the fullness of time and the course of human events, the namesake of New Orleans' airport, regrettably, according to some people, was sent to the penitentiary. For most cities the situation would have been embarrassing to say the least—but not to New Orleans. Eventually she changed the name of the airport, but more for the sake of the conventions than because of any personal feeling in the matter. A great deal of New Orleans saw no reason whatever for changing the name, and while that doesn't entirely explain the city it is typical of it.

Not long ago a porter at one of the Pontalba Buildings said to an acquaintance of the writer:

"Mister Blank, it's a funny thing—but how come people are always writin' an' sayin' about how N'Awlins is a very interesting city? Now I ask you, do you see anything interesting about it?"

"Why, yes," Blank said with a certain degree of natural surprise; "in some ways very much so."

"Well," said the porter, "I've lived here all my life an' *I* don't see anything interesting about it!"

May the reader who has come thus far have escaped the same boredom!

INDEX

A

Acadians (Cajuns), 8, 63
Adair, General, 132
Adams, President John, 108
Aetna (steamboat), 163
Agriculture, 23, 26–29, 34; truck gardens, 40; *see also* Crops
Airport, 325
A. L. Shotwell (packet), 198
Alabama (vessel), 158
Algiers, 7, 10–11, 152; ferry, 274
Almonaster y Roxas, Don Andreas, 71, 95–97, 203; his daughter, 71, 203, 283
American Barge Lines, 308
Antoine, Father, 90–91, 136
Architecture, 97, 187, 319, 323
Arkansas Post, 77
Arkansas River tract, 28, 30, 40
Artists and writers, 279–80
Asbury, Herbert, 49; *The French Quarter*, 49n.
Atchafalaya Bay, 31
Athanase, Father, 15, 16
Aubry, Charles, 58, 61, 64–66, 68
Augusta (vessel), 211

B

Bailey, Capt. Theodorus, 237–39
Baird, General, 257

Baldwin, Leland D., 201
Balize, 267
Baltimore's first export, 73
Banana trade, 9–10
Banks, Gen. Nathan P., 255–59 *passim*
Bar, Captain, 7
Barataria Bay, 139–41, 144–45
Barnum, P. T., 204–5
Barrows, Captain, 249
Basin Street, 285, 316
Baton Rouge, 85, 161; British in 1812, 147; in Civil War, 241
Batture, 169; riots, 137
Bayou Bienvenue, 149
Bayou Manchac, 53, 70, 85
Bayou Mazant, 149
Bayou Pierre, 133
Bayou St. John, 28, 123
Beauregard, Gen. P. G. T., 206, 249, 258, 284
Beauregard Square, 192
Bell, Captain, 233
Bell, Maj. Joseph M., 245–46
Belle of the West (packet), 197
Bellechasse, council appointee, 120
Béluche, Laffite aid, 140, 149, 157
Benjamin, Judah P., 206, 258
Bienville (Le Moyne), 7, 16–18, 24–32 *passim*, 39, 46, 59; Indian troubles, 44; nephews, 63, 67; and Ursulines, 37–38

Index

Bilbao agents, 80
Biloxi Bay, 16–19, 26, 29
Black Code, 35–36
Boisblanc, Hardy de, a planter, 63
Bolivar Point, 6
Bollman, Dr. Julius Erich, 132
Boom periods, 193, 196
Boré, Étienne de, 98, 120
Borgne, Lake, 17, 53, 147–49, 225, 302
Bosque, Suzette, 134
Boudousquié, opera manager, 205
Boundaries, 86, 91
Braud, a printer, 67
Breton Sound, 139, 269
Bribery, 93
British: in American Revolution, 76–84; and Confederacy, 249; incite Indians, 51; and Louisiana Purchase, 52–55; and Napoleon, 110, 112; and Spanish trade, 24–25; trade, 60, 70; in War of 1812, 142–56; Western posts, 53, 59–60, 80–81, 85
Britton, Barkley, 229
Brooklyn (ship), 226
Brown, Captain, 274
Burial, 185, 213
Burr, Aaron, 121, 125–33
Burr Conspiracy, 125–33
Butler, Andrew J., 243, 253–54
Butler, Gen. Benjamin F., 203, 226–35 *passim*, 236–57, 259; and foreign policy, 249–52; poor relief, 247–49; profits made, 243, 253–54; recall, 255–56; and slavery, 252; Woman Order, 244–45, 254–55

C

Cabildo, 28, 72, 95, 203
Cable, George, 135, 228, 278; quoted, 317
Cadillac, La Mothe, 24–25
Café des Emigrés, 287
Café des Exiles, 287
Cajuns (Acadians), 8, 63
Caldwell, Captain, 233
Caldwell, James H., 190–91
Calvé, Julia, 205
Camboden Castle (vessel), 211
Canadian entrants, 16–17

Canal Street, 10, 11, 103, 290, 321
Canals, 152, 153, 154, 185, 301–2; proposed, 269–73
Canby, Gen. E. R. S., 257
Cantrelle, council appointee, 120
Capuchin order, 36–37, 49, 56, 90
Cardenas (vessel), 251
Caresse, Pierre, 63, 67
Carmelite order, 36
Carolina (vessel), 150
Carolina families, 7
Carondelet, Baron de, 96, 101–4, 123
Carpetbaggers, 246, 258, 261–63, 284
Carrollton, 189, 239
Cartagena goods pirated, 139
Casa Calvo, Marquis of, 113, 118, 136
Cathedral, 72, 95, 136, 203
Catholic Church, 15, 20, 43, 136, 179, 287; and Judaism, 36; various orders, 5, 15–16, 36–38, 49, 56, 90, 95, 98; work and expenses, 36–37
Cavalier, Robert, 5
Cemeteries, 185, 213
Chalmette, Plain of, 153, 156, 229–30, 235
Charity Hospital, 38, 71; in epidemic, 212
Charles III of Spain, 80
Charlevoix, Father, 32
Chartres Street, 31
Chauteague (Le Moyne), 16
Chickasaw Bluffs, 130
Chigizola, Laffite aid, 158
Churches and religion, 36, 179–80, 183; lotteries, 180; and slavery, 179; *see also* Catholic Church
Circus Square, 192
City Hall, 206
City of Louisville (packet), 295
Civil War, 172, 222–56; antebellum period, 216–21; financial factors, 222–23; New Orleans captured, 231–35; poor relief, 247–49; post-Civil War period, 257–67; transports returned, 243
Claiborne, William C. C., 114–36 *passim*, 156–57, 167, 177; Laffite troubles, 139–47; marriages, 134
Clark, Daniel, 100, 113, 116, 120, 127–28, 135

Index

Index

Index

Index

Index

Index

Index

The Seaport Series

A FAIR AMOUNT of the history of any country can be traced in the histories of its seaports. Here, in these places, where for a little distance the rough sea seeks shelter from the land, came the first sea-rovers, seeking new lands. After them the tides of commerce, the lusty waves of immigration. No land, anywhere, no matter how staid, how sedately governed, but can trace a gaudy pedigree in the story of its seaports. This is especially true of America. Every port large enough to attract a deepwater vessel makes a warm, bright spot of color in the pattern of America's past. This book is one in Doubleday Doran's Seaport Series. We plan to publish books in this series from time to time until the stories of all of America's major ports have been told, fascinating chapters in a nation's history.